The Gospel of Thomas

For the first time, this volume offers a detailed commentary of The Gospel of Thomas, a work which has previously been accessible only to theologians and scholars. Valantasis provides a fresh reading of the Coptic and Greek texts, with an illuminating commentary, examining the text line by line. He includes a general introduction outlining the debates of previous scholars and situating the Gospel in its historical and theological contexts. *The Gospel of Thomas* provides an insight into a previously inaccessible text and presents Thomas' Gospel as an integral part of the library of early Christian writings, which can inform us further about the literature of the Judeo-Christian tradition and early Christianity.

Richard Valantasis is Associate Professor of Early Christian Literature at Saint Louis University. His recent publications include *Constructions of Power in Asceticism* (Journal of the American Academy of Religion). Ordained as an Episcopal priest, he has served parishes and a women's monastery. He conducts adult education and other retreats for the laity.

New Testament Readings

Edited by John Court
University of Kent at Canterbury

The Gospel of Thomas

Richard Valantasis

London and New York

First published 1997
by Routledge
11 New Fetter Lane, London EC4P 4EE

Simultaneously published in the USA and Canada
by Routledge
29 West 35th Street, New York, NY 10001

Reprinted 1999, 2000

Routledge is an imprint of the Taylor & Francis Group

© 1997 Richard Valantasis

Typeset in Garamond by Routledge
Printed and bound in Great Britain by TJ International Ltd,
Padstow, Cornwall

British Library Cataloguing in Publication Data
A catalogue record for this book is available from the British Library

Library of Congress Cataloguing in Publication Data
The Gospel of Thomas/Richard Valantasis (New Testament readings).
Includes bibliographical references and index. 1. Gospel of Thomas –
Criticism, interpretation, etc. I. Title. II. Series.
BS2860.T52V35 1997   96–6808
229'.8 – dc 21   CIP

ISBN 0–415–11621–X (hbk)
ISBN 0–415–11622–8 (pbk)

for
Edward T. Rewolinski
linguist, scholar, friend, spiritual brother,
and companion on the way

Contents

Series editor's preface

This volume has every right to stand on its own, as a significant contribution to the study of the book of the New Testament with which it is concerned. But equally it is a volume in a series entitled *New Testament Readings*. Each volume in this series deals with an individual book among the early Christian writings within, or close to the borders of, the New Testament. The series is not another set of traditional commentaries, but designed as a group of individual interpretations or 'readings' of the texts, offering fresh and stimulating methods of approach. While the contributors may be provocative in their choice of a certain perspective, they also seek to do justice to a range of modern methods and provide a context for the study of each particular text.

The collective object of the series is to share with the widest readership the extensive range of recent approaches to Scripture. There is no doubt that literary methods have presented what amounts to a 'new look' to the Bible in recent years. But we should not neglect to ask some historical questions or apply suitable methods of criticism from the Social Sciences. The origins of this series are in a practical research programme at the University of Kent, with an inclusive concern about ways of using the Bible. It is to be hoped that our series will offer fresh insights to all who, for any reason, study or use these books of the early Christians.

John M. Court
Series Editor

Preface

This book actually began about fifteen years ago in a conversation with my academic mentor George MacRae, SJ. I had spoken to him about beginning studies toward a doctorate at Harvard and I wanted to work with the newly discovered documents from Nag Hammadi. Our conversation focused on the need to listen carefully and to construct even more articulately the theology of the texts discovered in that astonishing library. These texts, we concurred, represent the theological and religious artifacts of people for whom they were extremely important and they (both the people and their texts) demand the highest respect by modern scholars–the same respect due to every religious artifact.

Most of our colleagues were busy placing these documents in their proper historical place among the known literature of early Christianity, formative Judaism, and the religions of the Greco-Roman world, and they were preoccupied with arguing about the texts' heretical or orthodox status. Their interest rested primarily in how these documents enable modern scholars to reconfigure the world of the early Christians and to understand these early Christians' interaction with groups that seemed to have been suppressed. Suppressed is the key word here, because these documents were believed to be a cache of *heretical* and *rejected* documents curiously preserved in the precincts of an *orthodox* Christian monastery at Chenoboskion in the Egyptian desert. That irony was lost on that first generation of modern scholars, because the literature found at Nag Hammadi seemed curious, strange, unfamiliar, and preserved in Coptic, a language not traditionally identified with Christian orthodoxy. My interest, as Fr. MacRae's, was to treat these tractates as important theological witnesses to communities of people whose theological expressions and writings were worthy of respect and serious historical-theological study.

Over the intervening years, I have continued to read and study these texts as part of the sources for understanding the historical-theological milieu of pre-established and pre-Constantinian Christianity. They have been a rich fund for theological exploration and articulation among a variety of groups of people whose theology remains distant from my own, and yet so closely aligned. The widely divergent Christianities evident in the Nag Hammadi Library blend theologically with the other groups such as Platonists, Hermetists, and philosophers to open a large window into the theological discourses of the early church and their non-Christian neighbors. Their theology, often preserved in a language in which it was not originally composed and very frequently translated by modern authors so as to make it sound exotic and peculiar, nonetheless stands as a witness to what at least some people thought worthy of preserving in the jar in which they hid their collection of documents. Their witness to the religious diversity of formative Christianity stands as an ensign to our own age in which religious diversity and conflict also seem to dominate.

In this book, I turn to the Gospel of Thomas, one of the many tractates from Nag Hammadi. It has been slightly over 100 years since the discovery of the Greek fragments and slightly over 50 years since the discovery of the Coptic tractate in the Nag Hammadi Library. This Gospel has been at the heart of heated debates about formative Christianity, both orthodox and heretical, for a goodly part of this century. As the recent surveys of scholarship indicate (see Fallon and Cameron 1988; Patterson 1992; Riley 1994), scholars studying this tractate have addressed the traditional New Testament questions such as its gnostic character, its genre, its antiquity in relationship to the sayings of Jesus in the canonical gospels of Mark, Matthew, Luke, and John, and its dependence upon other religious traditions in the Greco-Roman period. Such questions confused both the scholarly and non-scholarly worlds by their technical and ideological frame. The argument in the academy has mostly centered upon this Gospel's fit in relationship to other gospel material, as opposed to what this Gospel says.

I turned to this Gospel first and foremost to understand what it says, its theology, and its particular understanding of the Christian life. As I worked, I also discovered that I was involved in rescuing the Gospel of Thomas from what appeared to be a difficult academic history during which the Gospel of Thomas was used both to solve previously articulated problems about the origins of gnosticism in the history of Christianity and to justify particular scholarly perspectives on the origins of Christianity itself. It is time simply to listen to this gospelspeak and to suspend briefly the questions that have preoccupied us all with this library. This simple reading means first of all reading the Gospel of Thomas as a theological document in its own right, and second it requires *not* reading the Gospel of Thomas in relationship to the synoptic traditions and *not* reading it in relationship to the fully developed gnostic systems of the second century. After the dust has settled (and I hope this commentary will help settle it), we all can begin again to locate this Gospel in its historical context and in relationship both to the synoptic tradition and to the theological movements of the second century. First, however, we must give this Gospel voice, as best as that is possible in a document so ancient.

The Gospel of Thomas has been a site for intense scholarly engagement: now it is time to set a new course, one more accessible to the general population and more measured for the academics. This book attempts to do that, first by presenting a consistent reading of the Gospel without reliance upon the traditional external historical, religious, and sociological material traditionally used to situate the Gospel, and second, by presenting a strong literary analysis of each saying. This analysis, so familiar in the work of George MacRae, hopes to establish a base-line, if not "zero degree," reading of the text for scholars while simultaneously enabling new and uninitiated readers to pick up the Gospel and begin to evaluate it (and others' opinions about it) on their own. In a sense, this commentary returns to the measured and balanced perspective of George MacRae (1960) who neither quickly rushed to establish parallels and sources nor sought too quickly to characterize its theology and perspective, and yet took the Gospel seriously in its own right.

Many people have been involved in supporting this effort. Saint Louis University, where the book was written, awarded me two Mellon Faculty Development Fund grants that allowed me to write during one summer and provided me the means another summer to travel to the Coptic Museum in Cairo to study the codex. Two Graduate School Research Awards allowed me not only the financial resources, but afforded graduate student assistance to pursue the project. Among those graduate students, I must especially recognize the work of Stephen Hoskins for assistance early on and for critical feedback: his willingness to learn about Thomas, and his enthusiastic questioning, set the stage for the complete rethinking of this commentary. Kevin O'Connor helped to survey the library resources and Gerasimos ("Makis") Pagoulatos spent a summer connecting this text to patristic sources. In the Department of Theological Studies, many colleagues provided moral support, among whom Dr. William Shea, Chair, graciously provided release time from teaching to finish the manuscript and questioned me enthusiastically about the text and its meaning.

I also thank Polebridge Press, the publishers of The Scholars Version of the Gospel of Thomas, who have granted me permission to use their translation as the English basis of my commentary. Their work in making ancient texts (both canonical and non-canonical) available to scholars and to the general public establishes a standard for academics and publishers alike. In almost every respect I encourage the colloquial translation of the Gospel of Thomas, even though at times I have chosen to translate in an alternative fashion; these alternative translations are noted in the text. The Scholars Version more than any other recent attempt in translation has tried to move the translation away from the bizarre to the familiar language of religious people. Their text of the Gospel of Thomas in *The Complete Gospels* edited by Robert J. Miller (1992) should be consulted for the more complete list of parallels to the Nag Hammadi Library and to the New Testament.

Thanks also goes to Richard Stoneman, my editor at Routledge, and to John Court, editor of the series, who together supported the task of making a commentary on a non-canonical gospel part of the series "New Testament Readings." I hope their efforts will eventually include a wide assortment of formative Christian texts.

After my penultimate version, many colleagues read the manuscript. My interdisciplinary research group (Brian Goldstein, Georgia Johnston, Matthew Mirow, Carol Needham, Hal Parker, Ken Parker, Marlene Salas-Provence, Fran Tucker, and Joya Uraizee) read and commented on the introduction with expected acumen. Critical and helpful responses to the whole manuscript were provided by my faithful and rigorously fastidious readers: Ellen Aitken, Janet Carlson, Stephen Patterson, Jennifer Phillips, and Edward T. Rewolinski. Their comments significantly advanced the clarity of the commentary. Although they often would have led me in safer directions, what follows in this book remains my responsibility. All of their assistance, however, is deeply appreciated.

It gives me great pleasure to dedicate this book to a long and faithful friend. My introduction to the Coptic Gnostic Library of Nag Hammadi took place during the summer (the date seems oddly irrelevant now that we are all older) that Edward T. Rewolinski was working on his doctoral dissertation on the Gospel of Phillip under our (eventually) mutual academic mentor, George MacRae, SJ. Every evening, over cocktails, Edward would read to my wife, Janet Carlson, and to me from his latest translation, using the outrageous sense of humor and knowledge of theology that he brought to all ancient texts. He initiated us both into the greater mysteries of these texts and opened for me new avenues of professional and academic interests. In addition to providing entertainment, we have stood together as a spiritual family for many years, beginning when I was in seminary and he was just beginning to study for his doctorate at Harvard University: we have traveled together, prayed together, read together, eaten and drunk together, translated together, and spent sporadic years living under the same roof at various times of life-transition. In his post-scholarly incarnation he became Janet's professional confidant and conversation partner on matters of business and finance. His presence transformed our lives, and we (Janet and I together) dedicate this book to him to honor him as a friend, spiritual brother, and colleague.

Abbreviations and symbols

< > Pointed brackets indicate a word implied in the original language and supplied by the translators of the Scholars Version.

[ ] Square brackets indicate words that the editors of the critical edition have restored where the text is not visible or is damaged. They are also used to correct scribal errors.

[...] Square brackets with ellipses between them indicate a lacuna or gap in the manuscript that cannot be restored satisfactorily.

[SV:] This indicates the Scholars Version. It is used to indicate the text found in the Scholars Version when I offer an alternative translation. Superscript numbers in the text refer to the Scholars Version versification system.

[Coptic:] This indicates the Coptic word upon which the Scholars Version has based its translation.

Lambdin: This refers to the translation of Thomas O. Lambdin in Layton (1989).

Layton: This refers to the critical edition of Bentley Layton in Layton (1989).

NRSV: The New Revised Standard Version of the Bible.

RSV: The Revised Standard Version.

NHLE: This refers to the *Nag Hammadi Library in English*, ed. James M. Robinson (3rd edn), San Francisco: Harper & Row, 1988.

P. Oxy: This abbreviation with the number that follows it refers to the publication number of the papyrus texts discovered at Oxyrhynchus in Egypt. Originally published by Grenfell and Hunt (1897 and 1904), the text used here is based upon Attridge (1989), found in Layton (1989).

Chapter 1

Introduction

The dry desert conditions in Egypt are ideal for the preservation of papyrus and other ancient writing materials. Two discoveries of papyri at two different sites in the Egyptian desert (Oxyrhynchus and Nag Hammadi) bear particular relevance to the Gospel of Thomas. Nearly 100 years ago Grenfell and Hunt discovered at Oxyrhynchus and published some fragmentary Greek papyri containing several sayings attributed to Jesus (Grenfell and Hunt 1897 and 1904). Although most of these sayings curiously did not have counterparts in the sayings already known in the canonical New Testament, these early Greek fragments were initially acknowledged simply as sayings unattested in the canonical tradition and unparalleled in other early Christian literature. They captured the imagination of scholar and layperson alike; their origin was unknown, but their significance was generally recognized.

Then, over 50 years ago, thirteen codices (ancient books constructed from papyrus sheets) were discovered at Nag Hammadi (Robinson 1979). These codices were written in Coptic, a dialect of Egyptian. Among the Coptic codices found in this collection (commonly called the "Nag Hammadi Library") were a number of different tractates of great interest to scholars studying the literature of early Christianity because the codices contained a number of tractates entitled "gospels" (such as the "Gospel of Peter," the "Gospel of Truth," and the "Gospel of the Egyptians") as well as a tractate (the second tractate of Codex II) entitled at the end "The Gospel According to Thomas." Scholars eventually linked the earlier unattested Greek fragments discovered at Oxyrhynchus and the Coptic tractate entitled "The Gospel According to Thomas" discovered at Nag Hammadi. The earlier Greek sayings of Jesus were nearly the same as some of the Coptic sayings from the Gospel of Thomas. From that time forward, the Gospel of Thomas became a permanent fixture in the search for understanding the origins and development of primitive Christianity. The desert of Egypt had preserved some Greek fragments and a complete Coptic version of a lost Gospel of Thomas.

Although these discoveries of Greek and Coptic sayings of Jesus attributed to the Gospel of Thomas were dramatic and exciting, the existence of such a gospel had long been known. Ancient Christian testimonia witnessed to knowledge of a gospel by this title and to ancient knowledge of some of the sayings that now are known to be part of the Gospel of Thomas (Attridge 1989: 103–12). Modern knowledge was dependent upon these later testimonies until these dramatic discoveries made in Egypt's desert. The discovery of new gospel material, especially that of the Gospel of Thomas, inaugurated an international quest in the general public and among scholars to understand anew the origins and development of Christianity.

The discovery of the complete Coptic version of the Gospel of Thomas caused a great stir for three primary reasons. First, New Testament scholars had theorized for many years that behind Matthew's and Luke's revision of the Gospel of Mark stood a collection of sayings, known simply as the Synoptic Sayings Source Q (Kloppenborg 1987: 1–40 provides a good history of the issue). This theory, known as the "two-source hypothesis," explains the literary relationship among the three synoptic gospels (Mark, Matthew, and Luke) and it maintains that the earliest narrative gospel was Mark's. Matthew and Luke used the majority of Mark's gospel as the basis for their own gospels, and then added one other major source (called the Synoptic Sayings Source Q) in addition to some of their own traditions about Jesus, to supplement Mark's narrative frame. The Synoptic Sayings Source Q that Matthew and Luke used was considered a collection of sayings of Jesus without any narrative frame. The content of this Synoptic Sayings Source Q could only be established by comparing the sayings common to Matthew and Luke and by then reconstructing the common text; the genre of collections of "sayings of Jesus" remained theoretical. With the discovery of the Gospel of Thomas in Coptic, scholars finally had an actual document in the same genre as had been theorized, an existent gospel composed only of sayings of Jesus in a collection of sayings. Although the Gospel of Thomas is not believed to be the source that Matthew and Luke used, the fact that many of the sayings from it directly paralleled sayings known from the common Synoptic Sayings Source Q added strength to the argument that such a source could have existed. The two-source hypothesis was in this way strengthened and renewed by the discovery.

Second, prior to the discovery of the Nag Hammadi Library, gnosticism could be studied primarily by reading the writings of those orthodox church writers (known as heresiologists) who described and copied parts of larger "heretical" works in their own anti-heresy literature in order to criticize supposed heretical beliefs. With the discovery of the presumed "gnostic" library at Nag Hammadi, church historians, historians of theology, and historians of religion finally had real and ancient gnostic documents that were not preserved by being embedded in heresiological treatises but that were both carefully copied and even more carefully preserved at a time when heterodoxy was being persecuted. These "heretical" writings would provide scholars with an original voice against which to evaluate the heresiologists' assessment of gnosticism.

Finally, people (both among the academic and general public) who were interested in alternative Christianities, gnosticism, and syncretistic religions, as well as people who were either tired of or bored with the traditional view of Jesus were captivated by the voice present in these sayings. Many thought that they could hear immediately the words of Jesus without the intermediary of the institutional church and its orthodox theologians.

It has been over 50 years since the discovery and interest in the Gospel of Thomas has not waned. Of all of the Nag Hammadi documents, this gospel has received the most interest and been the subject of the most writing. It has been at the heart of a general debate about the historical Jesus, the status of the canonical view of Jesus and his sayings, and religious journalistic speculation. It has also been heatedly debated by European and American scholars.

A DESCRIPTION OF THE GOSPEL OF THOMAS

The Gospel of Thomas is a tractate preserved in two ways: a fragmentary set of Greek papyri; and a complete Coptic text written in a "particularly fine script" (Turner and Montefiore 1962: 11). The physical evidence (that is, the actual papyrus and codices) dates from about the year 200 CE for the Greek and the middle of the fourth century CE for the Coptic. The scholarly consensus holds that these two sources provide evidence for an earlier gospel written originally in Greek in Syria (Koester 1989: 38), most probably emergent from the

Greek-speaking Jewish–Christian community (Quispel 1957; MacRae 1960) in Syrian Antioch (Desjardins 1992).

So what is this gospel that has been discovered in two different places, two languages, two versions, and from two different times? The answer to that question is not easy. The Greek fragments found at Oxyrhynchus and the Coptic version found at Nag Hammadi have both similarities and differences. The Coptic sayings comparable to the Greek do not seem to be a direct translation of the same Greek text, and the Greek seems to witness to another version of the gospel than the one on which the Coptic translation is based. So there is not really a singular gospel, but two divergent textual traditions. This situation makes a precise and well-delineated description of the Gospel of Thomas problematic, because the Gospel of Thomas may refer to a number of different elements in its textual history.

To answer the question about the exact referent, Edward Rewolinski (1996) has outlined clearly the various layers of the possible texts that may make up the gospel. These layers at once make the problem more complex and more simple: complex, in that the layers show the stages of the tractate's development; simple, because it allows me to locate a specific layer or phase of development for this commentary.

There are seven layers at least. First, there are the original sayings of Jesus that probably circulated orally and were repeated by various followers of Jesus in their own ministries. These sayings constitute the original field of possible sayings from which those in this particular gospel could have been selected. Second, there is the author of this particular collection of the sayings of Jesus who collected and then wrote the sayings down and published them. Not all the sayings of Jesus were recorded, rather the author or collector selected from those available. The second layer offers an opportunity both for an intentional selection of sayings from among the oral texts and for the adjustment of these sayings to suit the author's purpose and perspective. Third, the author's collection of sayings was probably used by various people and communities who would have read them, perhaps used them liturgically, and produced other copies of the gospel. In this process those people and communities probably adapted the sayings to their life-situations. This was a common practice in ancient Christian literature, especially in gospel literature, and it can safely be assumed to have occurred here and at any other stage in the transmission of the gospel. Fourth, these community adaptations of their text of the gospel would effect another text: the communities that produced the texts of the gospel would reproduce the text currently *in use* in their communities and pass them on to others who would not know in what way the texts had been adjusted. Therefore, the subsequent text would reflect the particular community's changes and show how they made their own adjustments to fit their own life-situation. Fifth, there is the last Greek scribe who influenced the text of the gospel in transcribing it (as in the fragments discovered at Oxyrhynchus); changes often occurred each time a scribe produced another copy. A number of scribes (in Syria as well as Egypt) transcribed their text of the gospel; the Oxyrhynchus fragments provide the physical evidence of at least parts of the gospel for which we have witnesses. Sixth, there is the Coptic translation of the text. In all likelihood, more than one person translated the gospel into Coptic. Translations involve an interpretative process because the translator renders into another language (here Coptic) what he or she understands the original text (here Greek) to mean. The process of translation itself, then, provides another version in Coptic of the Greek text that came into the hands of the Coptic translator. And seventh, there is the last Coptic scribe who produced the text that was hidden in a jar in the fourth century only to be discovered at Nag Hammadi nearly fifteen centuries later.

Each one of these layers could safely be called the Gospel of Thomas, but clearly each one refers to a different production, version, or edition of the gospel that the author wrote. The gospel could refer to the original core of sayings, the author's originally published collection, the Greek editions used by any number of communities, the Greek edition to which the Oxyrhynchus fragments witness, one of the Coptic translations, or the final Coptic version that was discovered. For the purposes of this commentary, the Gospel of Thomas refers to the authorial level only as it can be discerned through the physical evidence of the Greek and the Coptic texts that have survived: in other words, this commentary looks to the text that the author originally created, but only to those versions that exist in one fragmentary Greek version and one (presumably) complete Coptic version.

The tractate that we call the Gospel of Thomas actually has two possible descriptions within the tractate itself (see Robinson 1971a; Meyer 1990). The Prologue calls it "The Secret Sayings that the Living Jesus spoke and Didymos Judas Thomas recorded." This designation would indicate that the tractate consists of a collection of secret sayings spoken by Jesus and recorded by Didymos Judas Thomas. The title found at the end of the tractate (as is customary in these documents) reads "The Gospel According to Thomas." Here the tractate becomes an example of the literary genre "gospel," and receives a title parallel to the canonical gospels in structure, namely a gospel "according to" an identified disciple authority in parallel to Mark, Matthew, Luke, and John. This second designation creates problems, because the content of this gospel differs from those other texts in the genre in that there is comparatively little narrative material in the Gospel of Thomas (see Wilson 1960: 4; but also Koester 1990a: 80–84). Despite what it might be called, the tractate consists of a collection of sayings of Jesus.

The sayings are not in any particular order (Koester 1989: 41–42): they are not organized by themes or topics; they are not organized with any discernible theological direction; they do not exhibit any particular logical or cohesive overall structure that holds them together (see Wilson 1960: 4–10; Patterson 1993: 94–102). The sayings are bound together by a diminutive narrative structure consisting mostly of the phrase "Jesus said." Some evidence exists that the sayings were originally preserved in oral communication (Haenchen 1961–62; Cameron 1986: 34), because there are words that link certain sayings in sequence (a list is provided in Patterson 1993: 100–2), even though that sequence does not display any theological or literary connection beyond the linking words themselves.

Not all the sayings are unique to this collection. There are three classes of sayings in the Gospel of Thomas: those that have a parallel saying in the synoptic gospels (Mark, Matthew, and Luke); sayings of Jesus attested elsewhere in early Christian literature, but that have no parallel in the canonical tradition of gospels; and hitherto unattested and unknown sayings of Jesus (MacRae 1960). Some of these sayings have parallels to other literature of the period, both religious and philosophical (Baker 1964 and 1965–66; Quispel 1981). Some sayings have distinct parallels to material in Paul's Corinthian correspondence (Haenchen 1961; Davies 1983: 138–47; Koester 1990b: 51–52; Patterson 1991). Most all of the sayings are attributed to Jesus, although other people (disciples, for example) also speak and ask questions of Jesus.

THE THEOLOGY OF THE GOSPEL OF THOMAS

The Gospel of Thomas, as a collection of sayings of Jesus, does not purport to be a systematic or even an organized theological tractate. A collection of sayings by nature cannot fulfill expectations of a systematic presentation of discursive theology, so that any description of its theology must emerge from the oblique references in the sayings. The theology of a collection of sayings must be constructed, that is, from such indirect and opaque elements as inferences, innuendo, connotations of words, analysis of metaphors, and other elements both non-theological and non-discursive. In constructing from these elements, the theology remains fragmentary: not every theological question that an ancient or a modern reader might ask will be addressed in a satisfactory or consistent manner. It must be made clear, however, that the Gospel of Thomas does indeed present a recognizable and articulated theology, but both the mode and the content of that theology differs from other theological discourses. The theology of the Gospel of Thomas, moreover, presents even greater challenges because some of its content (the sayings parallel to canonical sayings) is familiar from the canonical tradition. This familiarity with other scriptural traditions tends to emphasize the normative status of the canonical tradition and to underscore the deviations and differences from that tradition in this gospel. Even with these difficulties it is possible to construct some elements of a theology characteristic of the Gospel of Thomas.

I would characterize this theology as a performative theology whose mode of discourse and whose method of theology revolves about effecting a change in thought and understanding in the readers and hearers (both ancient and modern). The sayings challenge, puzzle, sometimes even provide conflicting information about a given subject, and in so confronting the readers and hearers force them to create in their own minds the place where all the elements fit together. The theology comes from the audience's own effort in reflecting and interpreting the sayings, and, therefore, it is a practical and constructed theology even for them. In communicating through a collection of sayings, moreover, the topics move rapidly from one to another with little meaningful connection between them. The sayings cajole the audience into thinking, experiencing, processing information, and responding to important issues of life and living without providing more than a brief time to consider the question fully. The audience's forced movement through and interpretation of rapidly changing topics and issues bases the theological reflection in cumulative experience emergent from their responses to the stimuli of the sayings. That is why it is performative theology: the theology emerges from the readers' and hearers' responses to the sayings and their sequence and their variety.

The community that forms around the collection of sayings is one created by the association of the readers and by their mutual experience of finding the interpretation of the sayings. The community developed in this gospel is not one analogous to a parish, or a church, or any other organized group of people with a structure and a charter. Rather, this community is a loose confederation of people who have independently related to the sayings and found their interpretation, who have begun to perform the actions that inaugurate the new identity, and who have become capable of seeing other people who perform similar activities. The community, in short, is a by-product of the theological mode, a loose conglomeration of people of similar mentality and ways of living, but who do not necessarily live together as an intentional community. This introductory overview of the theology of the gospel will focus upon this performative aspect.

The person of Jesus

In the gospel, Jesus pronounces a number of sayings to his disciples. Actually, it is more complicated than that. In these sayings, the narrator presents Jesus as a character speaking to an audience, and at one point (Saying 111) the generally diminutive narrative voice breaks out of its hidden presence and asks "Does not Jesus say...?" as a direct address to the implied audience of the gospel. The narrator indicates that these sayings come from Jesus ("Jesus said"), so that the narrator adopts the voice of Jesus as its own. Jesus is the character the narrator has created to transmit the sayings.

This narrativized Jesus pronounces sayings. He functions primarily as a voice, and the gospel provides little information about his identity, his intellectual or emotional life, or any significant biographical information about the major events of his life. One time in the sayings, Jesus describes his emotion at the empty world full of spiritually blind people (Saying 28: "My soul ached for the children of humanity"), but beyond that readers are not admitted into Jesus' emotional structure. Moreover, Jesus' mother and brothers are mentioned (Saying 99), although Jesus generally rejects the legitimacy and centrality of family bonds (Sayings 55 and 101) in favor of a redefined society (Saying 99) which is the group comprised of those who hear his sayings. The gospel affirms that Jesus appeared in the flesh to do his work in the world (Saying 28), and that he did not understand himself to be a philosopher, an angel, or a teacher (Saying 13). The most significant theological factor about the Gospel of Thomas is that it contains no information about the passion, death, and resurrection of Jesus. The only mention of the crucifixion occurs in an indirect reference to his disciples carrying a cross as does Jesus (Saying 55). Beyond these few elements, Jesus' life remains opaque.

The preceding examples provide a negative appraisal of the person of Jesus from the absence of biographical information. A more positive appraisal may be constructed from Jesus' function as the chief speaker in the narrative. The gospel presents Jesus as "the living Jesus" (Prologue) who is "the living one in (the audience's) presence" (Sayings 52 and 91, my parentheses). This gospel portrays Jesus as immediately accessible to the hearers of the sayings; his voice is that of a fully engaged speaker and guide who speaks the sayings to his followers (Saying 38). The readers of these sayings, then, connect not to the narrative of Jesus' life (as in the canonical gospels of Mark, Matthew, Luke, and John), but to his living presence as a person speaking directly to them.

Jesus entered the world as a fleshly being precisely in order to assist people to change their way of living (Saying 28). Consequently, Jesus' mission revolved about presenting hidden mysteries (Sayings 17 and 62), reorganizing the meaning of discipleship (Sayings 3, 31, 34, 61, 101), calling people who live in the world to a sober and full life (Saying 28), enabling people to drink from the bubbling well of his spiritual direction (Sayings 13 and 108; also see Sayings 45 and 114), encouraging people to manifest their interior and spiritual selves (Saying 70), and leading the worthy to rest (Sayings 50, 51, 60, 90). This mission may be best summarized in Jesus' saying: "Look to the living one as long as you live, otherwise you might die and then try to see the living one, and you will be unable to see" (Saying 59). The immediacy of Jesus' active speech underscores the urgency of the message to choose another mode of life.

Jesus is also constructed as a mystagogue (Saying 17), a revealer of sacred knowledge to seekers, who discloses the mysteries to those who are worthy (Saying 62). This mystagogic Jesus describes himself as the light, the "all" found in every place, the one who is the origin and destiny of all creation (Saying 77). As a bearer of secret wisdom (Prologue), Jesus is portrayed as a divine figure who not only permeates all life, but enables true vision to occur (Saying 37), and who guides people to the fulfilling of their deepest desires (Saying 51). Moreover, Jesus' presence becomes merged with the seekers so that there can be no distinction between Jesus and those who follow him (Saying 108).

Performances

Exploring what Jesus tells his readers to do in these sayings provides the most productive way of understanding Jesus' mission. Jesus instructs the readers in a new way of living, and his instructions advocate certain actions or performances that are appropriate to that new lifestyle. Jesus' sayings function at the heart of the new life; this means that the interpretation of the sayings is the key to the reformation of life. Saying 1 encapsulates this central performance: "Whoever discovers the interpretation of these sayings will not taste death." Jesus' voice, and the content of his speaking, define the means of becoming a new person (Sayings 38 and 52) and guide seekers to various discoveries that transform life (Sayings 5, 80, 91, 110).

In addition to these more sublime instructions, Jesus also provides very practical guidance. His followers are advised: to reject pious acts such as fasting, praying, almsgiving, dietary restrictions (Sayings 6 and 104), and circumcision (Saying 53); to have no worry about food and clothing (Saying 36); to renounce power (Saying 81) and wealth (Saying 110); to lend money to people who will not repay it (Saying 95); to endure persecution, hatred, and hunger (Sayings 68 and 69); to practice privately the death-dealing relationship with the outside world (Saying 98); to love the other members of their community (Sayings 25, 26); to hate father and mother, sisters and brothers (Sayings 55 and 101); to manifest their interior and saving worth (Saying 70); to work on the reformation of their own life before helping others (Saying 26); to drink from Jesus' mouth so as to be united with him (Saying 108); to strip off their clothing without shame and to stomp upon them (Saying 37); to fast from the world and to observe the sabbath as a sabbath (Saying 27). This list exemplifies the specific performances these sayings advocate for the construction of an alternative way of living. They show the breadth and variety of factors involved in Jesus' message. The readers, both by performing these actions and especially by interpreting the puzzling sayings that Jesus speaks, become new people capable of living a new kind of life, and the contours of that new personality are carefully developed through Jesus' advocacy of specific actions.

Subjectivity

This new person (the subject, or subjectivity) that Jesus promulgates in these sayings may be constructed more specifically. The distinction between the newly envisioned identity and the dominant opposing identity finds its expression most dramatically developed in two major areas: gender and singularity. This person has become in essence a third gender, a person no longer fitting in the cultural categories of male or female, but one who is now a fully integrated person with a body whose parts are replaced by newly understood parts in a sort of ascetical reconstruction of the meaning and signficance of each member of the physical body (Saying 22). This third gender does not simply transcend the old male and female genders, but transforms both completely into a third gender identity that revolves about that integration. Jesus metaphorizes this integrated personality as that of a "single one," a solitary, a person who lives alone and who combines the characteristics of old and young (Saying 4). This integral person lives in unity with other solitaries in a recreated or redefined family environment (Saying 16). This single person is elected to live as a solitary (Saying 23 and 49) and as a solitary is capable of miraculous powers over the physical world (Saying 106). The metaphorized "single one" makes concrete and defines the new third gender that replaces the former dual-gender paradigm.

The sayings further characterize this subjectivity. The person envisioned in these sayings is immortal: the seeker will not taste death (Sayings 1, 11, 18, 19, 111) and will reign forever (Saying 2) as a person of superlative gifts and power. The subject advanced by Jesus benefits from a form of pre-existent existence (Saying 19) that originates in light and returns to the light (Sayings 24 and 50) and that manifests an eternal and invisible image (Saying 84). This person lives in the world in a detached manner as a passerby (Saying 42) or even as an homeless itinerant (Saying 86) and yet clearly understands the distinction between the world posited in these sayings and the surrounding mundane world (Saying 47; see also Sayings 56, 110, 111). This subject works hard at finding the interpretation of the sayings, but finds the difficult work a source of life (Saying 58). Jesus' sayings construct a sort of divinized person united to Jesus through his mouth (Saying 108) who is of higher status than Adam (Saying 85) and who is worthy to enter into the most intimate relationship with Jesus in the bridal chamber where all the other solitaries live (Saying 75). The ultimate goal for this person is to find the rest (Sayings 50, 51, 60, 90) that comes from having learned the secret and hidden realities of life (Sayings 5 and 6).

The opponent, or the opposite type of subjectivity, also receives attention. These opponents are considered drunk and empty people (Saying 28) who are strong, but who can be defeated by the seekers (Saying 35). They live in a world that the seekers must reject (Saying

110) because it is analogous to a carcass (Saying 56). These opponents ought to be interpreted not as a specific group of people, but simply as all others who do not engage in the search for meaning that these sayings promulgate.

In contrast to this opponent, these sayings work at constructing a new and alternative subjectivity. Through reading the sayings of the Gospel of Thomas deliberately and consecutively, the readers gradually come to understand not only the new identity to which the sayings call them, but also the theology, anthropology, and cosmology that support that new identity. Although the contours of this subjectivity may be generally (and cursorily) described, they cannot ultimately become clear without a careful and close reading of each saying in the context of all the sayings in the collection. A number of scholars have developed summaries of this gospel's theology (see Gärtner 1961; Kaestli 1979: 389–95; Davies 1983; Koester 1990a: 124–28; Patterson 1993: 121–57), but ultimately no summary will be able to capture the interactive and intellectually challenging process of hearing the sayings pronounced by Jesus and finding their interpretation. One can only understand the theology developed through these sayings by beginning the difficult task of searching and finding their interpretation. This attentive reading is, after all, the suggested strategy presented by the gospel itself.

THE DATE OF THE GOSPEL OF THOMAS

Assigning a date to the Gospel of Thomas is very complex because it is difficult to know precisely to what a date is being assigned (see Rewolinski's description page 4). Scholars have proposed a date as early as 60 CE and as late as 140 CE, depending upon whether the Gospel of Thomas is identified with the original core of sayings, or with the author's published text, or with the Greek or Coptic texts, or with parallels in other literature. The physical evidence (the Greek fragments from 200 CE and the later Coptic codex) does not really help, because these versions provide more information about the actual production of the texts, rather than about the publication of the first Gospel of Thomas by its author. The fact that these two versions also differ from one another indicates that changes in the gospel occurred at some intervening time during both the production of the texts and their translation. Moreover, it is difficult to provide a date for a collection of sayings, because a collection, like any list, can be changed over time without any evidence of addition or subtraction being visible to later readers. A collection may thus contain material much older than the first collecting of that material, and it may include material that later scribes considered sufficiently important or consistent to add.

An eclectic series of factors, then, must be considered in order to assign an accurate date to the tractate we have received as the Gospel of Thomas. Those factors include the following: comparing the Gospel of Thomas to other early Christian literature; an analysis of the way in which the gospel communicates through sayings of a wise person; that is, an analysis of the mode of discourse in the gospel and its genre; an attempt chronologically to locate the gospel in the context of the production of early Christian literature; and finally, a comparison of the gospel to other synchronous literature of the period. In the end, I argue that the Gospel of Thomas was composed during the first decade of the second century (100–110 CE), and that this gospel (together with the synchronous Gospel of John and Letters of Ignatius) form part of a common theological discourse at the turn of the first century.

The first means of dating the Gospel of Thomas emerges from a comparison to primitive and formative Christian literature. Parallels with other New Testament literature (especially the Synoptic Sayings Source Q) and sections of authentic Pauline literature suggest that parts of the material collected in these sayings comes from the period of Christian origins and reflect some of the earliest written forms of the sayings of Jesus from around 60 CE (Koester 1990b). The parallel parables seem to indicate that the version preserved in the Gospel of Thomas comes from the earliest, and least edited, level of the sayings of Jesus (see Turner and Montefiore 1962: 40–78; Cameron 1986). Other comparisons with the Synoptic Sayings Source Q indicate that many sayings in Thomas come from a source equally as early as that source (Cameron 1986; Patterson 1993: 18–71; cf. Schrage 1964). The occasional Pauline parallel indicates that some of the material reflects primitive Christian concerns (Koester 1990b: 50–53). The dating of the Gospel of Thomas by means of the oldest core of sayings suggests an early date of 60–70 CE.

The later date (140 CE), one which I find more problematic, is suggested by comparing the content of the sayings with the theological content of later forms of gnosticism. Gnosticism is a theological and spiritual movement that advocates salvation through a particular knowledge ("gnosis") provided by a savior, in the content of theology, and through specific mythologies of creation and redemption. Gnostic theology is often characterized as dualistic with regard to the relationship of the physical to the spiritual (see Rudolph 1977; Filoramo

1990). Historically, gnosticism as a Christian movement is documented in the second century CE (Wilson 1960: 14–44); however, as a religious tendency or phenomenon, gnosticism is suspected to exist in other religious and philosophical writings of the first century BCE and the first centuries CE (see Bianchi 1967: xxvi–xxix). Valentinian and Sethian Gnosticism give evidence for the fully developed systems of gnosticism, while some wisdom traditions of Second Temple Jewish writings, some Greco-Roman philosophy, and Paul's early Christian communities provide evidence of the developing gnostic movement (see Bianchi 1967; Layton 1981). These early Jewish, Christian, and Greco-Roman gnostic movements have been seen as precursors to the fully developed Christian gnosticism of the second century CE. The scholars who want to identify the theology of Thomas as "gnostic," begin with the assumption of its gnostic nature and then proceed to justify that characterization through establishing parallels with the theology and mythology of later and fully developed gnosticism (Grant and Freedman 1960; Schoedel 1960; Gärtner 1961; Cullman 1962). These scholars employ the categories of the known anti-gnostic literature and correlate them to the newly discovered Gospel of Thomas (see Gärtner 1961). Almost every one of these scholars acknowledges, however, that the Gospel of Thomas does *not* contain any of the known systems or theologies of gnostic writers (see Wilson 1960: 11), and yet they will insist that the document comes from the same period of historical theology. In the end, the terms "gnostic" and "gnosticism" have become increasingly difficult to use because there is such a wide discrepancy between the theological statements of the heresiologists who have defined the categories and the texts of supposed gnostic documents that the terms no longer aid interpretation. Recent surveys of scholarship provide important guidance to understanding this problem (see Fallon and Cameron 1988; Patterson 1992; Riley 1994). The application of a mid-second century CE date to the gospel fails to convince: there simply is no evidence for the fully developed gnostic systems in the Gospel of Thomas.

James Robinson (1971a) and John Kloppenborg (1987) developed a more productive comparative-literary strategy that has been followed by a majority of scholars working on the Gospel of Thomas today. This strategy identified the genre of the Gospel of Thomas and of the Synoptic Sayings Source Q as a collection of sayings of a wise person, and then it located both the Gospel and the Synoptic Sayings Source Q within the stream (or trajectory) of writings in that genre beginning with the Hebrew Scriptures, continuing with the intertestamental literature, and ending with early Christian literature. Kloppenborg has located the genre and the form of these collections in the wider context of the ancient Near East.

Some background information will help explain the import of these observations. The genre of the sayings of the wise and the larger tradition of wisdom arose among the court scholars, or professional scribes, of the ancient Near East (see Wills 1990: 22–38). These ancient scholars used short, pithy sayings as a means both to teach the skills of writing and to instruct the scribes in the mores of the court. When these wisdom collections were gathered together and published they became the nucleus of social and ethical formation for people living in any community. In the Hebrew Bible, the best examples of this genre of literature are *Proverbs* and *Ecclesiastes* ("the church's book" because it was so popular among Christians; the teacher is *Qoheleth*). These biblical books (and many other Jewish and Christian ones as well) attest to the gradual organization by theme so that the wisdom of the ages would be more readily learned and applied. In the Hellenistic Jewish period (c. 250 BCE until 70 CE), this literature flourished, and the numerous early Christian translations into demotic languages (such as Syriac, Armenian, Coptic) indicate its popularity among Christians. Later in the Christian period, monks continued to produce literature in this genre, culminating in the *Sayings of the Desert Masters* (see Ward 1975). The specific genre of the sayings of the wise, as well as the wisdom tradition itself, has a very long history in Jewish, Christian, and Greco-Roman literature.

By locating the Gospel of Thomas within this stream of wisdom literature as a collection of the sayings of Jesus, the wise person, both Robinson and Kloppenborg have provided the parameters that determine the precise intellectual location of the gospel (see Patterson 1993: 94–110). The gospel's location in this tradition does not produce a precise date, but it does provide the information with which to begin to compare this gospel to other wisdom literature and other collections of the sayings of the wise.

The first important point of comparison relates to the earliest of the witnesses to formative Christianity, the letters of Paul. The wisdom orientation of the gospel connects with a discourse about wisdom found in Paul's first letter to the Corinthians (see Robinson 1971b: 42–43; Koester 1980: 248–50; Patterson 1991). Again, Helmut Koester (1990a: 50–53) identified the similarities between the Gospel of Thomas and 1 Corinthians. Paul argues against the understanding of Christianity as initiation into a mystery, as his opponents seem to have understood baptism (1 Corinthians 1–4). Koester argues that Paul countered the hidden mysteries of his Christian opponents with a proclamation of the crucifixion as the hidden mystery (1 Corinthians 2.1). More important for the Gospel of Thomas is the mere presence of this conversation in the 50s CE, because it mirrors the understanding of Jesus and his wisdom found in the Prologue of the Gospel of Thomas: "These are the secret sayings that the living Jesus spoke. . . . " The mode of discourse in Thomas' Prologue replicates the "mystery" language of 1 Corinthians. That kind of wisdom discourse among followers of Jesus begins in the 50s CE (as Paul's letter indicates) and continues well into the middle of the fourth century (as the *Sayings of the Desert Masters* attests). Now, however, there are two important elements (the wisdom tradition and Paul's letters) that pull the date of the Gospel of Thomas more toward the last quarter of the first century (for a summary of the arguments see Fallon and Cameron 1988; Patterson 1993: 113–18).

A correlative way of dating the Gospel of Thomas is to attempt to place this tractate into the context of the production of literature in the formative period of Christianity prior to the third century. John Dominic Crossan (1991: 427–34) has stratified the Jesus material according to chronology. The First Stratum, 30–60 CE includes (among others) the authentic Pauline letters, various fragmentary Oxyrhynchus papyri (P. Oxy. 1224) not in the Gospel of Thomas, The Synoptic Sayings Source Q, a Miracles Collection attested to in Mark and John, an Apocalyptic Scenario, a Cross Gospel now found in the Gospel of Peter, and the earliest layer of the Gospel of Thomas. During this period the material in the Gospel of Thomas that is parallel to these other early sources was recorded. Crossan's Second Stratum, 60–80 CE, includes (among others) the Gospel of Mark, a Dialogue Collection (now found in the Dialogue of the Savior (Nag Hammadi Library tractate III, 5), the Signs Source for the Gospel of John, and some material in the Gospel of Thomas. Crossan's Third Stratum, 80–120 CE, includes (among others) the writing of the Gospel of Matthew (c. 90 CE), Luke (also c. 90 CE), and the first edition of the Gospel of John (c. 100, but no later than 125 CE for which we have the earliest extant papyrus attestation). Crossan's Fourth Stratum, 120–150 CE, includes the redaction of John's Gospel, the writing of Luke's second volume commonly called Acts, the Pastoral Epistles and the Catholic Epistles (among others).

For purposes of comparison, I would like to adopt Crossan's stratification and focus (after some comments on the earlier ones) on the Third Stratum, the period in which the first edition of John's gospel was produced. The First Stratum contains important information about the early Jesus followers of a wide variety: those who collected sayings, others who were oriented toward the miracles, still others fascinated by the apocalypse, and others in the Pauline community who were living out a new form of universal Judaism. These communities in various ways related to a living Jesus, one speaking in the sayings, one immediately available in the miraculous manner of Moses' deeds to save the people of God, one present in the meal, one manifest in the community that formed his Body and that transgressed boundaries of gender, race, and class. This stratum, in short, is characterized by a wide diversity of forms and understandings of Jesus, those identified with him, and manners of living out the diversity in community.

I agree with Burton Mack (1988: 318–24) that Mark was the one, in Crossan's Second Stratum, to write the document that held all the diversity together. The narrative of the biography provided the skeleton upon which a wide variety and even disparate sorts of Jesus material could be placed. This narrative strategy put limits on the often conflicting and immediate understandings of Jesus from the earlier generation, and produced a more acceptable biography of a secret messiah in the prophetic tradition. In order to get all the disparate parts to fit together, Mark had to place narrative controls on the material he was presenting and organizing.

In the third period, Matthew, Luke, and John begin to offer criticism of Mark's earlier project. Matthew and Luke in different ways argued that the material placed in the Markan narrative account was insufficient: it was too scant in relationship especially to the sayings of Jesus (which Mark for the most part avoided) and to some other particular material which they themselves knew (some of which appears in the Gospel of Thomas). They wanted to complete the Markan picture with the addition of a strong tradition of Jesus as sage from the extant collection of his sayings. In accepting the narrative structure of Mark, however, Matthew and Luke had to submit to his controlled presentation of Jesus. The emergent structure of the community, organized around the biography of Jesus and the appointed disciples, remained, but now supplemented with a few other traditions and with a great body of sayings of Jesus variously organized. Their revision of Mark moved the churches of their time and place back toward the origins of the Jesus movement in the relationship of a listener or seeker to a sage.

John, at a slightly later time, knew the earlier work of the synoptic gospels and was not interested in pursuing their theological agenda.

Rather, he "understood his task to be the fresh interpretation of the Jesus traditions current in his own church in the light of the passion narrative" (Koester 1992: 28). Koester interprets John's project as benign, as a reinterpretation. I would argue that John *rejected* the Markan strategy even as revised by Matthew and Luke as a betrayal of the original mode of living among the early Jesus people and the earliest understanding of Jesus as the living voice in the community. John's efforts, then, functioned as a radical and early renewal movement intended to return to the original ways of the first Christians by pushing the strategy of his immediate predecessors more strenuously. John envisioned the origins of Christianity as a time of open community, without authorized leadership, when Jesus spoke to the community openly and enigmatically at the same time (for a description of that early community see Schüssler-Fiorenza 1983: 160–241; Crossan 1991: 227–426). John's effort in writing his gospel was to return to that formative and original understanding of the Jesus movement. Like the Gospel of Thomas, the Gospel of John has been identified with the gnosticizing tendency of this community in formative Christianity (see MacRae 1960).

The writings of Ignatius, Bishop of Antioch, are synchronous with the Johannine project. Ignatius composed his letters between 100–118 CE (Schoedel 1985: 4–7) while traveling as a martyr from Antioch to Rome. Along the way, Ignatius wrote letters to the churches of Smyrna, Ephesus, Magnesia, Philadelphia, Tralles, and Rome and to an individual, Bishop Polycarp. These letters contain incomparable information about Ignatius' theology, understanding of the church and ministry, sacraments, and his relationship with Jesus as a martyr (see Schoedel 1985: 1–31). Ignatius' project revolved about a complex and rich understanding of the way in which Christ was present in the community. By invoking the charismatic and organizational traditions of Paul (Koester 1982: II, 281–87), Ignatius promoted the hierarchical organization of the church on the model of the imitation of Christ and his first followers. This imitation of Christ was actually two-fold: the community in structure was to imitate the structure of Christ surrounded by his apostles and followers, and the imitation of the passion and death of Christ modeled the life of those condemned to death as martyrs. Just about the time that John attempted to renew his community by a return to the original and earliest modality of understanding of Jesus' relationship to his followers, Ignatius attempted to guide the church into further hierarchical reformation by the promulgation of the church offices of bishop, presbyter, and deacon as a means of replicating the presence of Christ in the community–a presence made manifest in the proper celebration of the eucharist and also in martyrdom as sacramental participations in the life and immortality of Christ. This pattern of revelation based upon an immediate access to Jesus either through martyrdom or through the structures of the church, and the centrality of the passion and crucifixion of Christ, mirror the activity of John's gospel.

In the early second century, then, between about 100 and 110 CE, there is evidence for understanding a watershed period of Christian living focused upon an intense interest in articulating the way Jesus is present and related to the community of his followers. On the one hand, Ignatius continues the development of a hierarchically organized church that refigures the dominant position of the major disciples around Jesus promulgated in the synoptic gospels; on the other hand, John attempts to circumvent this hierarchical and sacramental system in the composition of the gospel that includes extensive dialogues of Jesus with his followers and that denies the sacramental system. The ideal type for John is the beloved disciple; the ideal type for Ignatius is the monarchial bishop.

I argue that at this particular junction there is a third option promulgated by the publication of the collection of sayings of Jesus as the Gospel of Thomas. Although there are no direct literary parallels between the Gospel of Thomas and the Gospel of John, their common thematic elements (such as light, life, truth) have long been noted (Brown 1962–63; Quispel 1969; Davies 1983: 106–16). Helmut Koester (1990a: 113–24, especially 119) has convincingly argued that these two gospels share a common tradition which they interpret in very different ways, while Gregory Riley (1995) is persuasive that the communities represented by Thomas and John were communities in a competitive relationship. Two elements emerge as important here: first, the Gospel of Thomas has material that comes from the earliest traditions of the sayings of Jesus; second, the Gospel shares theology and perspective with the Johannine community (although that common material is often very different, and even polemical). The Gospel of Thomas, then, connects to early Christian literature in two ways: some of its contents parallel the material in the Synoptic Sayings Source Q from primitive Christianity; some of the way in which that material is developed parallels the work of the Johannine community.

I maintain that the author wrote the Gospel of Thomas at this point (100–110 CE), at the same time as John's gospel and Ignatius' letters, as part of the debate about the renewal of the church and about the way that Jesus relates to the community of his followers. All three of these texts situate the believer in intense relationship with Jesus, each revolving about a different center. John's gospel connects the early sayings with the passion narrative, but with a discursive Jesus who speaks as a living, discursive voice in the midst of the community. Ignatius articulates a vibrant and mystical understanding of the church, the eucharist, and martyrdom as means of connecting internally and socially with the immortal life Jesus provides. The Gospel of Thomas connects the hearer and seeker to the very voice of the living Jesus speaking in the midst of an interpreting community. The living Jesus of the Gospel of Thomas and of the Gospel of John have similar positions in relationship to their respective communities as revealers of sacred wisdom. This revisioning of the relationship of Jesus to community in the first decade of the second century CE has often been identified with a gnosticizing tendency within formative Christianity, so that at various times in the history of scholarship John, Thomas, and Ignatius have been scrutinized as gnostic writers. This tendency, however, does not primarily relate to a gnostic theological construction, but to a renewal movement emergent at this time to reconsider and reformulate the relationship of Jesus to the churches as a foundation for Christian living.

On the basis of this analysis, then, I place the composition of the complete Greek version of the Gospel of Thomas somewhere in the years 100–110 CE influenced by the same dynamics that produced both the Gospel of John and the Letters of Ignatius. Wilson (1960: 146–47) has already noted this constellation of Johannine theology and Ignatian chronology as a likely milieu for the production of the Gospel of Thomas (see also Davies 1983: 18, 100–2). It is certain that some of the material of the Gospel of Thomas comes from the First Stratum (30–60 CE) and there is always the possibility that one of the copyists of the Coptic version included sayings other than those contained in his archetype. With both these provisions, I would date the Gospel of Thomas to 100–110 CE.

In the context of John and Ignatius, the Gospel of Thomas probably appeared to be somewhat "old fashioned" in its approach. I say this because, on the one hand, the gospel presents very early material and a goodly number of sayings that are found in the Synoptic Sayings Source Q; on the other hand, the Gospel of Thomas works with those sayings in a way more similar to John's gospel, but without the development of extended dialogues or discourses. Another way of articulating this is to recognize that contemporaries of the author of the Gospel of Thomas were working with the tradition in different ways: like Thomas, John's gospel looked to the sayings, but developed them into discourses; like Thomas, Ignatius reformulated the earlier image of the church as a closely knit community around Jesus as a model of contemporary ecclesiastical structure around the bishop. Both these contemporaries move in different directions with the traditions, while the Gospel of Thomas continues the tradition already used by Matthew and Luke a few decades earlier to revise Mark. The Gospel of Thomas simply presents an older tradition of relating directly to Jesus through a collection of his sayings. Its "old fashioned" appearance, then, is based upon first its use of a genre of writing that had already been subsumed into the Markan outline by Matthew and Luke and second its refusal to advance the sayings genre by the development of discourses as John had. Certainly by the middle of the second century CE, the genre of wisdom literature as collection of sayings among Christians appeared anachronistic (Davies 1983: 13). The Gospel of Thomas would sound even more out of date as the ecclesiastical orientation of the Fourth Stratum took shape. Even John's gospel would fare poorly when the dominant ecclesiastical structures of Acts, the Johannine redactor (that is, the ecclesiastical writer who added material to an earlier version of the gospel), and the Pastoral and Catholic Epistles were to emerge. In the end, both John and Thomas were superseded by the Ignatian model of church in which there was little room for the intimate, interpreting communities of these sayings-oriented gospels.

THE GOSPEL OF THOMAS AND ASCETICISM

I argue, then, that in the first decade of the second century CE three different and conflicting interpretations of the Christian's individual life were promulgated and competing. Three different and alternative Christian identities emerged at the same time as a last attempt at renewal before the hierarchical structures of the church became dominant. The Gospel of Thomas promotes an engaged and immediate experience of the living Jesus gained through the interpretation of the sayings (Saying 1). The Gospel of John promotes a similar Christian person but modified by reference to the passion and death of Jesus: these revelations connect with the death and resurrection of Jesus (see Koester 1992: 28). Ignatius promotes a Christian person in imitation of the life (in the church) of Jesus and participation in his death. Thomas' kind of person alone hearkens to the days of immediate presence of Jesus without any need to engage in imitation either of Jesus or of the disciples; John and Ignatius work with the passion and attempt to reduplicate the experiential basis of that immediacy (John through the discourses; Ignatius through the participation in the death of Jesus through martyrdom), but Thomas is satisfied simply to present the interpretation of the sayings as the only necessary experience (Mack 1993: 181).

Another way of talking about this way of promulgating a new identity within a religious movement is to analyze it as asceticism. The word "asceticism" itself derives from the preparations that athletes performed in order to be capable of rigorous athletic competition. By extension, I understand asceticism to include all the actions, called performances, that are required to build a new identity, called a subjectivity (Valantasis 1995a). When John, or Thomas, or Ignatius begin to describe a new kind of person and to promote a different identity within the larger confines of Christianity, they also must speak of the means of activating or creating that new identity so that members of this smaller community may learn how to make that identity real.

At the heart of asceticism is the desire to create a new person as a minority person within a larger religious culture. In order to create a new person, there must be a withdrawal from the dominant modes of articulating subjectivity in order to create free space for something else to emerge. A redefinition of social relationships must also emerge from the new understanding of the new subjectivity, as well as a concurrent change in the symbolic universe to justify and support the new subjectivity. These are all accomplished through a rigorous set of intentional performances (Valantasis 1995a).

All three of these turn-of-the-century writings reflect ascetical interest: in relationship to three different models, they attempt to construct an identity alternative to the dominant and prevailing one. John's subject receives the revelations of Jesus in the discourses, but awaits a correlative transfiguration or glorification through the death and resurrection of Jesus (Koester 1992: 28). Ignatius finds the new person at once obedient to the bishop as to Christ and promotes a charismatic understanding of leadership as immediately expressive of Jesus' presence to which the believer must submit. The Gospel of Thomas promotes an interpreting and questioning subject who connects with a living Jesus by engaging with his words and sayings through which interpretation the believer finds the eternal life which all three (John, Ignatius, and Thomas) propose. Each of these texts exhibit in their own way the ascetical agenda appropriate to the kind of spiritual or religious formation that they propound.

Reading these texts, and especially the Gospel of Thomas, as ascetical texts offers an important lens through which to categorize and analyze both the content and the mode of communication within them. The main focus of the Gospel of Thomas revolves about instruction to a reader who in all likelihood functions as a member of a group of readers formed from among other readers. The sayings in the gospel provide a means of instruction to the reader by encouraging the reader to interpret them (Saying 1). These sayings construct and reconstruct the understanding of the identity of the readers/interpreters, they suggest alternative ways of living in society, and they develop an understanding of the world and the wider environment that supports the new way of living. This process constitutes an ascetical system within the text. Reading the text as an ascetical text helps modern readers to understand the import and significance of the way of living promulgated in the gospel; that is, it constitutes a convenient strategy for reading the gospel in order to discover on its own terms what kind of person and what kind of identity the text posits and constructs. As a reading strategy it also assists in understanding how social relationships change for this new identity, and how theological and philosophical systems have been developed to support it.

The ascetical nature of the Gospel of Thomas has long been recognized (Grobel 1961–62; Turner and Montefiore 1962; Quispel 1965; Frend 1967; Koester 1990a: 128; Patterson 1993: 166–68). Early literature, however, identified this asceticism with the negative aspects, with "enkrateia" or the arts of self-control (Quispel 1965; Frend 1967; Richardson 1973; Kaestli 1979): they identified the acts of self-denial as being in themselves ascetical. These negatives included, as one scholar put it, the renunciation of wealth, family, and sexuality (Kaestli 1979: 393). The ascetical orientation of the gospel, moreover, was read as a counterpoint to the gnostic orientation of the sayings, so that the Gospel of Thomas was read as either being "encratite" *or* gnostic (see Frend 1967; Richardson 1973). This choice, in fact, misleads because a text may be both ascetical and gnostic (Richardson 1973: 68). My perspective on asceticism looks not only at the negative performances (rejecting wealth or sexuality), but primarily toward the positive articulation of the new subjectivity that the gospel presents ("becoming a single one," for example). This positive perspective promotes a constructive reading of the text, so that all performances (whether negative or positive) are interpreted in the context of the larger project of creating an alternative identity within a larger and more dominant religious environment.

It may just as well be that, with the emergence of the hierarchical structure of the church as normative, asceticism, with its intense orientation toward the development and articulation of an individual subjectivity, became marginalized and problematized so that not only gnostics, but also professional ascetics emerged as counterpoints to hierarchical structure. This may be seen to be the case beginning with the "widows" in 1 Timothy 5.3–16, and continuing through Athanasius' battle with the ascetic followers of Arius and Hieracas (Elm 1994). What became problematic was not gnosticism, but unmediated and non-hierarchical practices (Brakke 1995) whether educational (as with Hieracas and Athanasius) or spiritual (as with the orthodox monks and Valentinian gnostic Christianity). The Gospel of Thomas certainly falls within the category of ascetic text, and its history in Coptic even identifies its production with a Pachomian ascetic community. Its ascetical orientation may have proven problematic to Christian leaders of the mid-second century and later, but its content shows little, if any, evidence of later gnostic mythology and theology.

The ascetical reading of the Gospel of Thomas provides a more neutral position from which to articulate its theological tendencies and to develop an understanding of the tractate in its own language: the articulation of the specific performances (primarily revolving about interpretation of the sayings), the particular subjectivity (often called "the single one"), the redefinition of familial relationships, the construction of a community awareness through mutual engagement with the sayings, and the positing of a smaller (perhaps esoteric) society within a larger and less aware cosmos. These elements reflect the ascetical and formative dimension of the Gospel of Thomas and they do not necessarily arise in the traditional categories of theological and scholarly research, but rather emerge from a close reading of the text on its own terms in order to move toward the definition of suitable categories for study from within the text itself.

MY PERSPECTIVE ON THE GOSPEL OF THOMAS

This ascetical reading strategy sets the stage for what I have attempted to achieve here. This commentary aims to appreciate the Gospel of Thomas as an example of one variety of an authentic Christianity which seems to have emerged at a critical crossroad of formative Christianity—the same crossroads that produced the Gospel of John and the Letters of Ignatius. I do not intend to make it fit into any of the later categories of orthodoxy or heresy, but to treat it as exemplary of one understanding and articulation of Christian living that was sufficiently important that it was preserved in antiquity and is studied in modern times. Through a close literary reading of the entire text, I aim to develop the theological perspective of the various sayings without bias (again) to later categories of orthodoxy or heresy. This strategy distinguishes the readings that follow from most of the precedent commentaries (Grant and Friedman; Ménard; Kasser; Fieger, for example).

Moreover, I am not interested in constructing the trajectory of Jesus' sayings, nor in writing a history of Jesus, but in constructing the perspectives and theology of the Gospel of Thomas. My focus rests not on the Jesus in these sayings, but in the theological and literary tendencies of the sayings themselves. There are two implications of this: first, that I read the entire corpus and not simply those that have parallels in the Synoptic Sayings Source Q and Paul; and, second, that I focus directly and primarily on the material as it is preserved in the tractate that has survived. That means that I am only interested in this gospel, and not how this gospel relates to other gospel materials or to other writings of early Christianity. There have been many scholars who have noted parallels both canonical, intertestamental, historical, biblical, philosophical, and gnostic; and their works may easily be consulted through any one of the major current surveys of scholarship (see Fallon and Cameron 1988; Patterson 1992; Riley 1994). My aim in writing this commentary is simply to present a consistent, literary analysis of each saying in the order in which they appear in the tractate.

I have not set out to provide a complete survey of pertinent scholarship. Nor have I attempted to engage the entire history of scholarship in argumentation for my perspective on the text. The interested reader may easily access the history of scholarship as well as capable summaries of recent research in review articles which have already been acknowledged. I have incorporated only the scholars whom I have found helpful in opening the text of the Gospel of Thomas to careful reading and study. These scholars, though not always ones with whom I agree, will be acknowledged as the commentary proceeds.

Some studies, however, deserve particular mention here. I have not attempted to reduplicate the recent and thorough work of Stephen Patterson (1993) in his *Gospel of Thomas and Jesus* which explains the relationship of the gospel to the Synoptic Sayings Source Q: his work carefully argues the independence of Thomas and thoroughly explicates the interaction with those synoptic sources. Three works in particular commend themselves for the comparative study of the parables of Jesus in Gospel of Thomas and the synoptic gospels: John Dominic Crossan's *In Parables: The Challenge of the Historical Jesus* (1973), Charles Hedrick's *Parables as Poetic Fictions: The Creative Voice of Jesus* (1994), and (in a more literary theoretical vein) Dan O. Via's *The Parables: Their Literary and Existential Dimension* (1967). These scholars fully explore the relationship of Thomas parables to the synoptic as well as explicating the meaning of the parables in general and in relationship to Jesus.

I have taken the lens provided by the author of this gospel seriously. If a community exists behind these sayings (Lincoln 1977; Riley 1995), it consists of those who have taken the interpretation of these sayings as their primary duty. Since it is an interpretative process that creates the community, that community need not articulate a homogeneous and singular theology. The sayings genre leaves ample room for diversity, disagreement, alternative and resistive interpretations, and even subversive readings by people within the various groups of readers who may not agree with one another. Moreover, these sayings could be used in a variety of organized communities: fourth-century monks could have found in them rich ascetical teaching; gnostic Christians would have found profound esoteric meaning; orthodox Christians might have thrilled to hear the parables without allegorical interpretation. Many people in many different kinds of communities could, and did, read these sayings and interpret them, but they cannot be assumed to share one common theology, perspective, or even interpretation of the sayings.

In my consistent reading, I have focused on the collection of sayings as a complete text. I have not looked toward the development of the material over the course of the period from roughly 60 CE until the dating of the Coptic manuscript, but I have looked at the material as a complete collection from the first decade of the second century CE. I presume that they would have been read as a collection, not as isolated sayings. The sayings, therefore, may be understood to refer internally to one another: a reader may assume that a statement made earlier may be alluded to later in the collection. The text, that is, takes precedence over the individual saying. My intention here is to construct the world from within the text and its sayings. In a sense, my commentary was designed to lay the foundation for subsequent research in the biblical and theological intertextuality of the Gospel of Thomas.

I have especially avoided the designation "gnostic" and any explicit articulation of gnostic myths or theologoumena. The precise meaning of such terms, and their significance for understanding, has become even more clouded since the mid-1970s. There seems no longer to be either a consensus about the definition, nor the referent, nor even the chronology and content of gnosticism. The gnostic character of these sayings needs the same sort of re-evaluation as the entire study of gnosticism in early Christianity. I have tried to explain the sayings without invoking either that body of research or that body of mythology.

Only occasionally have I introduced the language of asceticism into my explanation (even though I believe it to be an ascetical text). The elements of my definition (such as performances, dominant and minority groupings, the construction of a subjectivity, attention to alternative social relationships, and attention to the construction of a symbolic universe) have provided an important lens through which the sayings have been read, but I have resisted making it the heart of my own reading.

I have begun with the Greek fragments from Oxyrhynchus. These have recently received little attention in the scholarly literature, and they have been virtually ignored by the popular press in their discussions of the Gospel of Thomas. I present these Greek fragments as a "Window on Thomas" to assist people from outside the theological disciplines as well as the general public to engage with the sayings of Jesus and their particular perspective on a limited corpus before proceeding to the fuller Coptic text. The Coptic text develops those literary and theological themes in greater detail.

The importance of the Gospel of Thomas to early Christianity is actually only beginning to be understood. The previous work has brought us all to the point that there is some need for a fresh start, a new and vigorous reading of these sayings. This commentary will, I hope, help to clear the way of old detritus, while also opening new avenues of interpretation. In the end, I hope my commentary establishes this gospel as a serious and articulate historical-theological source that not only deserves our respect, but also deserves to become part of the unofficial canon of texts studied to create a history of primitive and formative Christianity before the Christianization of the Roman empire.

Chapter 2

A window on the Gospel of Thomas: the Greek fragment texts
The evidence of P. Oxy 654, P. Oxy 1, and P. Oxy 655

It is not easy to pick up the Gospel of Thomas and to begin to read it with comprehension and understanding. This Gospel, a collection of sayings of Jesus, presents a very different world to anyone who would understand early Christianity–a world sufficiently foreign to contemporary religious and philosophical discourse as to baffle and confuse the modern readers. It is for people today a kind of unprecedented conversation in which they are ill-equipped to participate. This "window" provides an entry into the world, theology, ethics and values, methods, and interests of the people who originally invested their energies in interpreting and understanding these sayings, so that it might provide modern readers with sufficient skills to enter not only the conversation *in* the Gospel, but also a conversation *with* it. This "window" allows the new reader of this material a short and relatively easy course in grappling with these difficult sayings.

This section, which I call a "window," uses the Greek fragments of the Gospel of Thomas. These fragmentary documents of various sayings of Jesus were discovered in Oxyrhynchus, an ancient city in the Egyptian desert 125 miles south of Cairo and about ten miles west of the Nile River (in modern times the city is called Behnesa), during an archaeological excavation. In 1897 and in 1904, these Greek papyri were published by B. P. Grenfell and A. S. Hunt. (Papyrus is an ancient form of paper made from the papyrus plant; in scholarly discourse, a papyrus (plural papyri) is a document written on a sheet of papyrus paper.) Until the discovery of the Coptic version of the Gospel of Thomas at Nag Hammadi, these sayings were not known to be part of a particular gospel, but were believed to be fragments of some lost gospel. When the Coptic version was discovered, however, these Greek texts were identified as an earlier Greek version of the same later Coptic text. These Greek fragments are identified in order of their publication as:

Papyrus Oxyrhynchus 1 (P. Oxy 1), Papyrus Oxyrhynchus 654 (P. Oxy 654), and Papyrus Oxyrhynchus 655 (P. Oxy 655). For convenience, I also identify their equivalents among the numbered sayings of the Coptic version from Nag Hammadi which have been assigned verse numbers as a convenient way to refer to the text.

The Greek fragments have been chosen for a number of reasons. First, there are not many of them, and, therefore, they constitute a small and consistent corpus of material that can be mastered more readily than the larger corpus of 114 sayings found in the Coptic collection. These twenty sayings and their Prologue present a manageable small collection for introduction and initial study, while presenting a version sufficiently close to the Coptic text to bridge knowledge from one version to the next.

Second, the Greek fragments are the earliest text we have of the Gospel of Thomas, but, because they are fragmentary, they have been relegated a lesser place in recent study than the more complete Coptic sayings. Scholars were quite excited about them when they were first discovered, and there has been much written about them, but they are not generally well-known outside scholarly circles, nor have they (unlike the Coptic Gospel of Thomas) received much current attention. So they are early, relatively unknown, and in a more accessible language. Their chronological priority commends them for special attention separate from the later Coptic translation and edition of the sayings.

And third, each of these papyrus fragments represents a cultural artifact of someone who, or some community that, found the particular sayings collected on those papyrus sheets important and significant, at least enough to copy and preserve them in writing. Their fragmentary state should not deflect their cultural significance: they represent distinct collections of material that (when compared to the more complete Coptic text) provide a window into the way these sayings were distributed and disseminated.

After working through this short course in the Greek window onto the sayings of Jesus from the Gospel of Thomas, the reader should be equipped to proceed to the larger Coptic collection. Some, however, may find in the "window" enough to satisfy themselves, and, therefore, may simply read the Coptic passages and interpretations which pique their interest. Others may find themselves wanting to understand the Coptic collection in greater detail. The window is open to either use.

P. Oxy 654.1–3a [Coptic Prologue]

These are the [secret] sayings [that] the living Jesus spoke, [and Judas, who is] also <called> Thomas, [recorded].

This brief Prologue orients the reader to what follows. It is a kind of "title page," a marketing device for letting readers know what is to follow. The title page, or Prologue, relates that the reader may expect sayings. Collections of sayings were common in antiquity (Kloppenborg 1987: 263–316): these collections provided a means for training people in specific kinds of education (as in scribal schools), or in philosophical traditions, or in mystical knowledge. Sayings, or aphorisms, were a common educational device.

The fact that these are secret sayings adds some specificity. Their secrecy at once explains the audience and the mode of expression. The audience, the proposed readership, the buyers, are not common people, or just anyone. These sayings have been collected for a particular, and entitled readership–one capable of entering into this conversation (Koester 1990a: 124–28). They are esoteric because they are not written as discursive descriptions or as a philosophical tractate, but as sayings. Sayings demand that the audience puzzle over their meaning, and, therefore, only the capable will understand them. Secrecy also defines the mode of expression: these sayings are difficult and challenging elements to puzzle about. The sayings do not speak plainly, or directly, but in a hidden way, a mysterious way about things that are at once obvious and riddling. These secret sayings of the living Jesus, then, present difficult and perplexing material to a select group of people (Kaestli 1979: 389).

The "living" Jesus presents these sayings. The sayings speak not of dead knowledge, nor of ancient knowledge, nor even of eternal knowledge, but a *present* knowledge. Jesus lives within the loosely confederated group in which these sayings operate; whoever puzzles through these difficult sayings encounters a living voice, a real person, speaking to them. This evokes presences, immediacy, life in a context in which the study of the sayings evokes the living presence of the speaker of the sayings.

The title page also mentions the recorder of the sayings, Judas, who is also known as Thomas. This identification of the recorder provides the lens through which the sayings of the living Jesus are viewed. Jesus does not speak directly, but through the recordings of Thomas. Thomas defines what the readers will know; Thomas determines what voice Jesus has by presenting some sayings, and, presumably, not recording or transmitting others. The readers hear Jesus, but that Jesus has been carefully defined (or edited) by Judas/Thomas. That particular lens constructs a pattern of authority in a very subtle way: Jesus speaks as a living presence, that living presence depends upon Thomas' recording, the readers' understanding depends upon Thomas. The readers of these secret sayings become followers of Thomas' understanding of the secret sayings of Jesus. The readers have been constituted as a "community" of people following the understanding of Jesus recorded by Judas/ Thomas.

P. Oxy 654.3b–5 [Coptic Saying 1]

And he said, "[Whoever discovers the interpretation] of these sayings will not taste [death]."

This saying presents the marketing goal: immortality. The speaker's identity remains ambivalent. Thomas could be presenting the readers with the rationale for his recording of these sayings of Jesus: he does not want the readers to experience death. Or it may be the living Jesus who presents the goal: anyone who understands the sayings of the living Jesus will never experience death. Either way, the ultimate aim remains some kind of life without death.

The deathlessness, however, comes from discovering the interpretation of the sayings. The achievement of the goal depends upon the readers', or, as they might be called now, the seekers', finding the right significance to these sayings. Not to experience death requires discovering the interpretation. The community that was posited in the Prologue, the one consisting of those who listen to the secret sayings and puzzle over their meaning, stands as the arbiter of this state without death, because interpretation involves a community's understanding and tradition of interpretation of the text. Those who enter this interpretative confederation will never die, they will be like the living Jesus speaking in the community, they will perpetuate forever the interpretation of Jesus which Thomas has recorded.

P. Oxy 654.5–9 [Coptic Saying 2]

[Jesus says], "Those who [seek] should not stop [seeking until] they find. [2]When they find, [they will be disturbed. [3]When they are] disturbed, they will rule, [4]and [when they rule], they will [rest]."

This saying identifies the readers with the seekers in the interpretative process. It advances an unusual progression: seeking, finding, being disturbed, ruling, and resting. The saying links the stages in a process that evolves through various stages: seeking and finding, finding and being disturbed, being disturbed and ruling, ruling and resting. The process is interactive, overlapping, dynamic. Seeking and resting define the two extreme poles in what appears to be a logical sequence (to seek to rest makes sense on its own). The mediate processes, however, surprise with their details. Finding follows seeking, but does not end the process; finding unsettles, rather than settling, the person seeking. That state of disturbance, moreover, does not debilitate the seeker, but empowers the seeker to rule. The progression toward understanding creates a complex process that inverts logical order so as to create a new understanding of formation. These seekers become empowered by their searching and finding, their disturbance and their ruling, and in that empowerment, they find rest, equilibrium, solitude.

The themes articulated here form the core of themes of the entire collection of sayings. The recurrence of rest, empowerment, disturbance, finding and seeking, punctuates the sayings throughout, so that such themes instruct us about the sort of goals and interests of the people who take these sayings seriously. These themes, in other words, provide the intellectual, spiritual, and emotional impetus to the engagement with the interpretation of these sayings.

P. Oxy 654.9–21 [Coptic Saying 3]

Jesus says, "[If] your leaders [say to you, 'Look,] the <Father's> imperial rule is in the sky,' then the birds of the sky [will precede you. [2]If they say] that it is under the earth, then the fish of the sea [will precede] you. [3]And [the <Father's> imperial rule] is inside you [and outside <you>. [4]You who] know [yourselves] will find this. [And when you] know yourselves, [you will understand that] you are [children] of the [living] Father. [5][But if] you do [not] know yourselves, [you live] in [poverty], and you are [poverty]."

The community these sayings posit experiences itself as fully empowered: its members do not need guidance. In fact, as this saying indicates, leaders often point seekers in the wrong direction, leading them to the heavens or the seas where nothing significant happens, and where other creatures more logically would function. So this saying encourages the seekers to ignore outside leadership and follow themselves into a kind of self-knowledge that reveals their adoption by God. For these seekers, self-direction marks true guidance: that which most leaders find only in objectification and exteriorization, the true seeker finds both within the self and outside the self. The interiority of the discovery of the rule of God correlates (and presumably precedes) any exterior experience of it. The desired reign of God cannot be located only outwardly (in the sky or under the earth), but also inwardly. Nothing circumscribes the rule of God or objectifies it: it is both within and without the person.

The statement about the interiority and exteriority of the rule of God leads to the development of a contrast based upon self-knowledge. The interior and exterior reality of the rule will be found by those who know themselves. The finding now becomes identified with self-knowledge, and that self-knowledge results in the self-understanding of the seeker as "a child of the living Father." The adoption by God emerges from a process of discovery of the self and its relationship with the rule of God. This beneficent situation contrasts markedly with its alternative. For those who do not know themselves, who have not discovered their true selves in relationship to the rule of God, they "live in poverty," and in fact become that poverty. The process of self-discovery, that is, does not remain neutral so that one gains an increment of knowledge or understanding which adorns an otherwise rich life. Rather, the knowledge itself becomes the wealth and its lack becomes poverty. The personal stakes for the seeker revolve about either a wealth or a poverty, becoming rich or poor. The starkly drawn contrast again provides a window into the emotional and psychological dynamic of those who read and interpret these sayings.

P. Oxy 654.21–27 [Coptic Saying 4]

[Jesus says], "A [person old in days] won't hesitate to ask a [little child seven days] old about the place of [life, and] that person will [live]. [2]For many of the [first] will be [last, and] the last first [3]and [will become one and the same] [SV: will become one]."

I have changed the translation here to conform with that of the critical edition (Attridge 1989: 126). Scholars Version simply says "become one." The Greek word *katantao* implies an arrival at, or result in, something, so that the sense here is that the old man and the young child will arrive at unity, or end up as one.

So much of the practice of interpreting these sayings revolves about inversion. This saying highlights two inversions: the preference of elders over youth; the priority of first over last. The way of life envisioned in this saying reverses the common social priorities, so that elders seek the advice of youth about the locus of life. The inversion extends, however, not simply to the discovery of the place, the locus of life, but the relationship confers life on the elder, so that it is the elder who finds and receives life through the young child. The specific situation of elder and youth becomes a maxim, "many of the first will be last, and the last first," which summarizes the experience of inversion.

But the experience of this inversion goes one step further. It is not only that the elder will seek out the youth, or that the last will be first, but that all of these result in some kind of unity. The final phrase "and become one and the same" points toward more than inversion, rather, to a process of collapsing opposites (such as old and young, first and last) into one. The distinctions ultimately resolve themselves into a state of non-distinction, plurality and opposites are transformed into some sort of unity.

The theme of unity combines with the rhetoric of inversion to pattern the experience in such a way that it does not operate simply in the mind as a mental construct, nor in the inverted society as a social relationship transgressive of societal norms, but rather it functions as an indicator of the meaning of the search. Those in these sayings who search will find themselves in this socially transgressive mode that will lead to the overcoming of the opposites, to the unity of self that fulfills.

P. Oxy 654.27–31 [Coptic Saying 5]

Jesus says, "[Know what is in front of] your face, and [what is hidden] from you will be disclosed [to you. [2]For there is nothing] hidden that [wo]n't [become] exposed, [3]and <nothing> buried that [won't be raised]."

This saying links knowledge and revelation in such a way that knowledge precedes revelation. For the seekers knowledge of the visible leads to revelation of the invisible and hidden. Knowledge leads to revelation and disclosure, so that the seekers in these sayings understand both apparent and revealed realities. This saying at once posits the existence of hidden, undisclosed things as well as visible and apparent ones: it speaks of both exoteric and esoteric understanding. For the one who has entered into the process of interpretation of these sayings, all the hidden things will be made manifest, but presumably for others, for those who have not entered into this process, they will remain hidden and undisclosed.

In a strategy common to collections of sayings, the two final verses of the saying have been attached by linking common words: the "nothing hidden" of the second verse attaches to the "what is hidden" of the first, while the "nothing buried" attaches to the "nothing hidden." The saying, then, forms an interlocking connection of three elements which develops a constellation of gradually less related themes. The second verse appears to provide a summary of the first saying, but that summary does not have anything to say about knowledge; it speaks only of revelation. The linking of the verses has caused the meaning to shift to a general statement that everything hidden will be disclosed. The final verse has nothing in common with the previous two, except the link that the word "nothing" provides. This last saying (that nothing buried will not be raised) makes a general statement parallel to the form of the previous statement, but now extending that discourse about revelation to include burial and resurrection.

The linking of these sayings in this fashion creates a connection larger than any one of the sayings. In this saying knowledge, revelation, and resurrection become mirrors of one another in a narrative created by their combination. The saying guides the seeker to understand that knowledge leads to revelation, because everything will be disclosed to the one who knows the invisible, and that it leads to resurrection, because the dead body which was made invisible by burial will become visible at the resurrection. A simple statement about paying attention to apparent things has emerged as a way to discuss a performative theology of revelation and of resurrection.

P. Oxy 654.32–40 [Coptic Saying 6]

[His disciples] ask him [and] say, "How [should we] fast? [How should] we [pray]? How [should we give charity]? What [diet] should [we] observe? [2]Jesus says, "[Don't lie, [3]and] don't do [what] you [hate, [4]because all things are apparent before] truth. [5][After all, there is nothing] hidden [that won't be exposed]."

This saying does not cohere. The disciples' question regarding ascetic and pious practices receives no specific answer. Instead, Jesus' response offers two sayings only tenuously connected to one another: the first saying relates a moralistic imperative not to lie or to do what one hates; the second offers an explanatory truism repeating the theological principle about revelation of the previous saying. The seemingly haphazard construction of the saying displays the compositional method of sayings collections in which (as in the previous saying) words interlock to conjoin sayings in order to force the seekers to produce a meaning to explain their correlation, or (as in this saying) a series of completely unrelated sayings are grouped together randomly perhaps based on the connection between verse 5 of this saying ("nothing hidden that won't be exposed") to the previous saying. In such a collection, this stylistic demands the construction of a narrative or some overarching theory in the reader's mind in order to make meaning of the conjoined, but thematically unrelated, sayings. The final meaning emerges from the reader's own construction which in turn is based upon each of the three elements and their correlation.

The first element questions the appropriateness of observing pious and ascetical practices: fasting, prayer, alms-giving, and diet (or lifestyle). These performances stand in the saying only as questions; they receive no declarative treatment or attention in Jesus' response. As floating questions, the saying neither rejects nor advocates these practices, but rather it problematizes such pious and ascetical performances. The moral injunction ("don't lie and don't do what you hate") makes this problematizing negative, because the juxtaposition of the question with this statement as the apparent answer implies that moral rectitude, an ethical posture that reveals the truth of ethical behavior, replaces pious and ascetical performances. The combination of this moral stance with the general principle expressed in verse 5 ("After all, there is nothing hidden that won't be exposed") universalizes the superiority of that moral stance over pious and ascetic acts; the interior, moral dynamic along with every other hidden dynamic of human existence, will be exposed.

The sequence of statements produced here suggests that pious acts and asceticism have little value in comparison with the proper moral posture, because that posture displays the true interior love and worth of the seeker. The interior performances of telling the truth and of only doing what one loves take precedence over external performances, because the interior ultimately will be revealed and published. No opportunity for hypocrisy and false piety remains for the true seeker. That message, however, follows from the combination of the three elements, not from explicit statements in the three elements of the saying.

P. Oxy 654.40–42 [Coptic Saying 7]

[... "Blessed] [SV: "Lucky] is [the lion that the human will eat, so
that the lion] will become [human. ²And damned [SV: foul] is the
human] that [the lion will eat...]."

A note on the translation: in an attempt to give the sayings a colloquial
and modern sound, the translators of the Scholars Version have used
the dichotomy of "lucky" and "foul." I prefer a clearer dichotomy
which the Greek text provides between "blessed" (Greek: *makarios*) and
"damned" (Greek: *anathema*).

The principle underlying this saying relates eating to identity and to
transformation: creatures that are eaten literally become those who eat
them within a strictly demarcated hierarchy of being, and, therefore,
caution must be exercised with regard to eating so that status in the
hierarchy either increases or remains static. The devoured lion becomes
blessed because, according to the principle and the hierarchy of being, it
would become human, that is, the lion would ascend to the higher
status. The negligent human whom the lion eats is damned because the
human will, according to the same principles, become a lion and be
degraded in the hierarchy of being (although this is based on the
assumption that the sayings are parallel in the fragmented papyrus text).

The playful language hides the complexity of the relationship of
eating to identity and transformation. The readers trip over the
playfulness into understanding that the world's hierarchy of being,
including animals, all strive upward, toward the higher forms of life.
Humans cannot assume their unchallenged and stable place in that
hierarchy: reckless people will find themselves demoted, devoured,
dead, while the vigilant will seize the opportunity to jump ahead. Under
this playfulness lies a strictly understood hierarchy that transcends
human pride and recognizes that all living creatures strive upward.

P. Oxy 655(d) [Coptic Saying 24]

³[...]"There [is a light within a person] of light, [and it shines on
the whole] world. [If it does not shine], it is [dark]."

This saying presents a theological truth that links illumination to
missionary witness. The light found within the person passes on to
illuminate the world. This light links the inner person and the world in a
process of illumination. The source of the light, however, remains the
person. Light does not come from the world, or from outside, to the

person, but from within the person to the world. The missionary impetus emerges from within the person and moves toward all the rest of the world: the missionary motivation does not occur by command (as in the Great Commission of Matthew 28.16–20), or even by dramatic external revelations (as for Paul in Galatians 1.11–12), but rather from the light existing within the person. Although this saying assumes the strict hierarchy of light, to human, and to world, the human still mediates that illumination to the world so the human being effects illumination in the world, and, therefore, retains an increment of value.

Two important themes meet in this saying: the orientation and valuation of light, and the high regard for the human being. These sayings tend not to deprecate human ability or status: those people capable of understanding and interpreting receive positive and enthusiastic treatment as people characterized as being filled with light. The light, and the presence of the light within them, marks the superior status of humanity in these sayings. Some people, however, do not exhibit the capacity for light, or freedom, or interpretation and they receive negative appraisal: the disciples find themselves frequently in this category.

P. Oxy 1(*verso*).1–4 [Coptic Saying 26]

[2][...] "then you will see well enough to remove the sliver from your friend's eye."

This fragment preserves only the second half of the saying because the papyrus itself has survived in very poor condition. The Coptic version relates this saying in its entirety: see the commentary on the Coptic for a fuller analysis (page 99).

This fragment, however, presents important instruction, for it argues that the seekers must prepare themselves first before they are capable of assisting their friends. The saying assumes no judgment between the friends, no animosity or hostility, but simply the ability, having cleansed and purged themselves, for friends to assist their friends: the issue revolves about the seekers' ability to improve their vision in order to assist others. The seekers' selves do not take priority over the friends, and collaboration requires activity for preparation. The Coptic version fills out the saying in its entirety, and its significance will be discussed there.

P. Oxy 1(*verso*).4–11 [Coptic Saying 27]

Jesus says, "If you do not fast from the world, you will not find God's domain. [2]If you do not observe the sabbath day as a sabbath day, you will not see the Father."

Note on translation: The translation here needs some comment. Scholars Version reads "fast from the world" while Attridge's (1989:127) translation reads, "fasting as regards the world." The Greek has an accusative of respect, so that, quite literally it would read: "fasting with respect to the world."

Sayings collections, such as found here, follow no set pattern of topical arrangement. Subjects merge and emerge fluidly, and often display differences of nuance and interest in the new environment, because the collections construct their meaning, not in the discursive relationship of sentence to sentence, saying to saying, but in the readers' or hearers' interpretation and puzzlement over each saying. Meaning emerges as much from "in between" the sayings, as from within them.

The question of fasting arises again. Some sayings reject the traditional ascetical practices such as fasting (see Saying 6, for example); here, however, the saying reinterprets fasting and connects it to another traditional pious act, the keeping of the sabbath. As with most of these sayings, there is a twist, an inversion, and revisioning that repositions the topic.

This saying posits that it is the world that satiates, and that true fasting functions in relationship not to food, but to the world. The seekers must carefully regulate their "intake" of the world in order to be able to find God's domain. The substitution of "the world" for "food" in the matter of fasting deflects attention away from the common understanding of fasting as the regulation of food and underscores the problematic status of the world among these particular seekers. Those who carefully regulate their engagement in the world will be equipped to find God's domain.

In this context, the statement about the sabbath begins to make sense. As a sign "sabbath" signifies rest, conversation with God, and obedience to the laws of God which take precedence over worldly activity. In this context, "sabbath" also articulates the "fasting from the world," since both advocate withdrawal and disengagement in order to focus upon God, the law, or spiritual matters. So then, for these seekers, observance of the sabbath properly as a sabbath will lead to the vision of God, but failure properly to observe the sabbath perpetuates engagement in the world. "Fasting with respect to the world" and "observing the sabbath day as a sabbath day" constitute equivalent signs of self-regulation with respect to worldly activities.

The mode of expression renders the sayings dramatically provocative. The substitution of expected categories with unexpected ones, as well as the juxtaposition of positive statements about pious acts with statements problematizing pious acts, provokes the readers and the seekers into thinking subversively. The provocative nature of the discourse, that is, seems designed to induce a certain stance toward the world and reality, one not dependent upon the understanding alone, but upon an experience of understanding elicited through provocation.

P. Oxy 1(*verso*).11–21 [Coptic Saying 28]

Jesus says, "I took my stand in the midst of the world, and I appeared to them in flesh. [2]I found them all drunk, and I did not find any of them thirsty. [3]My soul aches for the children of humanity, because they are blind in their hearts and [do not] see, [for...]."

Most of the sayings in this collection of sayings do not provide self-referential information about the speaker of the sayings. In this saying, however, Jesus discloses his understanding of himself and of his mission as a mystagogue, a divine figure who has entered the world in order to lead others into the divine realm. This mystagogue stands in the midst of the world–a world that these sayings seriously problematize, and the mystagogue appears to the world "in flesh," bodily,–again a status this community has problematized as lower on the hierarchy of being than things spiritual. Jesus announces that he stood in this problematized world.

The expression "took my stand" invokes a particular kind of entrance into the world and into the flesh, because it does not speak in the language of human generation or in the traditional language of divine figures who descend into the world. Jesus simply relates that "he stood" in the world and appeared bodily, employing an opaque metaphor for his position. The metaphor implies an increment of distance, in that Jesus does not say metaphorically that "he entered" the world nor that he "became flesh," but rather that he "took [his] stand" so that his relationship to the world denotes a solid presence, but without involvement. This distance, moreover, connotes an increment of hostility: Jesus remains one outside, unencumbered by apparent reality (but not appearance), and a kind of alien guide for those in the world (Jonas 1963: 48–99 explores these and the following themes).

What Jesus found revolves about two metaphors. The first characterizes people in the world as drunk, people who have overindulged in their engagement in the world to the point that they have lost their senses. Jesus balances this metaphor with an equally damning one: they were not thirsty. Not only were these people satiated and deluded, they did not yearn for the things that Jesus the mystagogue could provide. The readers and interpreters of these sayings would understand these negative characterizations as applying to other people, the majority of people who do not share the passion for these sayings and their meaning. By a reverse logic, the seekers in these sayings would understand themselves as those who are thirsty and sober, a small group of people who have retained their senses and their direction. The majority of people "in the midst of the world" do not belong to this select group.

The rarity of those who thirst causes Jesus anguish. "My soul aches for the children of humanity, because they are blind in their hearts and do not see. . . . " The drunken and satiated world ought not simply to be left to its own devices: its decayed status causes anguish for Jesus, and presumably for all the seekers, and reveals its inherent blindness to the possibilities that Jesus the mystagogue holds out.

This saying shows the complexity of the world in which these sayings operate. The "world" remains a highly problematized and delusory place that thwarts seekers' attempt to find their true lives, and yet the world cannot simply be dismissed as insignificant. Jesus takes his stand "in the midst of the world" and aches for the blind people in it, but he does not reject the world. The world at once locates the place of enlightenment and the problem which enlightenment solves. These metaphors and mythological narratives emphasize the destructive nature of the world, drunkenness, and satiation.

P. Oxy 1(*recto*).22 [Coptic Saying 29]

³[. . . comes to dwell in this] poverty.

This very fragmentary piece (similar to Saying 3) draws attention to the theme of "poverty" in these sayings. Poverty describes both an ontological status, that is, it describes the state of a person's being in which lack of riches (whether actual or metaphorical or both) or resources dominate. Poverty also describes a social status within the world: the poor are those people who have identified themselves with others who engage fully in the decayed world. Poverty metaphorizes the world and those who live in it. That metaphorization, however, lacks the sort of binary opposition found in such opposites as spiritual/physical, worldly/heavenly, and sets out the possibility of those people who dwell in poverty rising to dwell in richness. Poverty does not relegate the poor to a permanently lesser status, but describes the reality of those identified with the world or committed to living in it.

P. Oxy 1(*recto*).23–30 [Coptic Sayings 30 and 77b]

[Jesus says], "Where there are [three, they are without] God, [2]and where there is only [one], I say, I am with that one. [3]Lift up the stone, and you will find me there. [4]Split a piece of wood, and I am there."

The playfulness of language forms an important part of the interpretative strategy of this text. Often that playfulness also includes inversion. Verses 1–2 here operate in that way. It seems to be an inversion of a saying of Jesus found in the Matthean special material (Matthew 18.19–20): "Again, truly I tell you, if two of you agree on earth about anything you ask, it will be done for you by my Father in heaven. For where two or three are gathered in my name, I am there among them." The Thomas saying offers a severe critique of that Matthean theology. Whereas the Matthean saying of Jesus emphasizes the collaboration of members of the community following Jesus by confirming and guaranteeing the success of their collaboration by God, Thomas subverts that collaboration and establishes the person who is "only one." Thomas argues that Jesus' true presence resides *not* with the two or three together, but with the person who is "only one." I would place the Thomas saying chronologically later than the Matthew saying, so that it reflects, not a Synoptic Sayings Source Q parallel, but an intra-community argument about the conditions for the presence of Jesus. The lifted stone and split wood further emphasize that the community collaboration is useless: the solitary need not collaborate, but may simply lift a stone or split a piece of wood to find the presence of Jesus confirmed. The Thomas saying successfully inverts the meaning and the significance of the Matthean tradition.

One of the most important articulations of the subjectivity of the seekers or readers of the Thomas collection of sayings is that of "solitary" or "singular one" or "one alone." This designation does not deny the presence or force of community (recall that interpretation is by nature communal), but rather fully empowers the solitary as the basis of enlightened living. The community evolves from an association of individuals who have heard the living Jesus, interpreted the sayings, and who associate with others of similar disposition and knowledge. That understanding of community explains the reversal of the Matthean saying: loose association, even in the name of God, does not lead to revelation, but rather revelation and enlightenment lead to the association of one individual with another.

P. Oxy 1(*recto*).30–35 [Coptic Saying 31]

Jesus says, "No prophet is welcome on his home turf; [2]doctors don't cure those who know them."

Almost as a gnomic correlative to the isolationism of the previous saying, this saying not only underscores that isolation, but also indicates that even if the seekers wanted to be recognized in their familiar communities they could not be. In the form of a "wise saying," Jesus uses the examples of an unwelcome prophet and of a well-known doctor as metaphors to characterize the life-situation and self-understanding of his listeners. They are unwelcome in their own familiar places, and they are too familiar to their community to be effective. The saying suggests that those who understand these sayings become a different breed of person while continuing to live in their own communities, and that simultaneous familiarity and estrangement isolates them. The original itinerancy of the early Jesus people has been recontextualized in these Greek fragments further to construct the subjectivity of the solitary (Patterson 1993: 158–70), so that the isolation that at an earlier time in the Jesus movement resulted from itinerancy has become a social isolation of those different from the common people among whom they live.

Without any narrative context as is provided in the synoptic parallels, this saying has no self-referential quality for Jesus, but constitutes an instruction to the disciples. Jesus describes the isolation of his followers as prophets rejected by those who know them and as doctors refusing to heal their acquaintances. Recognition functions in both images, but in one as the basis of rejection of the followers, and in the other as the basis of refusal of salvation and assistance. In both cases, Jesus problematizes the presupposed relationship of the followers with the communities in which they were known prior to their association with Jesus.

P. Oxy 1(*recto*).36–41 [Coptic Saying 32]

Jesus says, "A city built on top of a high hill and fortified can neither fall nor be hidden."

Jesus metaphorizes the movement as a city with two primary characteristics: it has been built on an elevated site and it has been securely established. The need for fortification suggests that this city has enemies who wish to attack it; the fact that it is built on an elevated site suggests a social, political, and religious superiority to other cities in addition to its strategic advantage over opponents. This metaphor correlates to the message of the previous two statements, and thereby suggests that even in isolation and solitude, invulnerability and visibility follow Jesus' seekers. The loosely configured community posited in these sayings lives in an elevated place: their social and religious location demands that others look up to them. The community operates as a city, an enclosed and reasonably self-sufficient environment that provides a haven and care for those who live in them. The fortification indicates that the community retains an increment of protection against opponents.

If these fortified persons are the ones who have come to the understanding of the sayings, they have been placed in a high and visible place. Their understanding and knowledge has not only elevated them, but made them invulnerable while at the same time making their position in the world visible and plain to see. Those achievements remain secure and public, the benefits from them cannot be removed, nor can the effects of them remain private. The solitary ones, then, have a public status, even though they remain socially isolated.

P. Oxy 1(*recto*).41–42 [Coptic Saying 33]

Jesus says, "<What> you hear in one of your ears [proclaim ...]."

This fragmentary saying points toward the public nature of the teaching. The reader does not retain the understanding of these sayings, this knowledge cannot be hidden on the top of the high hill as an esoteric knowledge, but rather must be proclaimed. The riddling nature of these sayings and their interpretation demands that the readers/seekers publish (literally making public) the knowledge gained.

The public nature of the proclamation ostensibly contradicts the riddling aspect of the interpretation of the sayings. That contradiction presumes that the loosely configured community posited in these sayings remains closed to outsiders. The group may, however, have strong preconditions and requirements for participation, while remaining generally accessible to anyone who desires the rigor and vigor of their way of life.

P. Oxy 655, col.i.1–17 [Coptic Saying 36]

[Jesus says, "Don't fret], from morning [to evening nor] from [evening to] morning, [about] your [food]–what [you're going] to eat, [or] about [your clothing], what you [are going] to wear. [2][You're much] better than the lilies, which don't card and never [spin]. [3]As for you, when you have no garment, what [are you going to put] on? [4]Who could add to your life span? That same one will give you your garment."

The core of this saying (with a parallel in the Synoptic Sayings Source Q 12.22–27) enjoins the followers of Jesus not to worry about food or clothing. In the present context, however, the focus of the saying revolves about the provision of a garment, rather than the itinerant dependence of the Jesus people upon the hospitality which God provides. The verses following the analogy to the lilies all point toward the question of the garment which will be provided. The referent of the "garment" eludes discovery, and there have been many theories about its meaning, but it is clear that the granting of a garment implies more than simply having clothing. The garment seems to have some more evocative, definite reference. In a later monastic environment it could easily have referred to the habit worn by monks; to the newly baptized, it could refer to their baptismal garment; to those in the nuptial chamber, it could refer to the bridal clothing. In any event, God provides the solitaries with their garments, and, therefore, the seekers ought not to worry.

P. Oxy 655, col.i.17–col.ii.1 [Coptic Saying 37]

His disciples say to him, "When will you be revealed to us, and when shall we see you?" [2]He says, "When you strip without being ashamed, [3][. . . and you will not be afraid]."

The discussion of the garment, or of the negation of garments, continues in this saying. Here we have the narrator's voice again, setting forth the disciples and quoting their question. That narrative interjection widens the horizon, again: the readers are no longer simply listening to the conversation between Jesus and his followers, we are now given specific information about who those followers are. The disciples ask a legitimate question, one that bears some increment of irony in this context. Jesus has been speaking, giving instruction, relaying information, and yet the disciples have not yet understood. Even in a sayings collection, it should be obvious that the revelation occurs in the sayings: the producers of manuscripts were quite aware of this, because that literary presence was the way that scribes were trained. So their question rings hollow, as does Jesus' response. The scribe writing this sequence has just copied the saying that God will provide the garment, and now Jesus is telling those who do not understand to strip off their clothing and not feel shame.

The environment created by these sayings has become a revelatory one: the sayings reveal the truth to those readers and those seekers who have engaged in the interpretative process. The disciples experience fear in their inability to understand; their clothing and the social garments in which they are wrapped prevent them from embracing the process.

P. Oxy 655, col.ii.2–11 [Coptic Saying 38]

[Jesus says, "Often you have desired to hear these sayings of mine], and [you have no one else from whom to hear <them>]. ^{2}And [there will come days when you will seek me and you will not find me]."

This saying relates a very positive message. The readers/seekers have been hearing the words spoken by the present Jesus, the living Jesus who alone can speak these words. The saying underscores both the desire of those seekers who yearn for understanding and the central role Jesus plays in providing this understanding. Yearning and listening define the role of the reader and seeker in these sayings.

Eventually those who find that for which they search will no longer need these sayings to guide them, they will seek for Jesus and not find him, not because he is hidden (they have the text of his sayings, anyway), but because they will no longer be dependent upon these sayings. The latter part of this saying, in other words, anticipates a time when the text itself, the collection of sayings, will no longer be necessary for finding Jesus, because seeking in the text becomes redundant to those who have achieved understanding. They will seek him there and no longer find him there.

P. Oxy 655, col.ii.11–23 [Coptic Saying 39]

[Jesus says, "The Pharisees and the scholars] have [taken the keys] of [knowledge; they themselves have] hidden [them. [2]Neither] have [they] entered, [nor] have they [allowed those who want to] enter [to do so. [3]As for you, be as sly] as [snakes and as] simple [as doves]."

This reference to "Pharisees and scholars," or "Scribes and Pharisees" as they are traditionally designed, stands as one of the very few references to specific figures in the entire collection, joining the more dominant reference to the disciples, Judas/Thomas, Matthew, Salome, Mary, and Peter. This saying stereotypically characterizes the "Pharisees and scholars" as "other." Some early Christian literatures present them as the foil to true believers and right practices. In a strategy that may reflect a highly ironic perspective, these traditional enemies of truth hold the keys to knowledge; the saying reverses the early Christian stereotype of the Pharisees and scholars so that now they possess the keys to knowledge–keys, unfortunately, which they have hidden. The irony continues in that though they have the keys to knowledge, they have neither attained it themselves, nor enabled others to acquire it. They thwart themselves and others in acquiring the very knowledge to which they hold the keys.

This situation constitutes a warning to the seekers in these sayings. The "As for you" indicates that the prior statements describe others not included in this direct address. True seekers receive warning to be shrewd and simple.

Chapter 3

The Coptic version of the Gospel of Thomas

The evidence of Nag Hammadi Codex II, Tractate 2

The Coptic version of the Gospel of Thomas consists of 114 sayings written in excellent Sahidic Coptic, a dialect of Egyptian. This Gospel continued to be translated and published from the time of its composition (c. 100–110CE) until this final, known Coptic version was produced in the fourth century CE. The Greek fragments and the existence of this Coptic version attest to this history of its translation and production. We are fortunate that whoever hid it in jars in the desert near Nag Hammadi thought it worthy of preservation.

The Gospel of Thomas is the second tractate bound into the second codex (or book). The other tractates bound together in the codex bear witness to the diversity of interests either of those producing or those buying the codex. The full codex in which it is found also contains the following: The Apocryphon of John (Tractate 1), a revelation dialogue between the Savior and the disciples about the creation, human condition, and salvation of humanity; the Gospel According to Philip (Tractate 3), a collection of short discursive treatments of primarily Valentinian Christian sacramental theology; the Hypostasis of the Archons (Tractate 4), a revelation dialogue that interprets the first six chapters of Genesis; a Treatise Without Title on the Origin of the World (Tractate 5), a sophisticated exploration of the nature of the cosmos, the nature of humanity, and the end of both; the Expository Treatise on the Soul (Tractate 6), a poetic narrative describing the fate of the soul in the world; and the Book of Thomas the Contender Writing to the Perfect (Tractate 7), a revelation dialogue between Jesus and his twin brother Thomas. No one knows the reason why these works were gathered into one codex. Their collection into one codex does not necessarily indicate that they were considered to be similar or related; it could be simply the documents requested by the purchaser of the codex, or it may be the library of texts that were used by the copyists to produce other texts; or it may have been a collection made by a person or community who saw them as related and central to their beliefs. Nothing within the codex itself indicates the relationship of these tractates, and therefore, every possible rationale remains speculative.

The Coptic version presents the most complete extant text of the Gospel of Thomas. There may have been other versions that did not survive; or texts still not discovered in modern times; or there may have been longer or shorter versions (there is no real way of knowing how much of the Greek text circulated). The sayings are not numbered in the original texts (all the numbering is a modern scholarly convention) and they are written in a continuous script without word division and without differentiating one saying from another. The scribal hand has carefully and artfully formed each letter to produce a handsome appearance on the page. The title of the Gospel has been placed at the end of the tractate: the preceding line has been filled in with an attractive graphic geometric design, and the title has been carefully centered on the lines with the words "The Gospel" on one line being centered over the words "According to Thomas" on the following. There are many Greek loan-words in the text itself; this may point toward the Greek version as the basis of the translation, although the Coptic language often used many Greek loan-words. The Coptic text is the version of the Gospel of Thomas to which most modern scholars and the media refer.

Prologue

These are the secret sayings that the living Jesus spoke and Didymos Judas Thomas recorded.

This prologue provides the reader with the first entrance into the world of the text: the voice of a narrator speaks directly to the readers in suggestive language about "secrets" spoken by a "living" speaker, introducing them to these mysterious characters and orienting them to what follows. This world evoked by presences and secret sayings, of recorders and living speakers, comes to the readers in a text: the text conjures these textual realities and makes them speak in the mind of the readers. The world it constructs captivates the readers, and reveals to them the world recorded by Didymos Judas Thomas.

What voices emerge from this textual world? The brief initial statement introduces a narrator who mediates among the reader, Jesus, and the recorder of the sayings: the text evidences a number of different and simultaneous perspectives on the material presented. The narrator's voice provides the primary discourse from narrator to reader: that narrative voice conveys the apparent direct address of Jesus to the reader. Even though that narrative voice recedes to an almost inaudible and simple declarative "Jesus says," it nonetheless dominates the discourse by intruding at almost every turn to position itself between Jesus' speech and the reader. The continual repetition by the narrator that "Jesus says" seems to defer to Jesus' voice, while actually underscoring the dominance of the narrator's control of the saying given. The narrator mediates and provides the context for the transmission of the sayings of Jesus, subtly, sometimes imperceptibly, sometimes by omission, but always by direct interjection. The narrator's voice dominates.

The narrator not only provides the medium for Jesus' sayings, but also displaces the voice of Judas Didymos Thomas who, presented in the third person, becomes simply a discursive authority, a designated repository, for the sayings of the living Jesus which the narrator presents. The displacement of Judas Didymos Thomas, as a kind of mentioned locus of authority, at once provides a place for that tradition, while rejecting its definitive status. In order of priority, the narrator's voice takes precedence over Jesus' and over the authority of Judas Didymos Thomas, because it is the narrator who tells the reader who speaks and who records. The text's primary voice remains the narrator's, Jesus' voice provides the message refracted by the narrative, and Judas Didymos Thomas' voice provides an authority counterpoised to that of Jesus.

The discursive voices also construct a reader of, or a listener to, the sayings as a primary character in the text. Both the narrator and Jesus address the readers directly, the narrator by direct intervention (so as to mean "Reader, this is what the living Jesus says"), and Jesus by direct address to the "you" of the sayings audience (one example among many, "As for you, [be as sly] as [snakes...]"). This constructed readership has important implications: the instruction and challenge of these sayings have their direct reference to readers, who do not passively receive the material which the narrator conveys as from Jesus' own mouth, but who function as active agents in the development of their own understanding and way of life. That is, the imperative of the text lies with the readers who really have been constructed as seekers after the secret sayings of the living Jesus. The message, delivered directly to the reader whether by Jesus or the narrator, emphasizes the central role of reader to the text.

Most scholars have ignored the narrative voice and focused directly
on the issues that most intrigue them: the sayings of Jesus and the role of
Judas/Thomas. They have looked to evaluate the authenticity and
antiquity of sayings, to construct a concept of the community behind
the sayings, and to locate these sayings of Jesus and their theology in the
context of early Christian theology and heresy. Although the sayings of
Jesus hold an important place, they remain mediate; and although the
role of Thomas and his community fascinates New Testament scholars,
it remains peripheral. Both these interpretative interests deflect
attention from the central narrative strategy represented in the actual
relationships of the voices embedded in the text itself. This narrative
strategy must be understood prior to an evaluation of both the sayings
and the community of readers preserving the sayings, because the
narrative itself mediates and filters the information provided about the
content and context of the treatise.

This scholarly rush to judgment has resulted in a serious distortion of
an important dynamic in the text: the relationship of the narrator to the
reader. By splitting the voices (narrator, Jesus, the recorder, and readers)
the readers relate most directly with the narrator who guides them,
identifies the speaker, and (very infrequently) provides perspective. Since
the narrative voice is minimal (often reduced simply to "Jesus says"), the
narrator invests the readers with the authority and power to listen and
to interpret for themselves: these readers need no intermediary to read
or hear or understand the difficult sayings of Jesus that are recorded
here. The diminution of narrative instruction strengthens the role of the
readers to understand and to construct for themselves significant
interpretations and narratives to relate the various disparate sayings of
Jesus that follow in the treatise.

This narrative strategy establishes the readers as collaborators with
the narrative voice in developing an environment for hearing and
understanding. The minimized narrative voice also emphasizes the
readers' relationship with the content of Jesus' sayings. Although the
readers mostly hear the "living Jesus," in fact, they attend to recorded
sayings under the guidance of an invisible narrator. The narrative
strategy, however, creates the illusion of immediate apprehension, that
is, an illusion of an unmediated speaking person in direct relationship
with the reader, and that illusion augments the importance of the
readers in receiving the sayings (see Valantasis 1991: 147–55).

This invisible narrator mirrors the secrecy of the sayings: "These are
the secret sayings. . . . " The narrator informs the readers that these
sayings have a restricted audience: the narrator grants the readers

entrance into a select group of those selected by the narrator to hear the secret sayings. The secrecy has two fields of meaning: the Greek word *apokryphos* implies that the sayings are obscure and difficult to interpret; the Coptic word *hêp* implies that few can read them because they are not readily available. These sayings present the readers, as the narrator points out, with difficult and puzzling sayings that will challenge them.

The sayings come from the "living Jesus" (Kaestli 1979: 389). They are secret and troubling sayings that come from one present in the community. The fact that Jesus is "living" draws attention to itself. It implies that for others, there are sayings from a "dead" Jesus, that is, their Jesus is not really present to them in speaking the sayings. But for this community, the one to which the narrator extends the invitation, their Jesus lives, speaks, and continues to challenge. The narrative world includes a Jesus fully present, speaking, and capable of being recorded and transmitted to others.

The recorder of these sayings also seems curious (Koester 1990a: 78–80 provides an overview of the problem). The recorder, whom the narrator acknowledges as a distinct and unified voice, provides the lineage for the sayings, but that lineage presents problems. The Greek simply has "Judas who is also called Thomas," a designation that seems to posit two recording sources which have been identified, that of Judas and that of Thomas. The double naming bears the significance of a double identity conflated. The Coptic uses the tri-focal name "Didymos Judas Thomas," a designation that reduplicates the synonym "twin" in Greek (*didymos*) and Syriac (*thoma*). The tri-focality identifies the tradition from the Greek (Judas and Thomas) with the one who is also the "twin" (Didymos). The title at the end of the treatise indicates that this is a "Gospel of Thomas," a naming that ignores both the Greek designation Didymos and the proper name Judas. The sayings originate with Jesus, and they find expression in the world which the narrator and the readers share, but they are transmitted under the authority of Judas, and of Thomas, and of the one who was the twin, all of which has eventually been subsumed under the generic name "Thomas" whose treatise is no longer identified by its content (the sayings), but by its redesignated genre of literature, a "gospel" (Meyer 1990 and Robinson 1971a discuss this problem).

The readers, then, have entered into a different and new world at the invitation of one who knows both the living words of Jesus and the authoritative traditions of Judas, also called Thomas. That narrative world presents difficult material from the mouth of a present and speaking Jesus, and it is the struggle with that challenging material that brings the reward, as the next saying relates.

Saying 1

And he said, "Whoever discovers the interpretation of these sayings will not taste death."

It is not clear who is speaking here. The narrator is ambiguous about the source: the saying could be Jesus' first saying presenting the goal or end for listening to the secret sayings, or it could be a statement from the repositor Didymos Judas Thomas explaining his goal for recording the sayings. From either of these sources, the saying clearly provides the readers with an expected gain for proceeding to listen: discovery of the interpretation defeats death.

In the narrative world constructed by this text the task of discovering the interpretation dominates as the central and critical activity for the readers. The readers do not aim toward the discovery of Jesus, or even of the community of disciples and followers of Jesus: rather the readers aim to discover the interpretation of the sayings. By its nature, "interpretation" is communal: one person interprets a "text" or a "comment" or something else that comes from some other source, or person, or community. The readers must discover the understandings of these sayings that the community has already articulated: they are not told to interpret, but to *find* the interpretation. The meaning of these sayings resides in a corporate understanding provided to new readers. The social group formed of those who read and understand these sayings has already provided the interpretative focus, which the readers must uncover, discover, or recover. The readers do not create the meaning, or provide the interpretation, but through their engagement with the sayings, they will discover their already established corporate meaning.

In this narrative world, all the figures (Jesus, Didymos Judas Thomas, the narrator, and the readers) are present, active, and alive in the community. Death does not prevent Jesus from speaking or Didymos Judas Thomas from recording. Similarly, death does not inhibit the reader from interpreting the sayings or from entering the narrative world. The goal articulated in this collection of sayings, however, does not culminate in a literary development, a mere discovery of interpretation: the intent is not to create a fictive world, but to translate the fictive world into "real life," a particular and actual way of living and experiencing. Once the readers have entered that fictive world and translated their lives into it, it becomes the real world, one in which they will no longer taste death.

Just as the emphasis is on the discovery rather than on the interpretation of the sayings, so is the result of that discovery an *experience*, rather than a state. This discovery results in "not tasting death." It could have been abstractly put: "whoever discovers the interpretation will achieve immortality," but it was not. Tasting death joins two unjoinable events in graphic detail: eating is a sensible activity, but in death there is no eating. The discovery of the interpretation leads to a significant and alternative way of experiencing sensible life and mortality so that in discovering the interpretation of the sayings, the readers become different sorts of people "who do not taste death." The new understanding of self, encapsulated in this discovery, provides the primary impetus for searching the meaning of these sayings. The next saying addresses that new subjectivity.

Saying 2

Jesus said, "Those who seek should not stop seeking until they find. ²When they find, they will be disturbed. ³When they are disturbed, they will marvel, ⁴and will rule over all."

As indicated above, the goal in this new narrative world to which the readers were introduced in the very beginning of these sayings does not involve simply the construction of a literary world. These sayings do not guide readers, as in a novel, to live in the fictional world for a time and then to leave it having experienced its narrative action. Rather, these sayings guide their readers into being different kinds of people, or, at least, they suggest to the readers that a different way of living exists and should be attempted. The alternative experience of self and world posited in these sayings indicates that these sayings aim toward the construction of an alternative way of understanding self and of living in the world; the sayings aim toward the construction of an alternative subjectivity. The construction of an alternative subjectivity constitutes a primary characteristic of ascetic literature where such a development of alternative subjectivities is a major goal of the ascetic practice (Valantasis 1995b). One goal of the process laid out in this saying, then, revolves about the construction of a new self through an ascetical activity and performances: through the performance of the sequence of seeking and finding, being disturbed, marveling, and ruling, a new person comes into being. That performative process creates a new person, one who begins with seeking, but ultimately rules over all.

The second saying, then, presents the ascetic sequence for developing that new subjectivity: seeking, finding, being disturbed, marveling, and ruling. The first two elements in this sequence present nothing unusual in formative Christianity: the seeking and finding construction recurs in a number of different collections of Jesus' sayings (The Synoptic Sayings Source Q 11.9–"Seek and you will find.") and in other early Christian literature (Gospel of Mary 4: 7). The traditional early Christian formulation offers a simple guarantee that the one who seeks will find without any other explanation or delimitation of possibilities. The simple theme of seeking and finding also recurs in the Gospel of Thomas in Sayings 92 and 94 (with a parallel in the Synoptic Sayings Source Q).

The last three, however, present startling information: finding leads to disturbance; disturbance leads to marveling which, in turn, leads to ruling. Clement of Alexandria cites in Greek a parallel to this ascetical sequence that he attributes to the Gospel of the Hebrews (see Quispel 1957; MacRae 1960: 64–69), and that formulation combines the elements from both the Greek and the Coptic version of the Gospel of Thomas ("He that seeks will not rest until he finds; and he that has found shall marvel; and he that has marveled shall reign; and he that has reigned shall rest." (Cameron 1982: 86)). The expansion of the simple guarantee in these sayings into a fully developed procession of experiences (being disturbed, marveling, ruling) specifically advances the development of an alternative subjectivity. The person in the traditional formulation in the Synoptic Sayings Source Q need do nothing but seek in order to find; but the person in this expanded saying embraces a series of experiences that lead toward full empowerment. To rule over all expresses an increment of empowerment, of fulfillment and arrival at the apex of the experience. The formulation in this saying provides the basis for a significantly more complex process of formation in which, unfortunately, the precise referent of "being disturbed" and "marveling" cannot be established. The interlocking events, one step (seeking) linking to the next (finding) which in turn links with the next (being disturbed) establishes a precise sequence that abandons the earlier stages in favor of the unfolding later stages. This abandoning of the earlier in favor of the later stages reflects the gradual formation and reconstruction of subjectivity in the sayings. Even without understanding the precise referent to each of the stages, the ascetical process clearly articulates a different understanding of self and relationships to others. The culmination in ruling posits a dominate stance in relationship to other people and to the world. This new person, the one who, upon discovering the interpretation of the sayings will not experience death, emerges from the gradual and dramatic transformation that began with a search, mediated by finding, being disturbed, and marveling, and culminating in ruling. The search begins in deficiency; the end results in empowerment.

The progression of stages reverses the readers' expectations, and such reversals are frequent tactics in ascetical literature. The seekers in these sayings are people who will indeed find that for which they seek, but what they find will at once disturb them and make them marvel at their experience, and finally bestow upon them a superior authority and power over others. Those who seek must expect transformation and redefinition into a type of person and a kind of social relationship that does not fit the normal categories of human existence. Their experience moves them in an alternative direction. It takes a different kind of person to be able to seek in this way, and the sayings intend quite specifically to create that alternative and different sort of person.

Although the quotation from the Gospel of the Hebrews combines all the elements of the sequence, the Greek and the Coptic versions of Thomas differ in the sequence of experiences in this process, and that difference provides a locus for constructing new meanings. The goal in the Greek version (and in the Gospel of the Hebrews) is "rest" and the Coptic version suppresses the rest and puts "ruling over all" as the final goal, a goal articulated as the penultimate stage in the Greek versions. Sometime in the chronological and theological interval between these versions, "ruling over all" supplanted "rest" as the final experience in the sequence, and with that supplanting, *activity* replaced *passivity* and *dominion* displaced *repose*. The Coptic version, moreover, added the marveling: the ruling subject is the marveling subject. This additional phrase draws attention to the self-experience and self-understanding of the ruler: the "marvel" predicates a subjective state comparable to the disturbance. The process has shifted to a balance of activity and subjective states (finding/disturbing, marveling/ruling).

The Coptic version may well be pointing toward two interlocking phenomena. First, the community posited in the processes may have experienced an increment of social dislocation so that the displacement of rest by ruling reflects the social corrective to that dislocation. In the third and fourth centuries CE, desire to correct that social dislocation would, under the sustained impact of heresiological persecution, have seemed reasonable. Second, the interiorizing of the process into a balanced program of finding/disturbing and marveling/ruling may reflect the reorientation of the formative power under the impact of a more prominent withdrawal from society. The divergence between Greek and Coptic versions creates a platform for the construction of meanings–meanings which here I am interpreting as social, but I do not necessarily exclude other avenues of interpretation.

Saying 3

Jesus said, "If your leaders say to you, 'Look, the <Father's> imperial rule is in the sky,' then the birds of the sky will precede you. [2]If they say to you, 'It is in the sea,' then the fish will precede you. [3]Rather, the <Father's> imperial rule is inside you and outside you. [4]When you know yourselves, then you will be known, and you will understand that you are children of the living Father. [5]But if you do not know yourselves, then you live in poverty, and you are the poverty."

Scholars have read this saying in a number of ways, as a "popular Jewish motif of seeking after wisdom in the furthest reaches of the universe" (Patterson 1993: 72), or as a midrash on Deuteronomy 30.10–15 which establishes a connection between the commandments, wisdom, and the interior status of the reign of God (Glasson 1976–77: 151–52 and Davies 1983: 41–46). All of these interpretations overlook the subject of the saying: "those who lead you." This saying problematizes leadership. Readers experience for the first time the irony and sarcasm possible in these collections of sayings. The narrative strategy has already invested the reader with a kind of full authority to find the community's interpretation of the sayings, a process that has guaranteed immortality. When we first hear about "leaders," they are giving bad information, directing the seekers' attention to the sky or under the earth. To follow such leaders results in getting lost. In contrast to such misguided leadership, Jesus directs the readers to understand their own empowerment: the imperial rule of God is found both within and without the seeker. True leadership directs the seeker inward to a new understanding of the self, and outward to a new understanding of the world in which God's imperial rule is manifest. The seeker guides the self into knowledge, requiring no external guidance other than the saying of Jesus that directs seekers to themselves.

The important point is not only that there is a new understanding of an empowered self, but also that God's imperial rule must be understood anew. The location of God's imperial rule is not in the heavens, nor is it under the earth (other creatures would experience the rule of God first, if this were the case), but God's imperial rule is within and without the person. The interior location of the imperial rule, as Patterson (1993: 71–72) argues, finds specific thematic parallels with Luke 17.20–21 ("for behold, the kingdom of God is in the midst of you") and perhaps with Matthew's "warning against those who would locate the kingdom in a specific place" (Matthew 24.26). The Kingdom of God in this saying, however, remains interior in that it emerges from self-knowledge and exterior in that it depends upon a self-awareness that leads to a new understanding of the mundane world.

This relocation of the imperial rule of God probably represents one side of an ongoing conversation among early Christian people about authority and power: some probably expected an apocalyptic rule of God inaugurated from the heavens (as Paul did in 1 Thessalonians), others may have experienced the church community itself as the inauguration of the reign of God (as Matthew did in his gospel), still others at once interiorized the rule of God and, therefore, reinterpreted its external significance (as in this saying).

This new awareness and understanding of the self develops from the kind of seeking mentioned in the previous saying. The readers, and the seekers, will find this understanding of the rule of God as they come to know themselves. Self-knowledge reveals the connection to the Father, not as an external adoption by a distant heavenly Father, but as "children of the living Father," a Father who is present and vital. The opposite of this self-knowledge is poverty: true wealth does not consist in anything but knowing self, poverty both as a state of being and as a condition of life follows from the refusal to seek.

All of these issues are intimately connected. The true self, the empowering strategy both of the narrator and of Jesus' sayings, the alternative understanding of the world, the redefinition of poverty both as ontological and social, the rejection of hierarchical leadership–all these conspire to create alternative understandings of self, relationships, and world. These alternatives work ascetically; they are a part of a systematic means of redefining and reorienting the seeker to the world (see Valantasis 1995b). They open the possibility of transformation and renewal through the interpretative practices outlined in the sayings.

Saying 4

> Jesus said, "The person old in days won't hesitate to ask a little child seven days old about the place of life, and that person will live. [2]For many of the first will be last, [3]and will become a single one."

Some groups in antiquity were fascinated by the role and function of young children; the children constitute a consistent sub-theme of a wide assortment of early Christian groups considered orthodox and heretical (see Meyer 1985: 538–39; Lelyveld 1987: 25–32). This saying about children revolves about a reversal of expectations: children ought to be led by adults, not to lead them; children ought to ask questions of adults, not to answer them; children need guidance to find their way to the place of life, not to instruct elders on the way. Inversion drives the saying, and finds concrete expression in the disparity between an elder "old in days" asking a "little child seven days old." This inverting strategy, however, goes one step further: the elder will indeed "live" as a result of being led by a child. The child leads toward life, not knowledge alone: the discovery of the locus of life from the child leads to life.

The rhetoric of this saying puts the example (verse 1) before the twin principles which inform it. The phenomenon of an elder asking a seven-day-old child finds its first theoretical expression in the statement: "For many of the first will be last." The beginning and the end will be inverted, the former will find themselves the latter, the older will become the younger. The principle elevates the strategy of inversion to the level of theological truth *for many*. This delimiting of the sphere of that truth of inversion indicates that it applies only to those who participate in the world in which that truth operates: it is not "for all," but "for many," for those elders capable of asking a youth, and for those babies capable of leading the elders to the place of life.

The phenomenon of the elder asking the seven-day-old child about the place of life finds its second theoretical expression in the phrase (verse 3) "and will become a single one." Interpreters have tended to remove this portion of the saying from the rhetorical context in which it has been written, and to make it an example of a doctrine of singularity revolving about some primordial state of unity (for a summary of those positions and an alternative suggestion, see Griffith 1995: 220–29; but note Klijn 1962; Buckley 1986: 95–101). This sort of interpretative strategy exceeds the boundaries of the rhetoric of this saying; this saying clearly provides an example and two explications of the theology which underlies it. The "one and the same" of the Greek version and the "single one" of the Coptic refer simply to the unification of the polarities old and young, elder and child, first and last. The principle states that divergence, difference, and distinction will ultimately meld into singularity, union, and solidarity so that what was once categorized as elder or child, or as first or last, will become singular and united. The presumption is that this unity applies as well *for many*, and not for all: it is a restricted principle, not a universal one.

The singularity or unity theme may well find its negative parallel in the injunctions against being double-minded or duplicitous in the exhortative literature of early Christianity. The counterpoint to such duplicity is unity. The canonical Epistle of James, for example, contrasts the acquiring of wisdom through confident asking to double-minded doubt, "for the doubter, being double-minded and unstable in every way, must not expect to receive anything from the Lord" (1.8 NRSV). Later, James exhorts: "Cleanse your hands, you sinners, and purify your hearts, you double-minded" (4.8 NRSV). Such themes abound in the Apostolic Fathers: double-mindedness indicates doubt, while single-mindedness indicates faith (see, for example, The Shepherd of Hermas, Mandate 9). The two being made into one in this saying need not invoke other systems than the ill-effects of division and duplicity on the seeking person.

This saying introduces singularity as the primary characteristic of the subjectivity promulgated in these sayings. In this instance singularity displaces categories of age and priority in favor of becoming "a single one." The performance that inaugurates this new subjectivity is the bold asking that brings life. That ascetical performance, thematized as a set of inversions (old/young, first/last) becomes the ascetical means for creating a new understanding of self and of relationships to others.

Saying 5

> Jesus said, "Know what is in front of your face, and what is hidden from you will be disclosed to you. [2]For there is nothing hidden that won't be revealed."

Again, the rhetorical organization of the sayings places the particular before the principle. The injunction simply advises the seekers to perceive (if not to understand) what presents itself to them. Jesus enjoins the seeker to be fully present to the moment in such a way as to understand and comprehend it immediately. The orientation of the seeker ought to be neither to the past, nor to the future, but toward the present alone. The statement does not really talk about any ontological status so as to imply that those who have knowledge understand the present, but relates a simple truth that good perception and understanding begin with what appears to the senses, and therefore true knowledge begins in a clear perception and understanding of the present moment.

The knowledge of the moment, of immediate perception and understanding, forms the basis for revelation. There is a play here between knowing the present things and receiving the disclosure of hidden things. The injunction discounts the search for hidden things, by assuring that those who see what is before them will also have the hidden things disclosed to them. The knowledge here does not revolve about secret, or hidden, revelations, but rather about immediate perception and understanding that will guide the way to revelation and disclosure. Things that are hidden will be disclosed to those who understand what the senses present.

The principle which commends this statement relates that "there is nothing hidden that won't be revealed." The statement presents a very positive perspective on the hidden things, without hint of paranoia, or of cosmic withholding of knowledge: hidden things will be revealed. In its context, that disclosure will only happen to those who keep their eyes open, who see what presents itself to sight; it does not seem to apply generally, but specifically to those addressed in the example.

The strategy of emphasizing the present and visible over the hidden and invisible argues against an esoteric provenance for these sayings. The "hidden things" and other revelations depend not upon some secret knowledge or process, but rather upon a simple understanding of the nature of apparent reality. Knowledge of visible reality guarantees the disclosure of hidden realities and revelations of hidden things. An esoteric system would begin with the opposite, with some key to secret knowledge that must first be discovered in order to unlock the hidden and mysterious revelations. Such an esoteric system finds no basis in this saying that actually suggests the opposite: knowledge of the visible leads to the revelation of the invisible. These sayings are not esoteric, they are available to anyone willing to begin to find their interpretation; those who find the interpretation are not members of a secret society with a knowledge available only to themselves, but rather they are those whose different understanding of themselves, society, and the world enable them to live in the world with new understanding.

Saying 6

His disciples asked him and said to him, "Do you want us to fast? How should we pray? Should we give to charity? What diet should we observe?"

[2]Jesus said, "Don't lie, [3]and don't do what you hate, [4]because all things are disclosed before heaven. [5]After all, there is nothing hidden that won't be revealed, [6]and there is nothing covered up that will remain undisclosed."

The most appropriate answer to the question in verse 1 seems to be found in Saying 14, verses 1–3. The explanation to this might be something as simple as the misplacing of a sheet or two of papyrus which separated verses 6 and 14. There is no way of knowing that for certain, but it seems reasonable given that these sayings do not follow a prescribed pattern. A production error of this sort is very possible. The interpretation that follows will, however, leave aside this speculation, having simply noted that there may be other avenues of interpretation possible.

The narrative voice presents the question from the disciples about the practical conduct of life revolving about acts of piety (fasting, praying, alms-giving, and eating regimens). In a literary environment in which the emphasis has been on the self-sufficiency of the seekers, the narrative intrusion, as well as the content of the questions, surprise the readers. The narrative intrusion infantilizes the disciples, grouping them together as in one voice for many people, and presenting an importunate series of demands for information. And the questions revolve about the performance of pious acts: regulating food, abstaining from food, giving alms, praying–a kind of orientation toward the development of a social lifestyle that the remaining sayings seem to ignore. The questions, therefore, suggest that the narrator has no sympathy for the questions, and the readers/seekers are not expected to identify with them either. At their base, they operate at the wrong level for those interested in these sayings.

The inappropriate status of the questions becomes evident with the response provided: the questions about action result in moral instruction ("Don't lie, and don't do what you hate"). The moral formation provides instruction about honesty and the positive impetus toward action. These function again at the level of the example, followed by the theological or spiritual principles which inform them: "because all things are disclosed before heaven." All three precepts revolve about the disclosure of hidden motives and invisible dispositions and present that principle of disclosure under three different categories: everything is disclosed before heaven; hidden things will always be revealed; and those things covered up will be disclosed. So the pious acts miss the point because it is the interior or hidden motivation and disposition that will be seen, not the inherent goodness of any activity or performance. The seekers cannot, like the foolish disciples who ask these questions, hide behind their pious activities.

The theme of disclosure and revelation has connected this saying with the previous one. The verbal connections probably explain their proximity to one another, but the theme nonetheless stands out. Those seekers who interpret these sayings expend great energy in finding ways to have the invisible made visible, the hidden manifest, and the secret revealed. The sayings work the various ways of seeking, here with the injunction to live a moral life, and in the previous saying with the emphasis on adequately reading the things that present themselves to the person. The theme will recur periodically throughout the collection, with a variety of strategies for acquiring such revelation and disclosure.

Saying 7

Jesus said, "Blessed [SV: "Lucky] is the lion that the human will eat, so that the lion becomes human. [2]And foul is the human that the lion will eat, and the lion still will become human."

This saying assumes a clearly articulated hierarchy of being: human beings live higher on the scale of existence than even the mighty lion. Within this hierarchy of being, the impetus to rise above the current status through eating also functions. In a kind of reversal of fortunes, the lion becomes food for the human, but through his death and consumption, rises to a higher place in the hierarchy. While playing with the inversion of description of the lion as human food, the same stable hierarchy is maintained: the lion who eats the human rises to the level of his food. By any measure, the hierarchy stands with human beings above lions and (presumably) other life forms. The rise and fall of people within the hierarchy of being follows from their eating habits. Eating becomes the locus for the articulation of progress.

Jesus describes this process as "blessed" for the lion, but polluted or fouled for the human. The lion who progresses upward in the hierarchy of being consistently benefits, even under the adversity of becoming some human's food. The human being locked in the cycle of the eating of meat, at least, cannot benefit in the same way: the human gains food or becomes food and in both these circumstances has identified with the lower rungs of the hierarchy of being.

To a greater degree, the interpretation of these passages depends upon the relative dating of the saying. If one imagines an early Jesus saying of this sort, then the table fellowship characteristic of the early Jesus movement would argue that even base people, far below the truly enlightened, when they enter into the community's table fellowship, are transformed by it. The saying, in this context, applauds the transformation of base into higher forms of life. If one assumes a later period, during the time of the formation of ascetic and monastic communities, then eating in itself becomes problematic (see Jackson 1985). The focus then revolves about the question of eating meat, as opposed to observing a vegetarian diet, and to carefully regulating a very small intake of food. The interpretation of the saying could move in either direction.

Saying 8

And he said, "The human one is like a wise fisherman who cast his net into the sea and drew it up from the sea full of little fish. [2]Among them the wise fisherman discovered a fine large fish. [3]He threw all the little fish back into the sea, and easily chose the larger fish. [4]Anyone here with two good ears had better listen!"

The parables present an interesting interpretative problem. At the literary level, this one consists of a narrative within a simile that is explained by a narrative: the narrator's voice ("And he said") introduces a simile ("The human one is like") that inaugurates another narrative ("a wise fisherman who cast his net into the sea"). The perspectives on the meaning of parables reflect the complexity of literary angles within them: they will bear more meaning than appears at first, and, they provide readers (and seekers) a rich field with which to play for meaning (see Crossan 1973: 4–36). The word "play" should be emphasized: in every one of these sayings, the meaning and the theological or spiritual principles which inform meaning have been carefully and directly stated. The introduction of parables shifts from that discursive modality to one that requires greater interaction and less guidance from the narrative. The parables provide time and space for play.

The simile itself attempts to define, or to compare, the "human one" or "the man" to a fisherman. The ambiguity of the term "the human one" contrasts with the specificity of the description of the fisherman.

The simile makes a definitive statement about the human condition: "The human one" resembles a "wise fisherman." The human condition signified as the "human one" has the grammatical article ("the") that indicates that this humanity is not just any human, but the ones who live in a special category of human beings, perhaps those capable of interpreting these sayings. That specific community reference to the human being as similar to a *wise* fisherman places the weight of the comparison on the description. Attentive readers, however, recognize that although the emphasis falls on the description, the import remains with the three suppressed elements (the sayings-narrator; Jesus' narrative; and the subject of that narrative, "the human one"). These voices seem to join with the voice at the end to say, "Anyone here with two good ears had better listen!" The suppressed elements find their voice in the injunction to pay attention: the readers and seekers (if they are as wise as the fisherman) will heed the understanding they might gain about their humanity, and especially about their humanity refracted through Jesus' sayings and preserved in Thomas' collection. That such an injunction to listen receives attention underscores that only select people will be able properly to gain from the parable, and only select readers or seekers will be able to understand what transpires.

The narrative that follows has simple elements: a fisherman caught a net full of fish, but when he found a large fish he threw back all the other small fish. The wisdom of a fisherman throwing away the catch and keeping only one large fish inverts normal expectations. This is a wisdom of a different sort. This wisdom operates with a different set of values and a different orientation toward professional accomplishments. The goal of this wise fisherman is not to eat the fish or to sell them, but simply to reject all the smaller fish when he has found the largest one. The value of the one big fish makes all other systems of valuing irrelevant. Such a narrative defines a wisdom alternative to the dominant norm.

The readers/seekers may be located at any number of different points: they may be the fisherman who has gone fishing for their true self, and when they found it all the other petty identities were thrown aside; they may be the fine big fish that is found by the great fisherman of human souls and cherished beyond all the other fish who seem smaller in comparison; they may be the smaller fish who have been swept aside by the dominant larger fish and thrown out to sea. The particular location finds added meaning in the play on such words as "wise," "small," "fine large," and "without difficulty," so that the significance to the readers/seekers takes on added meaning, surplus expression, by playing with the adjectives and adverbs. The meaning would also slide along a scale depending upon when the parable was being interpreted: later monks would experience and cherish the fine large fish as a sign of their election, while the early Jesus movement might see the catch against the traditions of the disciples and the miraculous catching of fish by Peter and the other leaders of the church (John 21.1–14; Luke 5.1–11). Meaning slides along almost endlessly.

The subtle narrative voices and parabolic subjects keep directing attention back to the interpretative community, the readers and the seekers who desire to understand their own human condition and to discover true wisdom. The truths expressed here, the playful exploring of meaning, take on their ultimate significance among these final voices that make the playful interaction with the parable possible. Those who are capable of understanding these sublimated voices ultimately will find themselves and the truth.

Saying 9

Jesus said, "Look, the sower went out, took a handful (of seeds), and scattered (them). [2]Some fell on the road, and the birds came and gathered them. [3]Others fell on rock, and they didn't take root in the soil and didn't produce heads of grain. [4]Others fell on thorns, and they choked the seeds and worms ate them. [5]And others fell on good soil, and it produced a good crop: it yielded sixty per measure and one hundred twenty per measure."

This narrative has a simple plot: "the sower went out, took a handful (of seeds), and scattered (them)." This common task (it is, after all, what would be expected of a sower) does not carry the interest of the narrative, because the focus resides with the multifocal aspects of the location of the seeds and the consequent fate of the seeds in that location. This "sower" functions multivalently: it could be Jesus "the Sower" who speaks in these sayings, or it could be the collection of these sayings that sows the seeds, or the interpreter of these sayings who sows the seeds, or the hearer of these sayings (as in the allegorical interpretation of the synoptic tradition of Mark 4.2–9, Matthew 13.3–9 and Luke 8.4–8). The ambivalence and multivalence of the sower allows for multiple interpretative strategies from the perspective of each possible referent.

The major emphasis of the narrative revolves about the places where the seeds landed and on the fate of the seeds that landed in each place. The narrative identifies four places that the sower scattered with seeds: on the road, on rock, on thorns, and on good soil. The seeds receive different treatment: on the road, the birds gathered them; on the rock, the seeds could not develop roots and so could not produce; among the thorns, the seeds were choked and so became food for worms; and in the good soil, the seeds produced in great measure. The narrative organizes these results in a kind of overlapping interaction involving agency and natural cause: the birds gather (as the worms eat); the seeds could not produce roots (on the rock) or were choked, or they produced abundantly. The first two results are simple: the birds gathered them, or they could not take root to produce grain; the first is a simple agent, the second, a simple natural cause. The third result mixes natural cause and agency, so that the seeds choked by the thorns were eaten by an agent. The last element results in a strictly natural result: seeds on good soil produced significant results. This complex interaction of elements again provides rich potential for interpretation: the seeds interact with other living agents and with the environment to produce different results. The emphasis remains on the complex interaction of seeds, agent, and nature.

Oddly enough, there seems to be no inherent negative judgment related on the various locations where the seeds were scattered. The narrative withholds judgment, while explaining consequence. Although readers (especially those trained to read through the synoptic allegorization in the parallel text (see Hedrick 1994: 164–86)) may value the seeds and production located in the good soil, the narrative itself does not necessarily indicate any comparative values.

The narrative thematizes the effects of diffusion: the narrative speaks of the effects of diffused activity. The proper subject of the narrative, as it is of the narrative itself, is the activity of the sower. The sower's work activates the various effects: by scattering the seeds over four different places, the sower activates four divergent responses. Those responses remain neutral: there is nothing unnatural or wicked about birds gathering seeds or worms eating them, nor is there anything surprising about seeds on rocky ground not being able to produce while seeds in good soil produce abundantly.

The sower creates a problem by not focusing sufficiently on the desired end. The lack of focus by the sower creates a situation in which four different aims result. The focused attention and deliberation of the sower would have produced one, solid result, signified here by the significant production of the seeds that fell on good soil. The singular goal and coordinated activity of the sower could have produced singular and significant results. The sower's inattention, or lack of care, or lack of knowledge, or indecision, or lack of direction created a situation in which the double-mindedness or duplicity inhibited careful results. Such a reading of the narrative connects it with a common theme of singularity and unity that pervades these sayings. A single-minded person will be able to focus attention and achieve the desired goal; a double-minded person who does not focus may eventually achieve the goal, but only while squandering attention in lesser goods, or derivative results.

Saying 10

Jesus said, "I have cast fire upon the world, and look, I'm guarding it until it blazes."

This saying articulates a subversive aspect of the mission of these sayings. The collection does not entirely revolve about the positing of an alternative way of living and conceiving of self; it also describes the social displacement and social reorganization that follows those personal alternatives. The violence of that subversion becomes evident here when Jesus announces in this declarative statement, that he has "cast fire" upon the world. The problematizing of the world which seems so much a part of these sayings carries with it an increment of destruction and violence. Although Jesus has cast this fire upon the earth, the fire remains weak and needy, requiring protection from its originator until it can take hold. That describes a subversive violence, one which begins very small and hidden, but which eventually erupts into full force destruction. Fire bears a double significance in this saying, a duality of meaning that underscores this twin role of violence and dependence: the fire that Jesus casts seems to relate to a judgmental use of fire, the metaphor of fire as an apocalyptic or eschatological tool, while the tending of the fire in the second half of the saying suggests the kindling of a small force that will be protected until it develops. The positive and pastoral role of the guardian of the fire balances the negative role of the fire itself, because this fire is not an instantaneous destructive one, but one that needs tending and care until it matures.

The articulation of such violence should not surprise readers, because it seems to be a corollary to the kind of loosely formed community which these sayings posit. Since these people are the ones who have ears to hear (Saying 8) and senses to perceive (Saying 5), they do not form the majority, but an entitled minority. They are, in fact, the fire that needs to be guarded and tended until they may mature. This community chooses their minority status: the conflict with the dominant religious environment in which they live enhances their own identity. The clearer the distinction between their minority and the dominant religious expressions of their day, the more violent and subversive will their opposition to it remain. Jesus' saying makes that opposition essential to the self-understanding of the readers and seekers, while also acknowledging that the opposition does not put them immediately in a place of power but in a place of fragility which demands Jesus' protection.

Saying 11

Jesus said, "This heaven will pass away, and the one above it will pass away. [2]The dead are not alive, and the living will not die. [3]During the days when you ate what is dead, you made it come alive. When you are in the light, what will you do? [4]On the day when you were one, you became two. But when you become two, what will you do?"

This saying revolves about a series of seemingly unrelated statements about the mutability of the heavens, the character of real living, the effect of eating, a question about living in the light, and another question about singularity and multiplicity of subjectivity. They sweep quickly across topics, in staccato fashion, leaving the readers (both ancient and modern) to puzzle over their relationship to one another. By the time one statement ends and another begins, the reader's mind must adjust to yet another topic, expressed in dramatic and startling language.

The communication of the saying, then, operates at two levels: at the level of discourse in which the staccato statements challenge rational reflection; and at the level of the content of each saying which may be taken separately from each of the others (they may even have existed independently prior to their collection here). The interaction of these two levels produces exactly the effect stated in Saying 2: they are disturbing and cause marvel; they invert known reality as they assert an alternative and contrary manner of understanding the world. The communication leads through disturbance and marveling to a kind of ruling, a higher perception and understanding, a more superlative mode of interpretation, than could be achieved by simple, declarative statements.

The mode of discourse operates with dizzying speed: Three statements link with two questions. The statements do not require the readers' involvement, but the questions speak directly to them. The illusion of distance in the first three statements collapses when the readers are addressed and expected not only to respond, but to define a mode of action in the final two statements. The repetition of the question "what will you do?" demands reaction, engagement, by violating the readers' space, by intruding into their safely defined distance from the saying, and by bypassing the narrative voice, to have the voice of Jesus directly address the readers/seekers. Here even the distinction between readers and seekers collapses, because the "you" cannot be carefully delimited to refer only to the ancient hearers/ readers, but must refer to any "you" that reads and interprets the saying. The discursive strategy, therefore, challenges by drawing the readers more and more into the mode of discourse and by forcing a relationship by addressing a direct question to the audience; the readers or seekers engage directly with the voice of Jesus, a voice which jumps out to them from the page.

The second level, that of the content of the sayings, also reflects a careful strategy for the redefinition and reorientation of reality. The statement that "this heaven" and "the one above it" will both "pass away" invokes the well-known binary construction of heaven and earth in which the "heavens" remain immutable and "the earth" signifies changeablity. But in the world created by this saying, all the heavens also will pass away (even though Meyer 1992: 73 suggests without textual justification that "presumably" the third heaven, the realm of God, will not pass away). The saying revokes the common tradition found in the synoptic gospels (Mark 13.31 and parallels) and in the Synoptic Sayings Source Q 16.17 that *both* heaven *and* earth will pass away but that Jesus' words will not. In the world of these sayings Jesus remains a living presence in the midst of worlds that pass away.

The statements about the true meaning of living also posits an alternative reality: the simple declaration that "the dead are not alive" seems like a truism until the following statement ("the living will not die") introduces the suspicion that the saying plays on the referents of the terms "living" and "dead." "Living" and "dying" take on different meaning in the world in which this saying operates: in this reality, the truly living will not die, and those who are dead were never really alive. The inversion of expectation realigns the categories so that "being alive" refers to something different than the normal categories. The same playful working of the dead being made alive by being eaten follows the same sort of redefinition of reality: in this world what becomes part of the body shares in the status of that body so that dead food comes to life by being assimilated into the spiritual person's body (see Saying 7).

The two questions pose an even greater challenge to the interpreter, but both of them end in a call for action, not for information or knowledge. The first ("When you are in the light, what will you do?") identifies a state of being (that is, being "in the light") with a call for action. Those who are in the light must act, they must in some way live out the implications of their enlightenment. This construction contrasts with the Greek fragments that identify "rest" as the ultimate goal for the process of discovery, a goal which the Coptic text suppressed. It does not surprise, then, that the highest status of the enlightened person demands activity. The performance of deeds follows the achievement of that superior status.

The second question actually combines a statement and a question. The statement (also addressed to "you") correlates singularity and multiplicity within the subjectivity of the audience: "On the day when you were one, you became two." The statement is a simple declarative statement about the past: when singularity was achieved, multiplicity happened. This may be a reference to the biblical circumstance of Eve being formed from the rib of Adam (Buckley 1986: 88), the one that became two in Genesis 2.21–24 and that become one again in marriage. It may also reflect an understanding of the sort of enlightenment which this community of interpreters posits: the point at which the singularity is achieved becomes the very moment when a double understanding emerges. One of those understandings relates to the new self understood within the world of these sayings, and the other self, the duplicitous one (literally) reflects the rejected world which that new self has left behind. The question which follows speaks of a temporally present event: "But when you become two, what will you do?" Now this question makes more sense, because it refers to the call for action necessary for those seekers who have come to the point of recognizing that they have a different self than the one the world has provided for them. This different subjectivity demands a different mode of activity.

The communication of this saying does indeed operate at (at least) two levels, but these levels intertwine to force the reader into other modes of thinking and living. The two levels (that of discourse and that of content) posit a new reality by forcing the readers to enter into the discourse and to live in a world where the heavens are not eternal, the dead are not dead and the living will not die, the process of eating transforms the food into living being, being a person of light demands action, and where the two competing subjectivities demand action. That it has required this much explication to understand the means of communication stands as a testament to the saying's complexity and depth.

Saying 12

The disciples said to Jesus, "We know that you are going to leave us. Who will be our leader?" [2]Jesus said to them, "No matter where you are, you are to go to James the Just, for whose sake heaven and earth came into being."

The question of leadership, problematized earlier in the collection, re-emerges with this saying. The narrator again introduces the disciples' statement and their question. The statement indicates that they believe that Jesus will not always be with them; the question asks who will lead them. The statement and the question conflict with the mode of presentation: with the emphasis on the empowering of the seekers through most of these sayings, the question of leadership has always had an ironic component to it (see the commentary on Saying 3). The community constructed through these sayings needs no leadership that they cannot acquire from Jesus directly and immediately: not only does Jesus speak directly to the people, but the interpretation of that speech enlivens the seeker (Saying 1), this is, after all, the "living Jesus" presenting his "secret sayings" (Prologue). So in the context of these sayings, this first verse bears some irony in that these disciples maintain that this speaking Jesus will not always be with them because he will leave.

Jesus' subsequent direction that they should "go to" James the Just points them in the direction of a recognized authority in the world, an orientation also disavowed in other sayings (Saying 3, for example). Jesus tells the disciples that those who need leadership find James the Just. It is possible that this saying originated with the person James the Just while he lived, but later (after his death) he became more a locus of authority than a person of authority. The qualifying statement ("no matter where you are"), however, seems to indicate that such leadership operates in the same way as the text: James the Just, like the text of this collection of sayings, will always be available in every place. James the Just, then, functions in the composition of this Gospel not so much as a person, but as a tradition, or an authoritative method, or some other authoritative agency for those who need such authority or leadership to thrive. Helmut Koester (1982: II, 152–53) has taken the contrast of this saying with the next as an indicator of a "politico-ecclesiastical situation in Palestine" in the first century CE:

> The contrast between Thomas and Jesus' brother James, which appears in Sayings 12 and 13 of the Gospel of Thomas, allows the conjecture that the author of this Gospel belongs to Christian circles which sought to strengthen and defend the right of the tradition of Thomas against the authority of James, without denying the latter's claim to leadership in ecclesiastical matters.

This use of James as symbol of alternative ecclesiastical power is certainly plausible. The symbolic presence of James the Just in this saying inaugurates a list continuing in the next saying with Simon Peter, Matthew, and Thomas. The narrator seems to advance Thomas over the revelations of James the Just, Simon Peter, and Matthew. James the Just and Thomas both receive advancement in this collection of sayings, but Thomas retains the highest priority as will now be seen in Saying 13.

The context of the entire collection points to the deficiency of such a need for leadership, and the appeal to James the Just represents a sign of weakness. That deficiency becomes clear in the description of James the Just as the one "for whose sake heaven and earth came into being." In the sayings in this collection, heaven and earth have been problematized, even to the point that the saying previous to this says that these heavens are to pass away (Saying 11). This contextual problematizing makes the statement both ironic and negative. This negative approach to leadership becomes even clearer in the next saying.

Saying 13

> Jesus said to his disciples, "Compare me to something and tell me what I am like." [2]Simon Peter said to him, "You are like a just angel." [3]Matthew said to him, "You are like a wise philosopher." [4]Thomas said to him, "Teacher, my mouth is utterly unable to say what you are like." [5]Jesus said, "I am not your teacher. Because you have drunk, you have become intoxicated from the bubbling spring that I have tended." [6]And he took him, and withdrew, and spoke three things to him. [7]When Thomas came back to his friends, they asked him, "What did Jesus say to you?" [8]Thomas said to them, "If

I tell you one of the sayings he spoke to me, you will pick up rocks and stone me, and fire will come from the rocks and devour you."

This small, narrated dialogue between Jesus and his disciples and between Thomas and Jesus' disciples functions at a number of different levels in a complex style with which these sayings seem consistently to present themselves. There are three parts to the saying: the conversation of Jesus with the disciples generally and Simon Peter, Matthew, and Thomas specifically; the narrative relating the private revelation to Thomas; and the conversation between the disciples and Thomas.

Jesus' request of his disciples immediately presents a problem. It seems strange that Jesus, who has consistently been providing sayings to the disciples, the seekers, and the readers, asks them to characterize him. With so much of the thrust of interpretation of the sayings moving beyond easy categorization, Jesus' request to be categorized, compared, and summarized strikes the readers as unusual. The self-knowledge promulgated for the readers and seekers does not seem to have been pursued by the revealer. Something more is happening here; the question contradicts the dominant theology in this collection of sayings. Its presence here suggests some sort of alternative reading.

The three responses to the question present three alternatives: Jesus is "like a just angel," "like a wise philosopher," or totally ineffable because he cannot be compared to anything. The first two responses locate Jesus within the spectrum of understandings of divine figures as angelic or as transcendently philosophical. These two understandings of Jesus operate within the spectrum of commonly understood religious figures. Thomas' response, however, addresses not the location of Jesus within known categories of revelation, but the mystery that surrounds Jesus and renders him beyond the categories. Jesus' ineffability takes precedence over any other categories of description.

Only this last characterization warrants a response from Jesus. Jesus begins by rejecting the title "Teacher" with which Thomas began his announcement of Jesus' ineffability (Koester 1990a: 123 discusses the Johannine parallels). Jesus denies the role of teacher, a role that here must be identified with the strategy of categorization that characterizes Jesus as angel or philosopher. Jesus is neither angel, nor philosopher, nor teacher. Having said that, Jesus proceeds to make a statement affirming the priority of Thomas' understanding: Thomas has drunk freely from Jesus' bubbling spring. Jesus' response is a mixed metaphor: one part of it relates to drinking and intoxication, the other part of it relates to a bubbling spring. The metaphor indicates Thomas has drunk too much of Jesus, that his characterization of Jesus as ineffable results from Thomas' too free an imbibing in Jesus' presence.

The metaphor of the bubbling spring or fountain may be part of the stock characterization of the relationship of initiant to the divinized spiritual guide, as it is in the Discourse on the Eighth and Ninth (NHC VI, 6: 58, 13–17; see NHLE 321–27), another document from the Nag Hammadi Library. Here the spiritual guide describes his vision:

> I have found the beginning of the power that is above all powers, the one that has no beginning. I see a fountain bubbling with life. I have said, my son, that I am Mind. I have seen! Language is not able to reveal this.
>
> (NHLE 324–25)

The combination of these two striking elements (ineffability and something "bubbling") seems to point toward a common metaphoric structure for spiritual guidance: the guide becomes a bubbling spring or fountain from which the initiant drinks; the experience of drinking from this bubbling spring or fountain cannot easily be described, it is ineffable. The correlative traditions in the Gospel of John of the living water for the thirsty, both to the woman at the well (4.13–15) and at the great feast (7.38) underscore the possibility of a cultural discourse about spiritual direction as metaphorized as active water, bubbling water that activates the revelatory process in the seeker. That all three of these texts have the same elements witnesses to the existence of such a metaphor for spiritual direction.

This first part of the saying sets up a hierarchy of understanding of Jesus among his disciples. Simon Peter and Matthew are the most dominated by common understandings of Jesus: their characterizations of him as angel and philosopher neither warrant a response from Jesus nor indicate that they know Jesus very well. Thomas' response takes precedence over theirs: Thomas has drunk from that bubbling spring and recognizes that language cannot articulate the experience. Thomas' understanding takes precedence over the other disciples' seemingly inappropriate attempt to categorize Jesus.

The narrative that follows this conversation describes what happened next: Jesus "took him, and withdrew, and spoke three sayings to him." Clearly this indicates a special revelation to Thomas, so that Thomas' positive response warrants also a private revelation. The language of "withdrawal" implies a sort of drawing back, retiring, rest: it certainly suggests that the special revelation requires a different locus, if not a different frame of mind so that the receiver of the revelation will be prepared to understand. The fact that the narrator states that there were sayings reduplicates the process of this collection of sayings: the narrator characterizes the process whereby special revelatory sayings are transmitted to particular people. It is a microcosm of the process whereby the sayings in this Gospel are being transmitted in a special textual locus to the readers/seekers. However, here the specific significance of the *three* sayings remains opaque.

The final dialogue between Thomas and the other disciples confirms the hierarchy of the statements and the priority of Thomas' articulation. The violence of the statement, together with the disdain for the disciples, underscores Thomas' superiority: the others would attack him and, thereby, destroy themselves. The revelation that Thomas has received in private both threatens the others and would become the occasion for their own destruction. The reference to fire recalls the "fire" which Jesus "cast upon the world" in Saying 10: these disciples who insist upon being a part of the world will find themselves calling forth the destructive fire by their own insecurity.

The names in these sayings (see Walls 1962) are part of the strategy that was first encountered at the beginning of this collection of sayings. Didymos Judas Thomas provides the perspective through which the sayings of Jesus may be viewed; by the end of the collection, however, the title simply identifies Thomas as the authorizing agent for the Gospel. This collection of sayings refracts Thomas' ideology, and, therefore, his perspective pervades. In this saying, Thomas' perspective contrasts positively with the perspectives of other disciples who use more worldly categories for interpreting the sayings of Jesus. These sayings are a locus of contestation and conflict, even though the perspective of Thomas assures both private revelation and a new locus of revelation.

The role of the narrative voice emerges here as an important element, for the narrative voice mediates the entire exchange. This saying provides one of the few places where the narrator's voice emerges to link a sequence of conversations. The narrator, ideologically identified with the priority of Thomas over the other disciples, orchestrates that priority by producing a relatively complex narrative sequence beginning with Jesus' question to the disciples and ending with Thomas' condemnatory statement to the other disciples. The narrator presents a saying in three scenes. The first scene presents the dialogue from which Thomas emerges as the designated revealer. The second scene consists entirely of narrative material ("And he took him, and withdrew, and spoke three sayings to him."). The narrator suppresses the sayings that Jesus spoke to Thomas, even though the readers have become accustomed to have sayings related to them. The suppression of these sayings augments the narrator's ideological alignment with Thomas, but also establishes that the narrator carefully controls the material the readers receive. The third scene returns to the model of the dialogue, but now Jesus has disappeared altogether and only Thomas remains to deliver the saying to the other disciples. From these three scenes, Thomas emerges as totally constructed by the anonymous narrative voice. The real subject of this narrative sequence does not revolve about Jesus' identity, but Thomas' authority as a spiritual guide and revealer. Moreover, by placing this saying immediately after the one in which Jesus points toward the authority of James the Just, the narrator corrects that earlier instruction: now James the Just simply becomes the leader prior to Simon Peter and Matthew, but just as secondary to Thomas. This narrative correction may, as Koester (1982: II, 152–53) has pointed out, reflect shifting authoritative ideologies in the early church.

Saying 14

Jesus said to them, "If you fast, you will bring sin upon yourselves, [2]and if you pray, you will be condemned, [3]and if you give to charity, you will harm your spirits. [4]When you go into any region and walk about in the countryside, when people take you in, eat what they serve you and heal the sick among them. [5]After all, what goes into your mouth won't defile you; what comes out of your mouth will."

Saying 14 seems also to be conglomerate, consisting of two parts: it addresses the issue of pious practice in the first three verses; and it redefines purity laws in the next two. There seems no obvious connection between these parts, although obedience to Jewish dietary rules may perhaps be categorized as one of the rejected pious acts.

The inversion of pious practices occurs with particular vehemence. Jesus does not simply reject such practices as useless or irrelevant, but rather he portrays them as completely detrimental to the seeker. Fasting invokes sin, rather than purity or sanctity; prayer brings condemnation, rather than communion with God or an enhanced personal strength; and charity simply harms the spirit, investing in the physical realm resources best bestowed on the spiritual. The saying provides no particular rationale for this reversal, not even a theology of inversion: pious practices harm. The observance of such practices, however, stands at odds with the primary orientation of these sayings toward the interpretation of the sayings of Jesus by the seekers: the needs of interpretation with its seeking and yearning for unity and rest do not mesh with the sense of accomplished good deeds brought about through fasting, prayer, and alms-giving. Seekers have neither time nor energy for that sort of completed and final practice. This may be articulated in another way: the asceticism of pious practices conflicts with the asceticism of interpretation in the tradition of these sayings, and the conflict probably relates as much to the religiously settled pious practices as against the itinerancy envisioned by these seekers.

The second part of this saying comes from the earliest level of sayings of Jesus, as the parallels in the Synoptic Sayings Source Q would indicate. In this earlier context, the saying promulgates an itinerant missionary lifestyle with a very simple profile: walk about, accept hospitality, eat what is provided, heal the sick. It provides a window on the formative period of the Jesus movement (Patterson 1993: 128–33). These verses envision a period in which members would be "on mission," traveling about the countryside, dependent upon the hospitality and fellowship of those resident there, and healing their sick. The missionary aspect of their lives involves the performance of mighty acts (healing) as well as eating among the poor. John Dominic Crossan sees an open commensality that "negates distinctions and hierarchies between female and male, poor and rich, Gentile and Jew" and that "would offend the ritual laws of *any* civilized society." Such offense, he argues, "was precisely the challenge" of open commensality (Crossan 1991: 263). The community of this Gospel of Thomas saying, however, finds itself in conflict: on the one hand, charity and giving alms are rejected; and on the other, their missionaries could not survive without charity and hospitality, the very acts rejected in the previous sayings. Holding those conflicting practices (the rejection of charity and the necessary acceptance of it while on mission) forces the hearer to a critical discernment about such practices, to prevent false security while providing for the wandering missionaries.

In this later version, however, another saying of Jesus combines with it, and that combination inverts the purity codes associated with eating. Clearly the observance of the eating purity codes could not be maintained by people who were itinerant and dependent upon others for hospitality and provision. The reinterpretation of purity from what is eaten to what is expressed by the mouth redirects the meaning of the injunction from the context of the earlier missionary exhortation: it is acceptable to eat whatever provisions are hospitably proffered because purity relates to the mouth's expression, rather than the food placed in the mouth. The missionary injunction has become, in essence, an example followed by the theological principle which underlay it (as it has been observed in earlier sayings). The missionary injunction has been swallowed up by a series of pious inversions revolving about fasting, prayer, alms, and now eating purity.

There may be one more avenue of interpretation of this theological principle. What goes into the mouth is food; what comes out of the mouth is speech. The saying values speech, discourse, over physical sustenance. The discursive practices favored over the pious ones reflects that value system: the search for the interpretation of the sayings takes precedence over the traditional pious practices. The value of the missionaries' work, moreover, even when dependent upon the hospitality and charity of others, relates to what comes out of them, healing power and revelatory words, not on their benefit to others' pious practices. This reading finds a thread of consistency running through sayings that apparently conflict.

Although such speculation often confuses the issue more than it advances understanding, allow me to speculate about the relationship of Saying 6 (verse 1) and Saying 14. Perhaps Saying 6.1 ("His disciples asked him and said to him, 'Do you want us to fast? How should we pray? Should we give to charity? What diet should we observe?' ") and Saying 14.1–3 ("Jesus said to them, 'If you fast, you will bring sin upon yourselves, and if you pray, you will be condemned, and if you give to charity, you will harm your spirits.'") were one saying that argued against the continuation of pious practices by people who were part of the Jesus movement, but at some point this saying was split between question and answer. Perhaps also independent originally were the missionary instruction to eat what is offered (Saying 14.4) and the statement about purity that defilement comes not from food, but from speech (Saying 14.5). This missionary guidance in Saying 14.4–5 provides an answer to the question in Saying 6.1 about the proper diet for the disciples to observe. When the missionary instruction was no longer definitive for the community preserving the sayings, it was transformed by changed context into a saying about eating, suffixed with the statement about eating purity. This complex was later added to the negative assessment of pious acts in Saying 14 in order to defuse the potentially offensive rejection of ascetical acts in Saying 6 and Saying 14 and to provide an interpretation of them that would relate to purity, and not to pious acts in themselves. The texts were combined and contextualized in a continual process of the revision and reproduction of meaning.

Saying 15

Jesus said, "When you see one who was not born of woman, fall on your faces and worship. That one is your Father."

This saying ends on a very positive note: the seeker potentially may see the Father. It describes that vision of the Father temporally in the term "when" which implies that it will indeed happen. The instructions given by Jesus apply to that time "when" the seeker sees the "one who was not born of woman." There seems to be no limit to the capacity of the seekers to fulfill their desires. The seekers have been fully empowered, and know that eventually at some point they will indeed see the Father.

The "one who was not born of woman" characterizes the ungenerated one, or the divinity not sullied by creaturely status. It inverts at least two other traditions about "the one born of woman" which come from the earliest literary remains of formative Christianity, and forms an intertextual reference to this saying: Paul's letter to the church in Galatia, and the Synoptic Sayings Source Q.

In Galatians 4.4–5, Paul writes: "But when the fullness of time had come, God sent his Son, born of a woman, born under the law, in order to redeem those who were under the law, so that we might receive adoption as children" (NRSV). Paul's dual characterization of Jesus as born of woman and born under the law underscores the physicality and humanity of God's son that forms a redemptive link with believers for their adoption as God's children. The narrator in this Gospel, however, has Jesus indicate that this one "born of a woman," that is Jesus, is not to be worshipped, but only the "one *not* born of woman." Only the Father should receive worship.

The Synoptic Sayings Source Q (7.28) also plays on the phrase "one born of woman" in a saying articulating the relationship of followers of Jesus to John the Baptist. This saying indicates that John is the greatest among those who have been "born of women" and that the least in the Kingdom is greater than John. This hierarchy of value places those in the Kingdom above John who, in turn, is above others who have been born of women. The low status of those born of women correlates to the high status of the one "*not* born of woman" in this saying in the Gospel of Thomas. The sayings may indeed be in conversation, even in an inverted way.

One other cultural intertextual reference, from roughly the same time frame in literary production, may be found in this saying, although this intertextual connection remains much more oblique. The birth narratives of both Matthew (1.18–25) and Luke (1.26–38 and 2.1–7), although differing from each other significantly in their orientations and narrative details, both emphasize the birth of Jesus to Mary as a locus of cultic and theological mystery and adoration. The Gospel of Thomas, however, rejects such a locus, and ascribes worship not to the one born of Mary, but to the Father. If these birth narratives form an intertextual frame, then they may, together with this saying from Thomas, point toward an early debate about the propriety of worship given to human agents, with Matthew and Luke affirming the practice and Thomas rejecting it.

The intertextual reverberations with early traditions that affirm Jesus or the members of the Kingdom as people "born of a woman" underscore the negative characterization such a status receives in this saying. Significance resides with the one not generated, not with the generated one. The identification of this figure with the Father seems tautologous in that it states that, unlike Jesus, the son "born of a woman," the Father is ungenerated and not embodied. When the seekers have found such a one, they have found the Father.

Having found the Father, Jesus instructs the seekers to perform an act of ritual adoration and worship called in Greek *proskynesis*. This liturgical and ritual bowing down before a significant figure ("fall on your faces") presents an anomaly here, because this collection of sayings by Thomas speaks very little about cultic activity and even disparages acts of piety. The cultus, although it may be assumed to have existed, holds no particular interest to this community. Even if the statement operated as a metaphor, it introduces an element of hierarchical distinction inconsistent with much of the theology of the collection: so much of the theology has been oriented toward empowering the seekers and disavowing authority and hierarchical structures. It may be, however, that those who prostrate themselves before the Father become equal to one another in that Jesus subordinates all people to the Father thereby rendering them equal before the Father.

Saying 16

Jesus said, "Perhaps people think that I have come to cast peace upon the world. [2]They do not know that I have come to cast conflicts upon the earth: fire, sword, war. [3]For there will be five in a house:

there'll be three against two and two against three, father against son and son against father; [4]and they will stand alone."

Again the theme of conflict arises. Jesus suggests that some have interpreted the life promulgated in these collections as a peaceful one. That perspective certainly makes sense: the images of peaceful activity pervade the activities of interpreting sayings, of striving for spiritual development, of withdrawal from the dominant society, of yearning for self-knowledge, and of forming a community with others seeking self-knowledge. A peaceful transformation seems a logical and reasonable consequence of such goals: the reflective quality and educative orientation of these sayings implies such a degree of leisure and peace.

The new way of living promulgated in these sayings, however, emerges from conflict, from dissents, from both metaphorical and actual "fire, sword, war." Since the subjectivity and mode of living developed in these sayings draws a sharp distinction between those who know themselves and those who do not, and between those inside the community and those in the dominant exterior world, conflict becomes the primary means of self-articulation and definition. The development of the subjectivity promoted here happens only in the conflict of the spiritual against the worldly, ignorance against knowledge, and inside against outside. The conflict actually advances the new understanding of self, society, and world, because it stands at the heart of the creation of something new. These conflicts function as instruments of formation, and cannot be avoided because they demarcate an area for a new subjectivity by drawing careful boundaries between the old way and the new.

Verse 3 presents the social implications of this conflict and shows the contours of old and new relationships. Common relationships in the family, or with a parent, do not establish the base community in which the new subjectivity develops. The seekers must withdraw from family, from parents, precisely in order to create an alternative society, based no longer on standard social arrangements (whatever they may be), but now upon those who have begun to enter the other world constructed by conflict. So social division follows the necessary personal conflict, because the social division, as the personal conflict, articulates the parameters of social solidarity. In a household, the conflict will divide; in a family, the relationships will be severed. Something new, some different form of social engagement, will follow the conflict.

The final verse (4) articulates the basis of that new social arrangement. It consists of those who "stand alone." The solitary people, those who have sought their own self-knowledge and who have engaged in the requisite personal and social conflict, will stand as the basis of this new community. The conflict strengthens the solitary and joins solitaries into groups of those who can stand and even who can stand alone. The plural form ("*they* will stand alone") leads to a solitary or unified community understanding so that the group appears as a corporate and unified entity consisting of multiple parts. The plural form ("they") need not refer to an organized community, but to a loose confederation of individuals who, through the conflict in the world and the family, become solitaries relating to other solitaries in similar life-situations. Unlike the Pauline parallel that articulates the church as the Body of Christ made up of many members (1 Corinthians 12.12–31), the emphasis here resides in the isolation of the communal experience and its differentiation from the dominant structure. This community emergent from conflict will "stand alone."

Saying 17

> Jesus said, "I will give you what no eye has seen, what no ear has heard, what no hand has touched, what has not arisen in the human heart."

This saying focuses on four negatives: the invisible ("what no eye has seen"), the inaudible ("what no ear has heard"), the intangible ("what no hand has touched"), and (to keep the parallel structure) the inhuman ("what has not arisen in the human heart"). These negatives characterize Jesus' gift to the hearer–a gift that cannot be apprehended from a common human experience nor understood from common human instruments of perception (sight, hearing, or touch). Jesus offers the hearer something that transcends human capacity. Patterson and Koester rightly link this saying to the collections of the sayings of Jesus (Synoptic Sayings Source Q 10.23–24) and to a letter of Paul (1 Corinthians 2.9) as a strategy of mystification of wisdom (Koester 1990b: 55–62; Patterson 1993: 83 and 233). In the present context, such mystification functions primarily in relationship to what Jesus provides: the emphasis in this saying points backward to the giver, Jesus, rather than to that which the hearer will receive. The four negative statements thus enhance the status of the giver while simultaneously providing the hearer and interpreter with a characterization of what mysterious realities the future holds.

This dynamic of enhancing the speaker while holding out

uncommon and mysterious goods to the hearer points toward another purpose of the saying: the creation of desire. Offering the invisible, the inaudible, the intangible as well as the supra-human as future potential gifts for the hearer constructs them as objects of desire. These things beyond human capacity, which will come to the hearer only because of the superlative status of the speaker, become goals, lures, and attractions toward the encounter and the understanding of things beyond sight, hearing, touch, and human desire. The message, then, does not revolve primarily about the status of the speaker, or even about the mysterious nature of the gifts, but rather about the creation of desire. Desire, the longing for something unattained or the yearning for something absent, informs this saying. Jesus offers the seekers something indescribable and beyond perception; Jesus offers the seekers the fulfillment of their most profound desires. Such a saying provides a window into the attraction of the sayings in this Gospel: the potential for the fulfilling of desire, of being a new person, of living a spiritual life, draws seekers to interpret them. It happens not only in the mind or the heart, nor only in vision or hearing or touch; the desire for something unattainable remains constant and informs the process of transformation promulgated in this Gospel.

Saying 18

The disciples said to Jesus, "Tell us, how will our end come?" [2]Jesus said, "Have you found the beginning, then, that you are looking for the end? You see, the end will be where the beginning is. [3]Blessed is [SV: Congratulations to] the one who stands at the beginning: that one will know the end and will not taste death."

This saying is complex. It presents a traditional wisdom saying in form and content (Patterson 1993: 198) that revolved about the theme of the immortality of the people in this community (Patterson 1993: 129). The structure of the saying consists of three parts: a question from the disciples to Jesus; a response by Jesus; and a macarism ("Blessed is") that appears to be independent of the previous dialogue, but summarizes its content. Jesus' response to the disciples' question consists of two elements: a question and a declarative statement. That Jesus questions the disciples directly ("Have you found") suggests an increment of irony or dismissal, while the declarative statement summarizes straightforwardly the message ("the end will be where the beginning is"). This dialogue has added the macarism that connects it to the previous discussion about the beginning and the end and to the immortal nature of those who understand. The literary complexity mirrors the complexity of the content that identifies the beginning with the end and with immortality.

The irony suggested by Jesus' answering the disciples' question with a question finds corroboration in the content of the question. The disciples ask "how will our end come?", and the question redirects the subject matter from the discussion of the "end" to a discussion of the finding of both the beginning and the end. The disciples' question presents one understanding of the end; Jesus' response redefines that understanding and links it to a theological premise that identifies the beginning with the end. The disciples' question gives rise to a larger theological issue, but also betrays the now familiar lack of proper understanding among the disciples. Even though they miss the point initially, they will receive further instruction about "the end" properly understood.

The saying presents a rich theological perspective relating to the goal and mode of living. The "end" about which the disciples ask presumably relates to their deaths. The irony in Jesus' response supports their misunderstanding. Jesus' response, however, argues that the proper "end" should be understood more accurately as "the goal," and he argues that the goal of human endeavor involves a return to the beginning. The beginning, however, exists perpetually: it is discussed in the present so that the end in the future will return to the beginning which presently exists ("the end *will be* where the beginning *is*"– my emphasis). The beginning, then, must be understood as a primordial place of origin that continues throughout time; the end returns a person in the future to that primordial point of origin. This saying presents a mythologized understanding of human origins and destiny common in ancient religion as a future return to a continually existent point of origin.

The saying also links this mythology with immortality in the macarism. The language shifts in the macarism to use code concepts: "to stand," "to know," and "not to taste death." The searching of the dialogue has been replaced with the macarism that blesses "the one who stands" at the beginning. The articulated goal of the dialogue (finding the beginning) has been transformed into a status in relationship to the perpetually present point of origin: the truly understanding seeker may "stand" at the beginning and will thereby receive two benefits, namely, knowledge of the end and immortality. This macarism takes the myth of seeking the end in the beginning and turns it into a theological statement about the seeker: standing at the beginning brings both understanding and immortality.

This macarism also invokes other theological principles in the Gospel collection. The final statement "and will not taste death" recalls the earlier Saying 1 that affirms that finding the interpretation of the sayings confers immortality ("Whoever discovers the interpretation of these sayings will not taste death"). The standing may be identified with the discovery of the interpretation of the saying. Moreover, the seeker's "standing" recalls the earlier stance of the believers in relationship to the hostile world (Saying 16) and the later stance of Jesus in the world to which he came (Saying 28). Such rich intertextual reference indicates that a complex theological process undergirds this saying and its meaning: the goal of human existence is to find the beginning which may be identified with the interpretation of these texts, to gain understanding and knowledge, to achieve immortality, to achieve a solid status with other seekers in the world and to imitate Jesus' stance in the world.

Saying 19

Jesus said, "Blessed is [SV: Congratulations to] the one who came into being before coming into being. [2]If you become my disciples and pay attention to my sayings, these stones will serve you. [3]For there are five trees in Paradise for you; they do not change, summer or winter, and their leaves do not fall. [4]Whoever knows them will not taste death."

Sayings have been linked here in the staccato presentation which has been described above (see the commentary on Saying 11). Such a conglomeration draws the reader's attention to the process of communication as much as to its substance, especially since some of the references in the sayings have no obvious connection (the stones that serve and the trees that do not change). The meaning of the saying, then, may reside in the manner of its communication. The sayings present four subjects: a statement about the priority of being, a comment about discipleship, a description of the five trees in Paradise, and a concluding statement about death. The final statement that "Whoever knows them will not taste death" may refer only to the five unchanging trees in Paradise, or to both the trees and the stones that serve. The ending statement on not tasting death invokes Saying 18 as well as Saying 1 in which the discovery of the interpretations of the sayings confers immortality. The reference in these sayings must then be understood as central and important, because the end result of this understanding equates itself with the goal of the interpretation of all the sayings.

This intertextual frame, however, frustrates modern readers. The association of one saying with the others forces the readers/seekers to find the common element, to search for the perspective with which they all cohere; the sayings provide no such common point of interpretation. The resolution comes only as the readers/seekers tease out the meanings themselves, and construct their own meta-interpretative connections. I propose that the elements of this saying construct a meta-structure of a mythology of discipleship. That mythology consists of the pre-existence of the seeker before (embodied?) existence, the ministration of inanimate objects that indicate the superior status of the seeker, the five unchanging trees in Paradise that exist for the benefit of the seeker, and an affirmation that the knowledge of this mythology confers immortality just as the discovery of the interpretation of the sayings does (Saying 1).

The first statement in the saying presents the concept of pre-existent existence in the form of a macarism: "Blessed is the one who came into being before coming into being." The macarism presents an anomaly: the blessing is upon the one who existed before existing. The statement articulates two levels of being: the being that was before coming into existence and the being in existence. It speaks of temporal precedence of a person's "coming to be," and yet such ontological categories generally do not connote temporal order. Generally in these sayings the distinction among categories of people revolves about their knowledge of the interpretation of the sayings or their understanding of the new way articulated in the sayings as opposed to those who neither interpret nor understand. Those who participate in the new community created from those who find the interpretation of the sayings receive all the benefits and blessings of the sayings. In this saying, however, another element is added to the anthropology: there is a pre-existent existence presented as a theological or philosophical aspect of anthropology. In adding this new element, Jesus refocuses the anthropology that has been presented in these sayings. This new element, the pre-existent existence, begins to construct another way of understanding subjectivity by articulating an ontological pre-existence in a way that suggests a myth of an already existent being entering the mundane world. The language of pre-existence and existence, that is, suggests philosophical speculation on the levels of being developed mythologically.

The saying connects this speculative philosophical myth of pre-existent existence to discipleship in the second statement of the saying. That statement links discipleship and mastery of the sayings with authority over nature. Jesus explains that his disciples, those who engage with these sayings, will receive the ministrations of these stones. These disciples will, as another saying puts it, "rule over all" (Saying 2) so that even the stones will minister to them. In the hierarchy of being set up in these sayings, humans have higher status than animals and stones, but in relationship to other humans, the true followers of Jesus have clear priority so that they receive the ministrations of those levels of existence that stand below them. Although some scholars have sought to connect this portion of the saying to canonical references to stones (see Ménard 1975: 106–7; Meyer 1992: 77), the connection seems more likely to relate to the question of higher and lower levels of existence. Those who both become disciples and who listen to Jesus' words will find themselves capable of being served by lower forms of life along a hierarchical scale that now includes stones, existent beings and beings that existed before coming into existence.

The statement about the five trees in Paradise seems to explain the meaning of the previous statement by the connector "for." The mythology as developed in this saying posits a gradation of being and a system of lower forms serving higher ones. This statement connects these gradations to a "paradise" or garden in which five unchanging trees stand, so that it forms a sort of parallel to the pre-existent existence in some other realm of living. The "five trees" exist for the benefit of the disciples, since they are described as "for you" in Paradise, and they are immutable because they are neither subject to seasonal change nor do they lose their leaves. This statement suggests an alternative world to the cosmic world that has been problematized in other sayings, and constructs a mythological place correlative to the place of pre-existence that never changes and that exists for the disciples' benefit. The statement simply posits the existence of this paradise without engaging the seeker in any way: there is no injunction to seek that Paradise, or to yearn for the Paradise, or to find the Paradise with its five trees. Just having knowledge of the trees suffices to confer immortality.

The final statement ("Whoever knows them will not taste death") with its significant intertextual frame can either refer to the saying on Paradise or to all the statements in this saying. The knowledge of the mythology developed here that organizes a hierarchy of beings and posits the existence of a paradise with five unchanging trees confers the same benefit as the discovery of the interpretations of the sayings

(Saying 1) and the standing at the beginning and knowing the end (Saying 18) since all of these sayings present the seeker as "not tast(ing) death." The immortal status of the seeker may be achieved through a number of different enterprises (interpretative, intellectual, and mythological). This saying develops one of those enterprises–one that does not receive other significant development in the larger collection. The riddling nature of these suggestive statements returns the reader/ seeker to the starting point: they present elements of a philosophical mythology that may have referent to other myths of paradise (see Ménard 1975: 107–8; Meyer 1992: 77–78) but that only make sense when the seekers begin to construct some meta-system to account for them. This may, in fact, explain the point of the saying.

Saying 20

> The disciples said to Jesus, "Tell us what Heaven's imperial rule is like." [2]He said to them, "It's like a mustard seed. [3]<It's> the smallest of all seeds, [4]but when it falls on prepared soil, it produces a large branch and becomes a shelter for birds of the sky."

This saying may be found in three versions: the Gospel of Mark (4.30–32), the Synoptic Sayings Source Q (13.30–32), and here in the Gospel of Thomas. This version seems to be the earliest and least reworked of them (see Crossan 1973: 45–49). It is a simple similitude encased in a simple narrative, although the simplicity of such forms of discourse does not mirror the sophistication of its mode of communication. The narrative presents the disciples' request for a comparison that would explain the Kingdom of God. Jesus responds to their request by comparing the Kingdom to a mustard seed and by developing the elements of the mustard seed that particularly demand attention for the comparison.

The simple narrative structure also points toward the way the similitude operates: understanding of the first element (here, the Kingdom of God) evolves from an analysis of a second (here, the mustard seed with its elaboration). The similitude creates meaning by conjoining these elements: it does not explicate or define the subject discursively, but rather depends upon a clear focus of energy and effect in the conjoining of elements. The energy of the comparison rests on the second element, on the comparative factor used to explain the primary subject.

The second element relates basic information about the mustard seed. It characterizes the mustard seed as a small seed that, when it lands in prepared soil, produces a large plant. This characterization does not simply relate the relative size of the seed to the relative size of the branch, because the factor of the state of the soil intervenes. The tilled soil mediates the growth of the seed and enables it to grow to a large size. The productive mustard seed requires prepared soil in order to produce abundantly. The result of this combining of a small seed and the prepared soil is two-fold: the mustard seed "produces a large branch" and that branch becomes "a shelter for birds". The first of these results follows naturally: a seed, falling into prepared soil, will produce well. The second, the shelter for the birds, functions at another level. The large branch produces this shelter as a by-product of its own growth, because the shelter for the birds bears no direct relationship to the growth of a small seed into a large plant or the location of the seed in tilled soil. The shelter for the birds is an unrelated benefit of the seed's cultivation in worked soil. Such an unrelated benefit, however, pulls the emphasis in the comparison away from the seed, the soil, and the branch and places it more squarely on the peripheral benefit that becomes the essential element in the comparison. The point of the similitude rests with the phenomenon peripheral to its subject: the shelter for birds gives meaning to the seemingly mundane and natural process of a small seed falling on tilled ground and growing.

The comparison provides an explanation of the Kingdom of God. In its natural dimension (if I may call it that), the Kingdom is something small which, when placed in a properly prepared environment, produces rich and strong results. The Kingdom does not necessarily produce such results anywhere, but only in an environment suited to its growth and development. In a sense, this is an internal argument about the reign of God, because it seems to assure that growth and development–provided the environment has been properly prepared. There is also an external argument about the Kingdom. Others who are not naturally part of the production and growth of the Kingdom benefit from its development. Outsiders to the natural process of the Kingdom find shelter; one does not need to be part of the reign of God in order to benefit from its presence. The reign exists as well for peripheral shelter and for peripheral people. Just as the emphasis in the similitude shifts to the peripheral aspect in its culmination, so does the reign of God shift toward the benefit of those not naturally or normally a part of its growth and development.

Saying 21

Mary said to Jesus, "What are your disciples like?" [2]He said, "They are like little children living in a field that is not theirs. [3]When the owners of the field come, they will say, 'Give us back our field.' [4]They take off their clothes in front of them in order to give it back to them, and they return their field to them. [5]For this reason I say, if the owners of a house know that a thief is coming, they will be on guard before the thief arrives, and will not let the thief break into their house (their domain) and steal their possessions. [6]As for you, then, be on guard against the world. [7]Prepare yourselves with great strength, so the robbers can't find a way to get to you, for the trouble you expect will come. [8]Let there be among you a person who understands. [9]When the crop ripened, he came quickly carrying a sickle and harvested it. [10]Anyone here with two good ears had better listen!"

This saying has a complex structure made up of many elements. It begins with a simple question and response between Mary and Jesus, and it continues through a short similitude of the children in a field (verses 2–4), the saying about the thief breaking into the house (verse 5), admonitions (verses 6–7), and it ends with some assorted sayings (verses 8–10). The shifts in subject matter (from the field, to the house, and then to the exhortations) and the shift in address (from Mary to a plural "you") indicate that this saying has gathered a number of different elements and attached them to a dialogue characterizing discipleship. There is no reason to suspect that each element develops some aspect of that theme.

The systems of solidarity within the sayings portray who may properly be considered "disciples." The form of Mary's request for a similitude for the disciples and the form of Jesus' response both treat the disciples from a distance, a "they" who are a third party not present. Mary asks about them as though she were not one of them; Jesus answers about them and then addresses the audience directly "as for you" thereby suggesting that Mary, the readers, and Jesus are a category apart from the disciples. The manner of speech creates solidarity between Mary and Jesus and those who are addressed directly–a solidarity that seems to exclude the disciples.

Jesus characterizes his disciples as "little children living in a field that is not theirs." This characterization at once infantilizes them and considers them as squatters on someone else's property. The tone of this characterization underscores that the disciples do not form part of the inner circle of Mary, Jesus, and those to whom the exhortation is addressed. Not dwelling in a land of their own, they are forced to return it to its proper owners. In a sense, this could mirror the theme of the alienation of the disciples from the world (Patterson 1993: 127–28) and that certainly would be consistent with the disciples' orientation toward the world. In another sense, however, this could be characterizing the "disciples" as those who are squatters on the true land provided to Mary and to those to whom the exhortation is addressed. There seems to be an argument about the nature of true discipleship operating in the tone of the saying.

The narrative of the children settling in someone else's field correlates two elements: their living in the field and their clothing. Just as the field belongs to another, so does their clothing, so that the children may return the field to the owner as easily as they remove their clothes. This does not positively portray the relationship of the disciples to their environment. Not only do they live on land that does not belong to them, as children, but they easily and readily strip off their identity as disciples and return it to the real owners of the land. In this reading, clothing signifies socialization: it marks one person off from another and thereby establishes social distinction; it covers the physical self with an appearance that signifies social location; clothing constructs social identity. These disciples live in a world not their own and their identity (signified in their clothes) is superficial. Their discipleship is a social and religious construction not essential to their true understanding.

The juxtaposition of this negative view of the disciples with the following statement on the thief and the house identifies the "disciples" of the earlier statement with the "thief" in this one. The owners of the house would here refer to Mary and those to whom the exhortation is addressed. They are the true disciples who defend their place of living from thieves. The shift in the discourse has moved from a negative characterization of the "disciples" to the positive description of the state of preparedness of the true followers who, knowing that the thieves are coming, prepare themselves and their possessions and prevent the thieves from entering. The contrast between these two stories portrays the dual understanding of discipleship.

The exhortation ("As for you, then, be on guard against the world.") at once generalizes the theme of the story about the preparedness of the true disciples by applying the moral to the readers/seekers, and it invites the readers/seekers into a second story. The world, which now becomes also the place where the (unworthy) "disciples" live as well as the arena problematized throughout these sayings, puts true disciples on guard.

The readers/seekers become an essential part of the story: "Prepare yourselves with great strength, so the robbers can't find a way to get to you, for the trouble you expect will come." The parabolic element has been discarded in favor of a direct warning, an exhortation delivered directly to the readers. This direct address opens the dialogue to include the reader, and it aligns the reader/seeker with the perspective of Mary who initiated the dialogue. That solidarity among these true disciples revolves about their preparedness and strength in the face of a conflict that Jesus announced earlier: the expected trouble will indeed happen, so the seekers must strengthen themselves and expect the conflict.

The concluding three sayings, although they seem to be tacked onto the preceding, ought to be understood as addressed to the readers/ seekers and to Mary. The first saying exhorts about a wise person in the midst of the community: "Let there be among you a person who understands." Among the true disciples understanding would be the norm, but this saying seems to indicate a particular function of "a person who understands" analogous to the Pauline gift of interpretation (see 1 Corinthians 14.13). This suggests a community office of "understanding" given to a person among the true followers. The statement about the harvesting of the ripe crop follows upon that of the person of understanding as though it is an elaboration of that person's duties. Since it seems so unrelated to any of the subjects presented in this saying, it must be taken as explanatory of the previous statement. The disciple who functions as the person of understanding must also assess when the ripened crop must be harvested. This disciple functions as both the one who discerns and the one who gathers the fruits of discernment in the loosely formed community of seekers. And finally, the familiar injunction is added, encouraging those who are capable of hearing to listen, so that importance is added to the closing statements in this saying.

This final injunction to hear indicates the seriousness of this saying in making the distinction between true and apparent disciples and in gathering the readers/seekers into the inner circle of true disciples. The complexity of the saying confirms the complexity of the themes presented and of the interaction of stories and exhortations. The relationship of each part to discipleship follows from the initial dialogue between Mary and Jesus, but carries the discussion much further into the life of the community.

Saying 22

Jesus saw some babies nursing. [2]He said to his disciples, "These nursing babies are like those who enter the <Father's> domain." [3]They said to him, "Then shall we enter the <Father'> domain as babies?" [4]Jesus said to them, "When you make the two into one, and when you make the inner like the outer and the outer like the inner, and the upper like the lower, [5]and when you make the male and female into a single one, so that the male will not be male nor the female be female, [6]when you make eyes in place of an eye, a hand in place of a hand, a foot in place of a foot, an image in place of an image, [7]then you will enter [the <Father's> domain]."

This saying is nicely complex. It consists of an "envelope" that presents the necessity of becoming like babies in order to enter the Kingdom: the top side of the envelope (verses 1–3) revolves about a statement Jesus makes about the children; the bottom side (verse 7) responds to the question posed by the disciples in verse 3. The content of the envelope consists of an elaborate series of temporal clauses that describe the state necessary for entry into the Kingdom.

Jesus announces that nursing babies resemble those who enter the Kingdom. There is no more elaboration about it than that, except that the connection between children and the Kingdom has already been met earlier (Sayings 4 and 21). The disciples, here again in their less attractive persona, resist the statement and ask if they must enter the Kingdom as babies, somewhat reminiscent of the response that Nicodemus gave Jesus to the announcement that one must be "born from above" (John 3.4). The answer provided at the end indicates that when the disciples have done all that has been listed in between, they will enter the Kingdom.

The becoming-like-nursing babies takes on a strange twist in the content of the envelope. Clearly this peculiar assembly of elements constructs an understanding of becoming like nursing babies. The intervening material recreates the body, that is, the body of the seeker becomes something different (see Buckley 1986: 89–91): it is trained and transformed into some other kind of body, so that, metaphorically, it becomes a baby's body which will grow up in a different way being nurtured on the breast-milk of a different parent. This recreated body begins the construction of a spiritualized body fit for those who enter the Kingdom, and it parallels other literature in which the body is constructed and transformed through asceticism (see Valantasis 1990).

This new body emerges from complex processes that involve a series of transformations. The list does not seem to be in any particular order, but includes the transformation of duplicity into singularity, the transformation of the inner and the outer mutually to reflect one another, the transformation of the upper and the lower, the transformation of binary genders into a new and unitary gender ("and when you make male and female into a single one, so that the male will not be male nor the female be female;" see Till 1958–59: 455), the replacement of various body parts (eyes, hands, feet) with transformed alternatives, and the replacement of an earlier image with a new one. Every level of human existence must be recreated and transformed in order to enter the Kingdom: gender, appearance, body parts, theological categories (the images) all take on new meaning in the context of the Kingdom. This new baby, the person who has persisted through all these processes of transformation, may enter the Kingdom.

More than any other saying, Saying 22 most specifically constructs the new subjectivity promulgated by this Gospel. All of the primary features of that subjectivity may be found in this saying. The new person must be singular, replacing duplicitous patterns of living with singular, focused ones. This singularity depends upon the mutuality and consistency of inner and outer, upper and lower aspects of human existence. The new person, then, presents a totally integrated self who has worked through the binary opposites to create a fully harmonious self no longer regulated by binary distinctions and the hierarchies inherent in them. This new person in fact constitutes a third gender that supersedes previous gender categories while at the same time negating gender: the new person both creates a "single one" from the male and the female and destroys the categories male and female so that they no longer function as valid distinctions. This new self also demands the recreation of the physical body and its theological signification. The former binary gendered understanding of the body and of its image must be replaced, part by part, with the unitary understanding of all the body parts now reconsidered as part of a unitary gender and as part of a new theological image which gives meaning to the new subjectivity. This saying promulgates nothing less than a complete ascetical recreation of human subjectivity in every dimension of its existence.

Saying 23

Jesus said, "I shall choose you, one from a thousand and two from ten thousand, [2]and they will stand as a single one."

The solitary subjectivity that has been presented throughout this collection of sayings has had an individual at the base. The community of people who engaged in the sayings consisted of individual people, solitaries, who banded together with other similar people, motivated by the same desire, and engaged in the same conflicts. Here Jesus suggests another form of that solitary subjectivity. It is a corporate subjectivity of solitaries ("they") who stand as a single one. Those very few chosen ones ("one from a thousand and two from ten thousand") together will stand as one person. Although each person is chosen separately, the community of those chosen consists of those people with sufficient similarity that they may stand in unity.

The content of this saying connects election, standing, and unity to the corporate subjectivity. The concept of election pervades these sayings, so that the interpreters of these sayings form a cohesive community who live out their manner of life uniquely in opposition to the world. The gestural metaphor "standing" expresses that election to a new and different life and articulates the bold physical stance in relationship to the world. The unitary corporate subjectivity, the singular "they" of this saying, points toward the unusual level of solidarity and power experienced by the members of this community. Such sayings indicate the cultic basis of the participants.

Saying 24

His disciples said, "Show us the place where you are, for we must seek it." [2]He said to them, "Anyone here with two ears had better listen! [3]There is light within a person of light, and it shines on the whole world. If it does not shine, it is dark."

This saying consists of two parts: the first (verse 1) states a request from the disciples; the second (verses 2 and 3) gives a saying (paralleled in the Greek fragments) about indwelling light and its function. The relationship between the two is not transparent, because the answer does not directly fit the question. The answer discusses the presence and function of the enlightened person's light and does not describe Jesus' present location nor the goal of the disciples' search that the disciples requested. This suggests that the question was developed to portray the disciples negatively. While so characterizing the disciples' concerns negatively, the saying simultaneously conjoins in a puzzling way Jesus' present location and the indwelling light among people of light. The puzzle revolves about the relationship of Jesus to the people of light as well as about the origin of Jesus in the light that dispels darkness. This conjunction hinges on the identification of both Jesus and the seeker with the "person of light" so that at once it reveals information about the members of this community and about Jesus.

The disciples' request lacks any real understanding: they demand to know Jesus' present location and posit the search for that location as their goal. This locative orientation contradicts the understanding portrayed throughout this sayings collection which tends to emphasize the interior and spiritual self-knowledge as the goal and the beginning of the spiritual quest (Sayings 3 and 18). To look for a place and to seek for a place argues that these disciples do not comprehend the reality that Jesus presents.

Indeed, the answer which Jesus provides to this question presents the expected understanding of the quest. Jesus emphatically ("Anyone here with two good ears had better listen!") insists that enlightened people have a light within them that illuminates the world. Without that illumination, the world remains in darkness. Jesus directs the seekers to shine in the world with the light that is within them. This mission of the illuminated ones does not have any place, but every place; it is not the end of the search, but the product of illumination itself; it does not operate in another place but in the very lives of the seekers. If seekers search for a place, even the place of Jesus' origin, they will not find what they seek. Correlatively, the locus of Jesus' presence, his origin, is in the lives of the true followers so that "a person of light" describes both Jesus and the seeker. The seekers found Jesus in the interior light with which they are illuminated and may interpret the sayings: if there is a place where Jesus may be found, it must be sought within the person.

Saying 25

> Jesus said, "Love your friends [Coptic: brother, singular] like your own soul, ^{2}protect them [Coptic: him, singular] like the pupil of your eye."

These sayings posit a strong sense of solidarity. Those who have been enlightened, those who have engaged with the sayings, form a strong community in which the relationship of the illuminated ones to one another becomes familial. The care for the spiritual siblings, therefore, becomes tantamount to care for the self. This care revolves about love as for one's own life, and protection as for a necessary and very delicate part of the body.

Solidarity among the participants in this community functions as the center of their ethic. Although individuals and their plight receive attention, the corporate identity and its consequent priority of spiritual solidarity has a greater value. This interplay between the friends (Coptic actually has a singular "brother"), on the one hand, and the soul and the pupil of the eye, on the other, suggests that this community has priority over the most precious parts of an individual's life (soul and sight), or at least, the corporate aspect of this community's life compares favorably with the highly valued aspects of human anthropology and embodiment. It also indicates the close connection between members of the community in that a "brother" (as the Coptic puts it) receives the same attention and protection as a cherished part of self.

Saying 26

Jesus said, "You see the sliver in your friend's [Coptic: brother's] eye, but you don't see the timber in your own eye. [2]When you take the timber out of your own eye, then you will see well enough to remove the sliver from your friend's [Coptic: brother's] eye."

The eye connects this saying to the previous one in a catch-word relation. The similarities are only verbal: the eye in Saying 25 is one element in a comparison; in this saying, the eyes become an occasion for talking about helping others who are a part of the community. The prior saying treats the corporate identity and its value; this saying relates to an individual's social interaction with others.

The underlying theological premise here suggests that one must have understood one's own failings and dealt with them by removing them before one may attempt to assist others in the correction of their sight. This self-preparation does not revolve about a purity system that stipulates that only the pure or perfect may engage with others. The system in this saying rather posits that an increment of personal work ("when you take the timber out of your own eye") prepares a person to assist others with the removal of their hindrances and impediments ("you will see well enough to remove the sliver from your friend's eye"). This rule applies to the members of the community who have banded together in the interpretation of these sayings (the friends; Coptic "brothers") not to everyone generally, so that the ministry envisioned here remains only within the community. It also speaks disproportion- ately in that the person who helps another must look at the enormous hindrances within the self in order to see clearly enough to remove a "sliver" of a fault in another member's life without stipulating that this process is mutual.

This saying provides an interesting window on the relationships of individuals to one another in the community. Each individual, by working through and removing major impediments and hindrances, becomes capable of assisting other members in their healing and working with their faults. Ethical formation, then, does not revolve about a system of measuring up to an externally imposed ideal equally applied to all members of the community, but rather it revolves about individuals working on themselves among others who are also working on their problems in a process of mutual self-formation and corporate transformation.

Saying 27

"If you do not fast from the world, you will not find the <Father's> domain. [2]If you do not observe the sabbath day as a sabbath day, you will not see the Father."

This saying consists of two conditional sentences: the first joins fasting with finding, the second connects the observance of the sabbath with the vision of God. The exact parallel structure of each condition, following one upon the other as they do here, makes a connection between the two sentences correlating both the two conditions and the two results. In this parallel structure to "find the <Father's> domain" becomes equivalent to "see(ing) the Father" and the ascetical discipline of "fasting from the world" becomes another way of articulating "observing the sabbath as sabbath." The saying balances its elements so carefully that the finding relates to the seeing, and the positive construction about "fasting from the world" conforms to the negative construction about the observance of the sabbath.

The balanced literary cohesion of the two parts also points to their similarity in content. To find the Kingdom demands a disengagement from the world: the discovery of the Kingdom demands the careful regulation of the process of intake that "fasting" denotes. Fasting practices signify both a severe restriction of intake and the prohibition of certain foods altogether, so that one who fasts may regulate the quantity of food (eating only once a day for example, or every three days) and the variety of foods (abstaining from meat or refusing to eat dairy products, or eating only bread). "Fasting from the world" denotes this same sort of careful regulation, so that the seekers regulate both the quantity of engagement with the world and the variety of involvement in worldly realities. The metaphoric transfer of meaning from "fasting" as a statement about food to "fasting" as a relationship to the world, redefines the nature and significance of the concept of "fasting." The metaphorization of the concept of fasting dismisses the literal under-standing (in respect to eating habits) and advances the newly posited metaphorical reality as the dominant meaning of the term, so that by displacing the older meaning the saying directs the seekers to the observance of the new meaning alone (Sayings 6 and 14).

On the surface, the observance of the sabbath would join the other pious practices which these sayings have redefined and dismissed (Saying 14). The performance of external practices holds no interest for the practitioners posited in this religious collection of sayings. "See(ing) the Father" results from the proper observance of the sabbath. Just as in the signification of fasting, so here the meaning of sabbath finds new expression. Sabbath normally signifies the day of rest in the observance of the law; here, by association with the previous statement and by being stylistically intertwined with it, the signification of "sabbath" shifts from its normal meaning to a sabbath with respect to the world. The observance of the sabbath as sabbath signifies the withdrawal into rest, the regular participation in the rest that has been articulated as a goal in these sayings. The sabbath observation, then, performs ritually the rest which animates the seekers' activity and which fulfills the seekers' desires. This sabbath rest is a prerequisite to the vision of God. To withdraw and rest from the world becomes the means by which the seekers will see the Father. Without the proper withdrawal and disengagement, signified both in the observance of the sabbath as such and in the fasting from the world, seekers will neither find the Kingdom nor see the Father.

The fasting from the world and the proper observance of the sabbath constitute ascetic performances intended to enable the seeker both to enter the Father's reign and to attain a vision of the Father. The disciplines necessary for these goals require redefinition in the context of the manner of living promulgated in these sayings: the fasting refers no longer to food, but to the world; and the sabbath no longer to a day, but to the theological category "rest." As redefined performances they promote a particular ascetical program with specific goals attached to each practice.

Saying 28

Jesus said, "I took my stand in the midst of the world, and in flesh I appeared to them. ²I found them all drunk, and I did not find any of them thirsty. ³My soul ached for the children of humanity, because they are blind in their hearts and do not see, for they came into the world empty, and they also seek to depart from the world empty. ⁴But meanwhile they are drunk. When they shake off their wine, then they will change their ways."

This cohesive saying develops a theme: it begins with Jesus' self-description as an enfleshed person in the world and ends with an extended metaphor of the people in the world as drunk. The phrase "I took my stand" (Lambdin: "I took my place") indicates agency: to enter the middle of the world and to appear in the flesh are within the realm of Jesus' volition. Jesus comes from another place than "the world" and his nature consists of something other than "the flesh: " Jesus adopts this location and this ontological status. The characterization of "the world" and "the flesh," however, receives no negative treatment as being either unworthy of Jesus' presence or a diminishment of Jesus' stature. It simply states a fact: one who was not in the world entered it, and one who was not embodied became flesh. Jesus speaks of his mission in the neutral language of simple description.

The characterization of what Jesus found when he entered the world, however, disrupts that neutrality. This drunkenness (unlike that free drinking which Jesus ascribes to Thomas in Saying 13. 5) indicates stupor and disorientation ("I found them all drunk"), with desire inappropriately satiated by the wrong systems of fulfillment ("I did not find any of them thirsty"). Drunkenness does not signify ontological corruption, but a temporary lapse, a temporary and passing over-drinking that quenches the thirst but ultimately does not satisfy. The metaphor works at showing these people in the world to be disoriented and misguided.

Again, Jesus' reaction does not condemn them, nor reject them permanently. This life-situation of the people in the world evokes compassion and sympathy in Jesus ("My soul ached for the children of humanity"): it is not their status as creatures that evokes compassion, but their disorientation. Jesus describes them as "blind in their hearts" and unable to see; they are "empty" both because of their involvement in their world and because of their vision of their own capacity while living in the world. The people to whom Jesus came lack vision, their desires reflect the vacuity of their worldly life, and they do not grow or develop while they live in the world ("and they also seek to depart from the world empty"). The human condition lacks substance, vision, power: humans are those who "for the moment" (as Lambdin translates it) are drunk.

That drunkenness does not describe the end of the human condition, because by Jesus' entrance into the world and into flesh he has created an opportunity for change. These disoriented and futile beings will be able to "shake off their wine" and repent (the Coptic uses the Greek loan-word *metanoiein*). The positive note on which this saying began finds, after so desultory a description of the human condition, a suitable ending in change of life and repentance.

Of all of the sayings in the Gospel of Thomas, this one most presents the traditional gnostic redeemer mythology. The theme of the savior's entry into a world of drunk and disoriented people, blind, empty, and needing to find their way back suggests that this saying articulates a classically gnostic theology (see Jonas 1963: 48–97). However, the presence of this saying in this Gospel does not mean that all the sayings are gnostic, but that some sayings articulate aspects of gnostic theology or mythology.

Saying 29

Jesus said, "If the flesh came into being because of spirit, that is a marvel, [2]but if spirit came into being because of the body, that is a marvel of marvels. [3]Yet I marvel at how this great wealth has come to dwell in this poverty."

This presents another riddle for seekers to consider: the relationship of flesh to spirit. The saying considers the categories (flesh and spirit, spirit and body, wealth and poverty) under the descriptive term "marvel" that in its continual repetition builds from "it is a marvel" to "that is a marvel of marvels" and ends with Jesus expressing his "marvel" at the entire relationship. The riddle, then, commends the consideration of the categories, not in their philosophical or theological dimensions, but as the wonderful expression of the relationship.

The saying that "if the flesh came into being because of spirit, it is a marvel" could characterize the situation of Jesus described in the previous saying where the spirit appeared in the flesh and began the mission for which that embodiment was destined. In other words, the flesh that comes to house the spirit may be self-referential for Jesus, as well as a characterization of his mission as the physical manifestation of a spiritual reality. That constitutes "a marvel." The "marvel of marvels" is that "the spirit came into being because of the body." This could characterize the role of the seekers who, because their bodies dwell in the stupor of this world, caused the spirit to be manifest among them. The body in the world calls forth the activity of the spirit; the body's needs occasioned the manifestation of the spirit. This "marvel" surpasses that of the previous one. The fact that this wealth (the spirit) dwells in this poverty (the flesh and the body) truly causes marvel. The wonders include the coming of Jesus, the finding of the spiritual self of the seekers, and the conjoining of this spiritual and fleshly body in the world.

The preceding reading has taken the statements as real conditions, as statements that bear no irony. However, if the conditions are not real, that is, if they grammatically articulate what cannot ever happen, then the statements about marveling become highly ironic. The meaning under these circumstances would change. The occasion of spirit causing flesh to exist is remarkable; what is more remarkable is that that spirit exists because of the body. Yet even more remarkable is the living of spirit in the body of poverty.

In both of these interpretations, the relationship of these realms (spirit and body) causes wonder precisely because they relate to one another. The flesh and the body operate in relationship to the spirit; the wealth of the spiritual realm lives within the poverty of the world. The wonder emerges not from the mere existence and priority of the spirit over the body and the flesh, but from their union in the world. The problematizing of the world does not denigrate it, but makes it a place of wonder.

Saying 30

Jesus said, "Where there are three deities, they are divine. [2]Where there are two or one, I am with that one."

The Greek version (see the commentary above, page 43) differs significantly from the Coptic. This Coptic form may provide an interesting window onto the theological speculations of the community that produced the final Coptic version of the Gospel sometime during the later third century. In a Christian environment, it would not be unusual to find a speculation on the emerging doctrinal formulation of the Trinity, and the affirmation of the divine status of each aspect of the Trinity. The development of the theology of the relationship of Father to

Jesus and to the Holy Spirit begins early in the biblical record and continues throughout the history of the formative period of Christian history, the period covered exactly by both publication and production of this Gospel.

This first statement may simply reflect an aspect of that conversation: "where there are three deities, they are divine" (Lambdin: "Where they are three gods, they are gods."). As a statement about the trinitarian conception of divine revelation, it stands as a tautology: three gods are gods. This (properly speaking) constitutes a straightforward theological statement and description of the workings of the divine personae where each person of the Trinity is understood to manifest divinity. Along these lines of speculation, then, the "two" or "one" could refer to the Father and the Spirit, or to either one of them, so that Jesus affirms that where the Father and the Spirit (or only one of them) is present, so is Jesus. I underscore that this is mere speculation, but it summarizes adequately the attribution of divine status to each element of the triune divinity that would have been known in third- and fourth-century Christian theological circles.

The first verse as it stands makes a theological statement about divine persons or figures, affirming that the three deities are indeed divine. Verse 2 makes a statement about the presence of Jesus: "Where there are two or one, I am with that one." This describes not simply theological principles or tautologies, but presences, and it may, therefore, open other possibilities for interpretation. The saying differentiates between the theological articulations of verse 1 and the locus of Jesus' presence in verse 2. Jesus attends to the small groups of people and to the singular person. This suggests that Jesus assures the small conventicles of two, and the solitary follower of Jesus through the interpretation of these sayings, that he will be present with them. Implied in this formulation may be a rejection of larger congregational meetings as in the dominant communities.

The manner in which the numbers decrease from three to two to one suggests that the theological content of the saying forms a secondary interest. The content of the saying seems more organized around the decreasing numerical progression with the emphasis upon the presence of Jesus, than upon any theological speculation about divinities. The three divinities, two divinities, and finally one divinity culminates with Jesus' presence, so that what may be operating in this saying is an affirmation of the divine status of the corporate and individual members of the community interpreting these sayings.

Saying 31

Jesus said, "No prophet is welcome on his home turf; [2]doctors don't cure those who know them."

In the canonical traditions of Mark (6.4–6a), Matthew (13.57–58), Luke (4.23–24), and John (4.44) these pronouncements refer to Jesus, and explain Jesus' rejection by those who know him and by those who lived nearby him. The announcement of Jesus' rejection as prophet and doctor to his own communities serves the narrative function of announcing beforehand the eventual rejection of Jesus both by those in the communities from which he came and even by his followers. These synoptic interpretations rely upon the narrative in which they are embedded to construct that meaning, so that each one of the pronouncements underscores the narrative theme of rejection. Divorced from that particular narrative, however, these statements have a more general presentation and they are spoken as a general principle. Without the narrative structure, that is, the saying describes the experience of the seekers in such a way that the thematizing of rejection characterizes the fate of those who read and interpret these sayings.

The saying presents an odd dynamic between the prophet and then the doctor in relationship to their communities. Outside of these sayings, the "community" of interpreters and healers has been positively presented: the corporate identity and divine status of each member creates a positive image of community as it is experienced by the seekers. But in this saying, community receives a decidedly negative characterization. In the community posited in this saying, prophets are not welcome and doctors cannot heal. Both these roles have a social base: the prophet who reveals the word of God to the community and the doctor who heals the sick perform specific functions within a larger community. This saying characterizes those communities as outsiders and others: these communities reject the work of the prophet in their midst and receive no healing from the doctor they know. The dual roles of prophet and doctor function in a hostile environment producing discord rather than enhanced community living. These social functionaries understand themselves as "prophets" in an inhospitable community, and "doctors" whose knowledge of others prevents their healing practice. These roles confirm an important and articulated identity constructed in a world that cannot accept or receive the gifts offered, so that it creates the distinction between true community and false, between those who can hear the prophets' words and those who cannot, between those whom the doctor may heal and those whom the doctor may not.

The key to this distinction of communities rests with the nature of knowledge. In the case of the prophet, false knowledge is based upon familiarity with the prophet; in the case of the doctor, the doctor's familiarity with the patient inhibits the ability to heal. The false community posited in this saying results from the identification of community with familiarity, with those well-known to a community. True community, although it is not developed in this saying, rests on some other basis which the readers of the text understand as those who read and interpret these sayings.

Saying 32

Jesus said, "A city built on a high hill and fortified cannot fall, nor can it be hidden."

This saying presents two different kinds of information about the city: a two-fold characterization as "built on a high hill" and "fortified," and a two-fold description of the city as one that "cannot fall" and cannot "be hidden." These characterizations, in fact, explain the city's fate: since it is both high and fortified, it becomes both completely visible and invincible.

Although the content of the saying relates to cities, the message of the saying refers to some other aspect of the life of the people reading and interpreting these sayings. Cities, as social institutions, signify the community under its corporate aspect: many people make up cities, even though they do not all relate to one family, class, or race. The city envisioned here describes the community of these seekers: their society has been constructed in a high place, and their society has been securely established. The visibility and the protection afforded by the society enable it both to sustain attack and to continue announcing its message. This city can neither be destroyed nor screen its mission from view. The city, then, functions as a metaphor for the high visibility and invincibility of the seekers whose corporate lives have been built in a well-protected and fortified high place. Such a metaphorized corporate description undergirds the public sense of the community's mission while at the same time guaranteeing them the ultimate protection and victory.

These sayings balance the authority and autonomy of the individual with the intensity and solidarity of the community that these individuals form. The isolation from society as a solitary builds a very strong community of people capable both of making their message visible and of sustaining attack. Membership in the community, however, does not guarantee the security, but rather that security and invincibility comes to those who have interpreted these sayings so as not to experience death. Those who have found the interpretation of these sayings become invincible, and their message cannot be cloaked.

Saying 33

Jesus said, "What you will hear in your ear, [SV adds: in the other ear] proclaim from your rooftops. [2]After all, no one lights a lamp and puts it under a basket, nor does one put it in a hidden place. [3]Rather, one puts it on a lampstand so that all who come and go will see its light."

There is a problem with this text that needs to be addressed first. It involves a common problem, called a dittography, where a scribe seems to have copied the same phrase twice without any reason. In the first verse, I am correcting the reading which has a dittography. The text says literally: "What you hear in your (singular) ear in your (singular) ear proclaim from your housetops." The scribal error has duplicated the phrase "in your ear." Lambdin translates the line without the dittography as follows: "Preach from your (plural) housetops that which you (singular) will hear in your (singular) ear." The Scholars Version notes the dittography but translates: "What you will hear in your ear, in the other ear proclaim from your rooftops" which does not make particular sense. I prefer simply: "What you will hear in your ear, proclaim from your rooftops."

As these sayings balance the individual and the corporate so that the seeker may understand the relationship of self to community, so they balance the esoteric and the exoteric so that the seeker may know both their true selves and their external mission. These riddling sayings have been presented precisely in order to make seekers/readers think about the relationship of interior knowledge and external mission. The form of the sayings has emphasized the playfulness of their communication: they should stop the seekers in their tracks and force them to consider alternatives. In this sense, the message of these sayings remains esoteric, they are reserved for only a few, and for that minority of people who risk engagement with riddles and the new life that engagement fosters. The public proclamation of the message counterbalances that esoteric quality. Since the world itself causes people, as some sayings put it

(Sayings 13 and 28), to become drunk and disoriented, and since the world itself seems to mitigate against the sort of search for self-understanding promulgated in the sayings, that world needs to be confronted with the reality of its own life and presented the option to create an alternative. The conflict spoken of in Saying 16 does not exist for its own sake, but in order to draw clear distinctions and, ultimately, to draw the world into a new understanding.

In addressing this balance between the esoteric and the exoteric messages, this saying emphasizes the latter. The seekers announce what they hear, and they announce it openly and dramatically. The quiet proclamation heard "in the ear" ought to be "proclaim(ed) from the rooftops" in a strategy that makes esoteric knowledge public information. Likewise, the light which illuminates the person and shines forth in the world cannot be hidden and cannot remain unseen. The light also makes esoteric knowledge open to public scrutiny. The shining light metaphorizes this public announcement: lighted lamps ought to shed light, not to be hidden, or else they would be vainly lighted. The illuminated seekers, like these lamps, ought similarly to reveal their illumination, so that others, outsiders, will be able to see by it. The seekers' mission revolves about making that knowledge, those heard and illuminating subjects, accessible to the wider public. The mix of esoteric and exoteric meet in the metaphor: the illuminated seeker provides a beacon of light to those who are disoriented and guides them to the truth; the secret knowledge heard in private becomes a subject widely and openly announced.

Saying 34

> Jesus said, "If a blind person leads a blind person, both of them will fall into a hole."

This saying describes a very simple process: that a blind person cannot lead a blind person or they will stumble. Again, this statement metaphorizes another subject, because the saying uses the category "blind person" not to make a point about the visually impaired, but rather to characterize those who lack spiritual vision.

The saying thematizes the lack of true wisdom as a process of disorientation. Those who are disoriented cannot lead others who also are disoriented, because they will not succeed. Both disoriented people will "fall into a hole." In the context of these collections of sayings, those "who can see" describe those people, the seekers or the interpreter of these sayings, who are capable of understanding by virtue of their discovery of the interpretation of the sayings. Sighted persons not only see, but understand what they see. Those who are blind, on the contrary, neither see nor understand, so that they continue to live without light and perception. The blind ones are those living in the world. When one person in the world attempts to guide another, both will fail; when one who lacks understanding attempts to lead another, both will fall; when someone without perception instructs another, both will remain in ignorance.

In the wider context of these sayings, the members of this community would understand the blind to refer to people outside their community and perhaps to those living in the dominant culture. This saying, then, would also offer a critique of leadership. A true guide must be one who understands, perceives, and knows the way well: guides who claim to be guides and cannot function properly as such will harm both themselves and those they attempt to lead. The presumption here remains that those involved in this community, in the sayings, in the search for the self, the lamps (Saying 33) and the fortified city (Saying 32), make the best guides and will lead those they follow to their goal.

Saying 35

Jesus said, "One can't enter a strong man's house and take it by force without tying his hands. ²Then one can loot his house."

This saying presents two distinct perspectives. The emphasis of the saying seems to focus on the first one, that of the person who cannot easily enter the strong man's house to loot it. This perspective portrays the difficulty of the thief in performing the thievery in the face of strong and prepared opposition (as in Saying 21). The second perspective, however, describes the thief's difficulty with a focus on the strong man's house and fate. The thief may enter the fortified house and loot it only by tying the strong man's hands. The saying ends with the thief's perspective, and that would indicate that Jesus contrasts the thief's role to the strong man's, and that he favors the thief.

The "strong one" in this saying possesses valuables worthy of looting, and, presumably, has fortified himself and his house in order to protect them. To remain effective, the strong man must be free to protect his house and belongings. The thief must understand this situation in order to accomplish his goal of plundering. Jesus does not seem to oppose or condemn this person, but merely describes his role and fate. This perspective on the strong man inverts Saying 32 about the fortified city: that city becomes inviolable, while this fortified individual may find himself bound and his house looted. Within the wider collection of sayings, then, there are two distinct forms of fortification: a corporate and communal fortification that becomes inviolable and that reflects the values of the corporate identity of seekers (Saying 32); and an individual and possessive fortification that remains vulnerable to the work of thieves who will both bind the person and loot the house. Within that two-fold distinction, the energy and focus of this saying rests on the thief.

The thief acts as the wise person who knows that the fortified household may only be taken by "tying the hands" of the owner. The thief's plan shows calculation and shrewd appraisal before beginning to execute his plan. This perspective dominates in the saying: the possessive and accumulative world will not be taken over casually, but only through shrewd planning and careful strategy so that those who do think they are invulnerable become vulnerable, and those who apparently lack resources will use their intellect to plunder the riches. The key to success among the seekers in these sayings remains their ability to understand, to plan, and to use their shrewdness to accomplish their goals.

Saying 36

Jesus said, "Don't fret, from morning to evening and from evening to morning, about what you're going to wear."

Clothing bears a dual significance in these sayings: it refers either literally to apparel or figuratively to some deficient religious status which must be removed (as in the next saying; see also Saying 21). Jesus admonishes the seekers to cast off concern for their clothing. This admonition may be that, in the first instance, the seekers should not worry about the clothes that they wear, or, in the second instance, that the seekers should disregard the external deficiencies with which they live. Interpreters (ancient and modern) cannot avoid both meanings in the saying, so that the saying enjoins dispassion about the seekers' apparel, or a correlative dispassion about the removal of the cosmetic overlay to the body. The comfort of not worrying, in either case, directs the seekers to what has more essential value and greater permanence.

The characterization of the seeker as not fretting, or more positively as being carefree, underscores the centrality of the theme of freedom in these sayings. The lack of anxiety about food and clothing indicates the freedom the seekers are generally enjoined to develop. They are people free of family responsibilities (Sayings 16 and 54), free of social and religious constraints (Saying 14), and free of normal social engagements (Saying 42). Their freedom, however, enables them to become a fortified city or a light on a table to the rest of the world (Sayings 32 and 33).

This saying contrasts with the previous one: the thief must plan and strategize, but this saying promotes disinterest and lack of concern. The playful interaction of these sayings (and the next) promotes an understanding of human existence that at once demands great care and specific attention while also demanding freedom from constraint and from social expectations. Only those who are within the community may understand the relationship of freedom to careful planning, because both remain necessary even if they appear contradictory.

Saying 37

His disciples said, "When will you appear to us, and when will we see you?" [2]Jesus said, "When you strip without being ashamed, and you take your clothes and put them under your feet like little children and trample them, [3]then [you] will see the son of the living one and you will not be afraid."

The question and the answer in this saying do not correlate exactly. As in other questions from the disciples, this one displays their lack of understanding about the speaker of the sayings. The ironic part about their question is that the person speaking to them is the Jesus who "took his stand in the midst of the world, and in flesh I appeared to them" (Saying 28). They do not understand who it is that speaks and who it is that appears before them: they speak directly to Jesus as though he were not present ("When will *you* appear to us...?").

The answer that Jesus provides for the question develops a chronology of revelation not based upon Jesus' work, but upon the preparation that the seekers will perform. Revelation must be preceded by a two-fold action: to remove the clothing without experiencing shame, and to take the clothing and stomp them underfoot as children do. Although it is possible that the saying intends to commend nakedness (there are traditions of naked ascetics and holy people in antiquity and early Christianity), the saying seems rather to commend both actions as symbolic. The stripping and the stomping on the clothes are performances which point toward another meaning. Earlier (Sayings 4 and 22) children functioned as a signifier of a new identity: the person of understanding begins living as a child who then can grow to maturity anew. The presence of the child here points this saying in that same direction. The stripping without shame positively signifies what the stomping on the clothing negatively articulates: the person of understanding must put off the old person and must repudiate the socialization of that old person in order to become someone new. In essence that person, by stripping and stomping, becomes a child who can grow to understanding afresh without socialized encumbrances.

With the removal of the former construction of self and the repudiation of its socialization, the seeker may see "the son of the living one" without fear. With this statement, the disciples' question would seem to be answered: they will see Jesus when they have prepared themselves. But is "the son of the living one" a description of Jesus or of someone else? In the textual world created by the Prologue, "the living one" is Jesus, so that (at least in this textual world) "the son of the living one" would be someone other than Jesus. The "son of the living one" could be a self-designation for a seeker who is oriented toward the interpretation of these sayings and the close relationship with Jesus that such an orientation produces. The revelation that follows upon these performances (stripping and stomping on the clothes) will prepare people to recognize others who have also performed these acts. The new behavior of the seekers (at once bold, apparent, and fearless) enables other seekers to recognize one another. In so recognizing one another, they have also seen Jesus who both appears in and is seen in those who are his true followers (see also the commentary on Saying 108).

Stripping off clothing appears in two sayings within very different contexts and with different implications. The same performance may have divergent meanings within the same ascetical system, because the purposes of the performances may be different. As in the case of the rejection of fasting as a spiritual discipline (Saying 14) and the promulgation of fasting as a positive performance (Saying 27), so here stripping off clothes has an alternative meaning. In Saying 21, the stripping of clothing functions within the brooding and threatening narrative of warning and receives a negative interpretation; but in this saying, stripping off the clothes signifies the positive performance necessary for revelation to occur.

Saying 38

> Jesus said, "Often you have desired to hear these sayings that I am
> speaking to you, and you have no one else from whom to hear them.
> [2]There will be days when you will seek me and you will not find me."

This saying articulates two different and yet correlative aspects of desire.
In the first part of the saying (verse 1) Jesus indicates that the desire for
hearing the sayings can only be satisfied by his speaking, because they
will not be satisfied by hearing these sayings from anyone else. This view
of desire underscores the unique perspective in these sayings and
emphasizes that they originate only in the living Jesus who directs his
speech directly to the seeker. The intimate relationship of seeker to
speaker of the sayings has a specific focus and direction. In the second
part of the saying (verse 2), the desire that involves seeking and finding
Jesus will be frustrated, because there will be times when even though
Jesus is sought, the seekers will not find him. Reminiscent of both the
search for wisdom (Meyer 1992: 86) and of the Johannine theme of
searching for Jesus and not finding him (Patterson 1993: 87), this saying
suggests that these sayings and their speaker are not always readily
available: they may be desired, but not necessarily found. Together
these themes of desire increase the desire: on the one hand, desire
becomes magnified by only having one source for satisfaction, one voice
and no one else's will be able to satisfy the desire; on the other hand, the
searching will not always result in satisfaction.

Desire so thematized is a common subject in the religious literature
of late antiquity (Meyer 1992: 86). Yet this saying presents an odd twist
to it. The saying focuses on the immediate presence of the speaker while
indicating that that speaker will not always be accessible. Such a
perspective among a collection of sayings so emphatically made
available for interpretation startles the reader. The response to this is
two-fold.

First, the particular voice given to Jesus in these sayings evolves from
a curious presence in the ebb and flow of sayings. The voice challenges,
directs, mystifies, expresses wonder, teaches, argues, metaphorizes, and
problematizes in a way that constructs the voice of Jesus very clearly as a
purveyor of divine wisdom and revelation in the enlightenment and
empowerment of individuals and communities. The narrator of the
sayings, however, has constructed that peculiar voice: the voice does not
speak to the reader/seeker except as mediated through the narrator.
Furthermore, when the voice does speak, it differs from the voice of
Jesus in any one of the four gospels, as it differs from the (albeit slight)

voice of Jesus presented in Paul's letters. The particular voice emerges from the collection of sayings that have been gathered and disseminated and mediated through a narrator. The narrator retains control by emphasizing that it is not the text itself that speaks, but the mediated text, the text made accessible through the narrative voice. That textual voice has not, and probably could not, be duplicated in any other environment. So the statement "you have no one else from whom to hear them" underscores the need for seekers and readers to acknowledge the narrative voice as the transmitter of the sayings of Jesus. Although the voice in the sayings in this text is the only one that will satisfy, only the narrativized collection of sayings will make them accessible.

Second, this textualized reading of the saying links also with the reference to desire. Desire encircles the text: desire gathers the readers and makes them seekers through the interpretation of the sayings; and the temporary absence of Jesus creates the desire that makes the collection of sayings even more precious. To seek for Jesus and not to find him challenges in the same way the sayings themselves do, presenting a riddle unsolvable or a presence unknowable or a marvel unspeakable. They construct the desire that gives power to the sayings and empowers the interpreter to seek and to yearn, in short, to desire. The desire must be fulfilled while the living Jesus is present, because there will be times when that yearning cannot be satisfied.

Saying 39

Jesus said, "The Pharisees and the scholars have taken the keys of knowledge and have hidden them. [2]They have not entered, nor have they allowed those who want to enter to do so. [3]As for you, be as sly as snakes and as simple as doves."

The polemic against the Pharisees and scholars, so familiar in the synoptic tradition, has only a very small place in these sayings. Although these sayings problematize leadership and authority, they do not differentiate particularly: all authority, including the scholars and the Pharisees, presents serious shortcomings and problems. Within the context of the problematizing of leadership, however, these scholars and Pharisees generally fare better than the correlative portrayal of the disciples in this Gospel. Jesus acknowledges that these Pharisees have knowledge which they have kept secret, and that acknowledgment places their knowledge on a parallel track to the knowledge and understanding promulgated in these sayings. The sayings do not define the nature of the knowledge that the scholars and Pharisees withhold, but their stance contrasts with the relatively open access to knowledge in this Gospel, which is open to anyone who seeks to find the interpretation of the sayings. The key to knowledge of both the scholars and the Pharisees, however, has been hidden, and having hidden it they neither benefit from it themselves, nor do they allow others to benefit from it. Their knowledge is dormant and secret, and, therefore, ineffective. The admonition to be "sly" and "simple," following on those statements, suggests that the knowledge of the interpreters of these sayings ought not similarly to be hidden: these seekers are to be sly as the quiet and slow-moving snake and simple as the carefree and ubiquitous dove. Recall the admonitions to speak from the housetops and to display the light openly (Sayings 32 and 33).

Saying 40

Jesus said, "A grapevine has been planted apart from the Father. [2]Since it is not strong, it will be pulled up by its root and will perish."

The first verse makes a simple declaration that posits the planting of a grapevine beyond the purview or location of the Father. The grapevine could refer to (at least) two different phenomena: the world or another religious community. If the grapevine refers to the world, then the world has been established apart from God. This suggests a sort of dualism between creation under divine authority and creation by some other authority (a dualism not normally expressed in the context of these sayings). This possibility exists, but does not to my mind, however, provide the best reading of the saying.

The grapevine could also refer to another religious community, one understood by the recorder of these sayings to be reprehensible and false. These sayings distinguish between varieties of authority and differing ontological statuses: sometimes, for example, the disciples seem disoriented and confused, other times they function as real transmitters of the meaning of the sayings; the same may be said of those who seek to understand these sayings and withdraw from the world. In either of these cases (and perhaps more), the understanding that some people exist apart from the Father (the drunk and the blind in Sayings 28 and 34, for instance) occurs with some regularity. This simple statement refers to those people, whoever they might be, who exist apart from the Father and whom the community finds unacceptable.

The judgment by the community on that unacceptability finds expression in the description of what will happen to that grapevine: its weakness will enable it to be uprooted and it will die. The truly invincible people who find their escape from death in the interpretation of these sayings, can never be uprooted and destroyed. The true seekers cannot be thwarted (as in Saying 32). Those unworthy or false seekers, however, will find that they may be overpowered, uprooted, and destroyed. Whoever these weak ones are, this saying condemns them to destruction, because, unlike the seekers, they are weak and vulnerable.

Saying 41

Jesus said, "Those who have something in hand will be given more, [2]and those who have nothing will be deprived of even the little they have."

Fairness does not figure as a value in these sayings. This saying portrays two different types of people: "those who have" and "those who have nothing." To understand the inequity requires the possession to be clearly articulated: the "haves" possess the knowledge of themselves, or have the interpretation of the sayings, or sight and sobriety; that is, they have whatever this community values most and that makes them superior to all other living creatures. The "have nots" lack this spiritual superiority, and therefore, even what little they have will be taken away from them, because the distinction between "having it" and "not having it" does not operate in grades, but in strict exclusion one from the other. To have, therefore, means to have entered into an entirely different way of living; not to have means to continue living in a deficiency that renders any available resources useless.

The oddity of this saying relates to what happens to each of these types of people. The spiritually superior will increase, while the deficient will lose everything. This configuration emphasizes the vast difference between the two categories and underscores the divide between them. The depletion or increase are not scaled, but absolute phenomena: if the seeker grasps even a little, that small understanding will increase significantly, while the one who lacks understanding will lose what little understanding that person ever acquired.

Saying 42

Jesus said, "Be passersby."

This short saying connects with the complex understanding of the seeker and of the social world of the seeker. Its simplicity deceives. The primary signification revolves about a quality of disengagement, of distance, of non-involvement in the world, so that the seekers pass by what surrounds them in order to live as solitaries and seekers after knowledge of themselves. The isolation of the seekers in these sayings attests to the centrality of this notion of individual as distinct from group identity.

Having articulated the meaning of the saying in terms of isolation, a further implication emerges. The disengagement with the world does not entail leaving it; withdrawal does not imply that the seekers depart from the world, but that they disengage from it. The saying advocates a form of engagement that recognizes the world as present, but chooses to bypass it, to move in another direction, to operate in another mode of existence. This posture with respect to the world mandates a freedom from it while maintaining a relationship to it.

Saying 36 recommended that the seeker "not fret" about food or clothing, and this recommendation pointed toward the freedom that the seeker should cultivate. By advocating that the seeker become a passerby to the world, this saying further develops that theology of freedom. Freedom involves not simply being detached from worldly concerns such as food or clothing, but also the more general detachment from the world constructed as something by which the seeker passes. It is a freedom, but also a freedom fully involved, yet not fully engaged, in the world.

Saying 43

His disciples said to him, "Who are you to say these things to us?" 2"You don't understand who I am from what I say to you. 3Rather, you have become like the Judeans, for they love the tree but hate its fruit, or they love the fruit but hate the tree."

Following the pattern well established in these sayings, the disciples propose a question that reveals their lack of understanding. Their hostile question challenges Jesus' identity in the sayings: "Who are you to say these things to us?" Their challenge indicates that they do not comprehend the connection between the revealer of the sayings and the content of the sayings.

There are some interesting ambiguities created by the narrator's omission (or refusal) to identify the responder to the disciples' question. Although the narrator presents the question as from the disciples and as directed to the speaker of the sayings, the question may actually be put to the narrator of the sayings whose perspective on Jesus dominates the entire collection. The hostile tone of the question contradicts the tone of all the other questions put to Jesus by the disciples in this Gospel. The implied level of hostility in the question "Who are you to say these things to us?" parallels that of the disciples' questioning Thomas about the three sayings that Jesus spoke to him in Saying 13. The narrative disruptions in this saying suggests a deliberate challenge to the source of the sayings, a challenge that includes the narrator as well as the speaker, Jesus. The question could challenge the voice and the authority of the narrator of the sayings or it could challenge Jesus.

This problem arises simply because the narrator does not identify the responder. All interpreters have assumed that the lack of the typical "Jesus said to them" represents a scribal omission. The lack of the statement, whether intentional or not, creates an ambiguity that directs attention to the text. The text presents these sayings as sayings of Jesus, and therefore proper understanding of the sayings leads to the correct understanding of the source of the sayings, the living Jesus. This is clear from the statement: "You don't understand who I am from what I say to you." The response points to the Jesus present in the sayings and, thereby, points the disciples to the textualized voice of the speaker. The readers become caught up in a discussion about a construction of Jesus' voice that the disciples cannot easily or readily identify with what they know.

Apparently in the voice of Jesus, the narrator draws a clear distinction between the fruit and the tree. The narrator presumably understands the narrative task in this collection to present the sayings (the fruit) that have come from the living Jesus (the tree). The disciples with whom the narrator engages prefer one over the other, either preferring the sayings over their source, or the source over the sayings.

The speaker associates this sort of distinction with the sort of distinctions made by the Judeans (Lambdin, "the Jews") whom the narrator characterizes as bifurcating the tree from the fruit and choosing one or the other. The speaker projects a current argument about fruit and trees onto another problem between Jesus and the Jews.

The two traditions (that of the Judeans and that of the disciples) have a natural and complex relationship. It could easily be characterized as one of fruit to tree, of Christian fruit to Jewish tree. The saying suggests that it is futile to differentiate such tree and fruit, loving one and hating the other. Even with animosity between the sibling religions, the mutuality and correlativity of the two traditions coexist inseparably. The reference to the Judeans may reflect a time when the mutual self-definition and distinction of Christianity and Judaism occupied sectarian interest. The debate in this saying between the disciples and the transmitter of these sayings, however, has been connected through this comparison to the debate between Christians and Jews. The debate between the disciples and the transmitter, moreover, characterizes the relationship of the minority position of the interpreters of these sayings to the majority position of the church.

In the final analysis, this saying addresses the question of the inherent relationship between the source and the product of a mutually interdependent process metaphorized as the production of fruit from a tree. This discussion, however, occurs in the context of hostile relationships. With this constellation of elements, a number of possible interpretations become possible; even more given the suppression of expected narrative expressions.

Saying 44

Jesus said, "Whoever blasphemes against the Father will be forgiven, [2]and whoever blasphemes against the son will be forgiven, [3]but whoever blasphemes against the holy spirit will not be forgiven, either on earth or in heaven."

This saying extends the systems of hierarchy to the persons of the Trinity, and establishes a hierarchy for forgiveness for blasphemy. It is an odd saying in this context, because it takes up theological and penitential categories seemingly incongruous with the content of the rest of the collection of sayings. The saying has parallels in the synoptic gospels (Mark 3.28–29; Matthew 12.31–32; Luke 12.10), but these passages only have two elements: the forgiveness available for blasphemy against the "son of man;" and the lack of forgiveness available to anyone who blasphemes against the spirit. The fully developed Trinitarian reference would indicate a later development of the saying, reflecting perhaps a theological development after the saying circulated in its binary form.

Another curious factor in this saying is that the hierarchy establishes the priority of the holy spirit over the Father and the son, so that the blasphemy against the holy spirit rates a more severe punishment than the blasphemy against the others. The question of forgiveness establishes the relative value: a blasphemer may be forgiven only in two out of the three occasions of blasphemy. The third, against the holy spirit, holds no possibility whatsoever of forgiveness. This incremental valuation of the spirit becomes even more pronounced with the specific reference to the Father and the son; it is a clear hierarchy and ordering of levels. The fact that this blasphemer against the spirit will not be forgiven "either on earth or in heaven" further underscores the fervor of the categorization.

This situation begins to make sense in the interpretative frame developed in this commentary. In this Gospel, the text conveys the spirit. The conveying of the spirit happens in two possible ways. First, the voice of Jesus mediated through the text makes present the living Jesus to those readers and seekers who attend to the sayings. Second, the content and the method of presentation of the sayings provide the means whereby the seeker/reader begins to puzzle and to find the interpretation that brings eternal life, so that the spirit is conveyed through the interpretative process. This statement about the unforgivability of blasphemy against the spirit may also be textual polemic against those who do not recognize the spirit in the voice of Jesus presented in the sayings, or in the sayings themselves. This could refer to those who would denigrate the voice and presence of the living Jesus found in these texts, a blasphemous statement that puts the person beyond the possibility of forgiveness, "either on earth or in heaven."

Saying 45

Jesus said, "Grapes are not harvested from thorn trees, nor are figs gathered from thistles, for they yield no fruit. [2]Good persons produce good from what they've stored up; [3]bad persons produce evil from the wickedness they've stored up in their hearts, and say evil things. [4]For from the overflow of the heart they produce evil."

The ascetical principle implicit in this saying correlates the exterior activity with the interior disposition of a person. The saying presents the principle in three forms: a statement about the relationship of fruit to the plant that produces it, a short positive statement of the principle, and a longer negative statement. Jesus says that grapes do not come from thorn trees or figs from thistles, and such a statement is logically true: the fruit grows only from plants capable of producing it. The positive statement of the principle, however, adds a further explanation (as though fruit were "stored up" in the branches of its source) that good people produce good from the good which they have stored up within. The negative statement repeats the statement, bad people produce bad from the bad they have stored up. The place of the "storing" is identified as the heart, and the fruit is speaking evil things. This is restated in the final verse so that the saying seems to be primarily concerned with the explanation of evil deeds and sayings rather than the positive statement about the production of good deeds and sayings. In its negative expression, this saying connects to the previous saying about the "blaspheming" against the holy spirit and posits an explanation for such blasphemy: those blasphemers have stored up evil in their hearts.

The seekers, then, are understood as the good persons who bear good fruit, while their opponents or the members of the dominant culture are bad persons producing bad fruit. There is a clear differentiation of good and bad people and the clear distinction of the fruit follows from it. Humans, whether good or bad, are metaphorized as plants bearing fruit consistent with their nature. Humanity, consequently, falls into clear and natural distinctions of good and bad discernible from their actions or fruits.

Saying 46

> Jesus said, "From Adam to John the Baptist, among those born of women, no one is so much greater than John the Baptist that his eyes should not be averted. ²But I have said that whoever among you becomes a child will recognize the <Father's> imperial rule and will become greater than John."

The hierarchy among human beings again emerges in the sayings. This time the hierarchy relates to the old dispensation and the new. John the Baptist was the apex of the old system, begun in Adam and finding its fullest expression in the Baptist. This old dispensation includes all those "born of woman," a descriptor which emphasizes the natural birth of these religious figures.

These referents to figures from religious history (John the Baptist and Adam) form part of a quasi-liturgical metaphor indicated by the gestural sign, averting the eyes. The averting of the eyes suggest that this is the posture or gesture of a less powerful person in the presence of divine or more powerful figures. The gesture acts out the relationship in a structured and clear manner that suggests a liturgical milieu for its performance. The liturgical posture metaphorizes the high standing of the seekers who need not avert their eyes from these important figures.

Jesus' statement about the children, however, displaces this old dispensation represented by these figures. There are two elements in his statement: about becoming a child, and about the superior status of one who becomes a child. This "becoming a child" replaces the system inaugurated under the sign "born of woman:" it is a kind of rebirth, reorientation, retraining that makes the old person someone new. That new person, that new subjectivity, has priority over the old, so that anyone who strives to become a child, to be recreated as a human, will recognize the reign of God. Those new persons, with their new understanding of God, become superior even to John the Baptist, the apex of the old dispensation. So within the hierarchy of human existence, then, humanity is divided into four: the worldly and the spiritual, the spiritual of the old dispensation and the spiritual of the new. This set of distinctions constructs the functioning anthropology implicit in these sayings.

Saying 47

Jesus said, "A person cannot mount two horses or bend two bows. [2]And a slave cannot serve two masters, otherwise that slave will honor the one and offend the other. [3]Nobody drinks aged wine and immediately wants to drink young wine. [4]Young wine is not poured into old wineskins, or they might break, and aged wine is not poured into a new wineskin, or it might spoil. [5]An old patch is not sewn onto a new garment, since it would create a tear."

This saying metaphorizes the relationship between the new person envisioned in these sayings and the old. The constant comparison of old and new, aged and young, characterizes the person of the old dispensation and the person of the new. The sayings gather under three headings: the number two; lore about wine and winedrinking; and a statement about sewing.

The sayings about the number two provide evidence for the strict bifurcation of the two worlds in which the person functions. One person cannot mount two horses: the world of those interpreting these sayings and the exterior world function like independent horses, and the seekers must decide which of them they will ride, because no one can ride both. The two bows provide a similar icon. The statement about a slave serving two masters (a saying with a parallel in the Synoptic Sayings Source Q 16.13) also strictly bifurcates the masters, suggesting that they are polar opposites, because in one action the slave honors one and offends the other. This polar opposition also characterizes the two worlds which vie for the seekers' loyalty and service.

The wine and winedrinking lore supports this understanding of the relationship between these two worlds. The desire for depth in taste, and the acquiring of that depth, will expel any desire for a less-developed taste. The aged wine presumably refers to the richness of the spiritual life presented to those who interpret these sayings, while the young wine refers to the lesser things of the world. The incompatibility of the old with the new picks up the force of the statements about the number two: the old and young do not mix in wine and wineskins because it would either break the wineskin or spoil the wine. Not only, as in the previous saying, are these two worlds bifurcated, but they are also detrimental one to the other and they cannot be mixed. The conflict of worlds, stated in other sayings, underscores this detrimental relationship. These worlds conflict and their relationship is not benign, but violent.

The garment statement summarizes all this. A new garment cannot support an old patch, the new subjectivity and identity cannot even be patched with the old. They are so different that the presence of the old would only ruin the new. These statements all support a clear demarcation of old from new. The new subjectivity must be clearly delineated from the old, and it cannot be either mixed into the old or patched onto the old ways of living.

Saying 48

> Jesus said, "If two make peace with each other in a single house, they will say to this mountain, 'Move from here!' and it will move."

This saying links the establishment of peace in a household with the exercise of power. In comparison to the other gospel traditions as in Matthew 17.20 (see also Mark 11.22–23), the ability to move the mountain connects with faith (see Ménard 1975: 150) so that the difference here relates to the origin of the capacity to move mountains: by faith or by the creation of peace. In relation to all the sayings in this collection about conflict and division in households, this linking seems unusual in that it seems to favor making peace over conflict: compare the attitude expressed here to Saying 10, on casting fire on the world; Saying 16, the conflict within the household; Saying 55, on hating father and mother; Saying 99 on Jesus' true brothers and sisters. This saying, however, posits the possibility of peace within a household: that is, those within the household who were in conflict may indeed establish peace among themselves.

Since the conflict with the world preoccupies seekers, this saying suggests that those seekers within a household who have both attained self-knowledge and who live together harmoniously will achieve a high level of power sufficient to move a mountain. This understanding of the harmony of spiritual people in the household emerges from the designation of the household as "a single house" (Lambdin: "in this one house"): the number "one" or "single" marks the household and this marking connects with the understanding of the seekers' subjectivity as singular or unitary. The household, then, that becomes like the seeker, that exemplifies the solitary and unitary subjectivity, will experience this extraordinary power.

The saying, moreover, presents the question of power obliquely through an example. It does not simply say that harmonious unity will lead to power, but that it will enable the two to move a mountain with a verbal command. The saying supposes that such a verbal command and its accomplishment signifies power, but the metaphorization of the process, the use of the example of moving a mountain, suggests also that these people will have authority over nature. The seekers who establish peace will have power not only to command and have that command obeyed, but to command the physical world and to have even nature obey. This power invokes the concept of "ruling over all" referred to in Saying 2.

Saying 49

> Jesus said, "Blessed are [SV: Congratulations to] those who are alone and chosen, for you will find the <Father's> domain. For you have come from it, and you will return there again."

This saying has three parts: a general macarism regarding the alone and the chosen; the application of that macarism to the readers/seekers in a direct address with an explanatory phrase that indicates that they will find the Kingdom; and a final characterization of the origin and destiny of the readers/hearers in the Kingdom. Each part of the saying develops one aspect of the lives of the hearers/seekers: the first part establishes that they are both elect and solitary; the second part links them with the elect and solitary and with their entrance into the Kingdom; the third part connects those hearers, now identified as the elect and solitary, with those whose origins and destiny remain in the Kingdom of God. It is a complex process of interlinking and identification of one group with another and with the theology of that group which is further complicated by the linguistic correlations of the term *monachos* ("alone") with Sayings 16, 49, and 75 (see Harl 1960; Klijn 1962; Griffith 1995).

The macarism portion of this marks the seekers under two distinct headings: those who are alone and those who are chosen. And it pronounces the blessing upon those who are both alone and chosen, so that the blessing would not necessarily relate only to people in one category, but to those who are in both: it suggests that to be a solitary does not necessarily automatically confer election. In theory at least, those who are *both* solitary and chosen will find the Kingdom, but, presumably, those who are only solitaries (without being chosen) and those who are chosen (without being solitaries) will not find the Kingdom.

The identification of the "you" who "will find the <Father's> domain" with these solitary and elect who are blessed provides an important window into the way these sayings construct an identity among those who are readers or hearers of the sayings. A reader or seeker understands three things from this second statement: they are *monachos*, they are chosen, and they will find the Kingdom. The two generalized categories ("those who are alone and chosen") become a descriptor of the hearer and seeker through the designation in the second phrase as "you". Those who are designated as "you" in the saying come to understand themselves as the elect and the solitary who will find the Kingdom.

The construction of identity continues in the third portion of the saying: "For you have come from it, and you will return there again." Those designated as "you" now understand themselves as having their origin in the Kingdom, and as having their goal to return to the Kingdom. The question of origin and destiny undergirds the process of election: those who have come from the Kingdom, and who continue as solitaries, are those who have been chosen to return to the Kingdom. The change in address accentuates the fact that the readers/seekers are those who "have come from it (the Kingdom)" and who "will return there again," that is, it accentuates their election from the Kingdom to the Kingdom through their solitude and the rediscovery of the Kingdom. The readers/seekers, for whom the Kingdom functions as origin and destiny, already have the status both of solitary and elected person through Jesus' simple direct address to the readers.

This somewhat simple saying provides important access to the process of the development of an identity. It shows how categories are presented simply, and then applied to the readers, and then further developed theologically so that the readers and seekers in the narrative begin slowly to understand themselves in alternative categories. The construction of these seekers and hearers as solitary, chosen, finding the Kingdom, and having their origin and destiny in the Kingdom sets the stage for their understanding of every other aspect of their lives. This identity replaces the common, or original identity, and creates the alternative subjectivity envisioned through the interpretation of these sayings.

Saying 50

Jesus said, "If they say to you, 'Where have you come from?' say to them, 'We have come from the light, from the place where the light came into being by itself, established [itself], and appeared in their image.' [2]If they say to you, 'Is it you?' say, 'We are its children, and we are the chosen of the living Father.' [3]If they ask you, 'What is the evidence of your Father in you?' say to them, 'It is motion and rest.' "

In these sayings, questions normally function as occasions of inversion or ridicule: they either mock the disciples (as in the following Saying 51) or they provide an answer that forces some alternative understanding (as in Saying 43). Here, however, the questions form a kind of exercise, or training, for those who might be questioned, because it gives the appearance of being a sustained and systematic presentation of the origins and goals of these seekers before outsiders. There are three related questions (itself unusual in these sayings) that posit an outsider, a "they," who will challenge the seekers or (if this is related to Saying 49) those whose origin and destiny is in the Kingdom. These answers, then, are for outsiders and people not sympathetic to the movement or its theology.

The first point regards the origin of these people. The question put to the seekers from without the movement asks "Where have you come from?" The response establishes that light is the origin of these seekers:

"We have come from the light." Three explanations of this light follow. First, the light from which they have come is the place where light created itself. This designation suggests a sort of primordial place of light when light preceded any other creation, and, therefore, may be part of the myth of the generation of light. It does not, however, refer to the Genesis account of creation, because in this Gospel light generates itself (or, as Lambdin translates it, "the light came into being on its own accord."). Second, light established itself in that place. This designation suggests that the light permanently set at bay the darkness: for light to be established it needs permanently to stand in opposition to darkness. It may also refer to the process whereby Jesus claims to have taken his stand in the midst of the world (the Coptic verbs are the same here and in Saying 28). The opacity of the statement does not preclude understanding the light as a barrier to the darkness. Third, the "light appeared in their image." This designation projects that light into the "image" of the seekers: that place where light originated and established itself is within the seekers, in their "image", in their portrait or likeness. What has been described as exterior as a place in the first two statements becomes interiorized as "image" in the third: the light that exists outside the person primordially images the light refracted interiorily.

Again in the setting of controversy, Jesus instructs that, should "they" question the seekers about whether they are the light (or the Kingdom?), the seekers should announce themselves as the offspring of light and "the elect of the living Father." Although in other sayings the status of the seekers is extolled, here the seekers place themselves in subordinate position, on one hand, as children of the light, and, on the other, as of incrementally high value, as the elect. The living Father, like the living Jesus who speaks in these sayings, has produced elect children who are entitled to find the Kingdom.

The final instructive question revolves about the evidence of their election. "They" will ask for proof that the Father dwells in them. The level of disbelief from outsiders of the elect status of the seekers surprises. This could be a point for the construction of the sociology of these readers and seekers, because here we find the kind of hostility from outside the community, and that hostility is identified with specific questions about the composition of the elect. The proof of their relationship with the Father involves "rest and motion." These two designators of the presence of the Father point toward two major themes in these sayings. Motion correlates to the levels of activity which these sayings promote: seeking and finding (Saying 1), desiring (Saying

17), loving, disengaging (Saying 42), unifying (Saying 22), making peace (Saying 48)–the seekers in these sayings exhibit a high level of activity. The goal of that activity, however, is rest, the disengagement from the vain activity of the world, the observance of the sabbath as sabbath (Saying 27). Both motion and rest mark the seekers as those who have the Father within them.

Although I argued above that these answers were intended to be given to the outsiders (the "they" of the saying), they also provide important information to the seekers in these sayings. The outwardly directed question becomes an occasion for this group's renewal and celebration of their own identity. The polemical aspect of these questions has been so diminished (simply to a "they") that these answers actually seem only to function with the interior group in mind. The explanation to opponents, that is, plays a secondary role to the primary role of the seekers gaining an understanding of themselves through the training this question-and-answer session provides.

Saying 51

His disciples said to him, "When will the rest for the dead take place, and when will the new world come?" [2]He said to them, "What you are looking forward to has come, but you don't know it."

Again the questioning of the disciples indicates that they do not understand. They put two questions to Jesus, one about the repose of the dead and the second about the new world. The first misses the point because the rest belongs not to the dead, but to those who have begun to interpret the sayings. The importance of rest as a consequence of living the life promulgated in these sayings affirms that rest is for the living, not the dead (See Saying 50.3, for example). Likewise, the new world has come to anyone who begins to interpret these sayings, or who enters into conflict with the old world, or who has begun to achieve self-knowledge, or has loved the spiritual companions more than self. The disciples understand these phenomena as future events which will be manifest and whose timing Jesus knows.

Jesus rejects the disciples' future orientation toward rest and the new world (see Patterson 1993: 208–14). The rest and the new world have already arrived, according to Jesus. Jesus states openly that the disciples do not understand nor recognize these realities, but prefer to wait expectantly for that which has already occurred.

This saying joins with other sayings that emphasize the immediate and present state of the fulfillment offered to the seekers in this Gospel (see Sayings 5, 59, 77, and 91). The tendency from the very earliest sayings has been to emphasize that life is realized fully before death (as in Saying 1) for those who seek the true meaning. The fact that Jesus presents himself as living in the community underscores that the present moment, not the past and not even the future, has a greater value for the people gathered through the interpretation of these sayings.

Saying 52

His disciples said to him, "Twenty-four prophets have spoken in Israel, and they all spoke of you." [2]He said to them, "You have disregarded the living one who is in your presence, and have spoken of the dead."

The theme of the fate of the dead continues in this saying. The disciples propose that the twenty-four prophets, presumably the entirety of the Hebrew Scriptures (according to 2 Esdras 14.45), have all pointed toward Jesus. The saying posits a hidden subject matter to the discourse of the twenty-four prophets, in the same way that the written text of this collection of sayings speaks on a number of different levels. The real subject matter of the Israelite Scriptures has been Jesus.

Jesus, however, rejects this construction. The claim that the Israelite scriptures created a discourse about Jesus displaces the reality of "the living one in your presence." Notice this living one, who has been identified with Jesus in the Prologue, does not speak of a living Jesus, but of a "living one." The voice of these sayings, the voice created by the recorder in the collection, remains a living voice, a living voice of a living person, not to be identified either with an historical person or an historical prophesy. The historical ones have died, but the narrative voice continues forever. The narrator portrays Jesus as rejecting the textualized prophesies of the Israelite Scriptures–these are dead writings–in favor of the narrator's own constructed "living" voice from the "living one" who speaks the sayings of Jesus.

Saying 53

His disciples said to him, "Is circumcision useful or not?" [2]He said to them, "If it were useful, their father would produce children already circumcised from their mother. [3]Rather, the true circumcision in spirit has become profitable in every respect."

This saying may follow on the general rejection of the Israelite Scriptures in the preceding saying. It problematizes the cultic practice of Jewish circumcision (as does Paul in his letters–see especially Romans 2.25–26). The disciples' query about the *benefit* of circumcision actually does not reject circumcision, but reorients it toward a spiritual understanding of the cultic practice. The argument, as Jesus presents it, problematizes circumcision as a human rite because God is capable of producing circumcision from birth. In contrast to this physical rite, inflicted by others on children, Jesus presents a "circumcision in spirit" as much more profitable. That spiritualized circumcision, reflective of the sort of interpretative strategies of the sayings, benefits the individual and it is controlled by the seekers, not by any external force, and it expresses their spiritual values. "In every respect" signifies that this benefit extends to the seekers as well as to their community.

The rejection of cultic activity, a consistent perspective in these sayings, has no boundary. There are not some cultic activities which are beneficial, while most are not (see Saying 14, for example). Even the most basic marker of group identity, the marking of circumcision for Judaism, cannot replace the construction of self and of community that emerges from the spiritual exercises advanced in these sayings. The true circumcision in spirit benefits, while physical circumcision implies the Father's inability to circumcise from birth.

Saying 54

Jesus said, "Blessed are [SV: Congratulations to] the poor, for to you belongs Heaven's domain."

Poverty generally has characterized life in the world in these sayings (as in Saying 3: "But if you do not know yourselves, then you live in poverty, and you are the poverty"), but here poverty appears to signify a certain freedom that results from the lack of resources (as fulfilling the mandate of Saying 42: "Be passersby"). Mendicancy, pauperism, and beggary form a basis of the lifestyle of these seekers (Patterson 1993: 163–70): their poverty indicates their lack of involvement in the world (Sayings 36 and 42, for example) and its pursuits in order to live without restraint and without debilitating responsibility (as in Saying 55).

The seekers and readers live in this poverty and find their blessing; the saying constructs them as "the poor" through the direct address to the readers. This direct address identifies the readers and seekers as those who are poor. In making this identification, however, the meaning of poverty must be expanded to include forms of poverty not based on economic status. The identification spiritualizes the referent to "the poor" because there can be no restrictions on the economic status of the readers. Anyone who reads the text has become "the poor" and in this way poverty becomes a more multivalent sign. The blessings of this now expanded understanding of poverty extend to all those who read and who seek through their reading and these blessings lead to the Kingdom of heaven: the poor find their provision in the heavenly domain made present to them in their poverty both economic and spiritual.

Saying 55

Jesus said, "Whoever does not hate father and mother cannot be my disciple, [2]and whoever does not hate brothers and sisters, and carry the cross as I do, will not be worthy of me."

The orientation of the preceding saying toward poverty also carries with it a disengagement from family. Here Jesus explicitly rejects as followers those who function within the normative social bonds of parents and siblings. The rejection, characterized as "hate," projects an increment of violence. The saying does not envision the construction of a super-social set of relationships which would provide meaning to the normal social patterns, but a totally different, if not opposite, social connectedness. Jesus accepts as followers only those capable of complete renunciation of familial relationships.

Jesus relates that those only who reject familial bonds and who carry the cross are worthy of him. This is a peculiar statement. This sayings collection does not refer to the passion, death and resurrection of Jesus in any narrative fashion. The presence here of "carry the cross as I do" raises the possibility that at least this saying may be aware of the tradition of Jesus' crucifixion: an awareness not found anywhere else in the text. Given the tendency in these sayings to metaphorize and also given the general distaste for cultic or liturgical activity these sayings evidence, it would seem more reasonable to identify the "cross" with the world. Those who bear the cross as Jesus bears it, are those who bear the world as Jesus bore the world, as a garment which would eventually be taken off.

Jesus holds out to these seekers two important results of their renunciation of family and familial relationships: to become his disciple and to be worthy of him. The new social arrangement among those renunciants not only defines true discipleship, but also true value.

Organized around a living and present Jesus, the disciples in these sayings live according to a different value orientation in contra-distinction to the world and to the family. Their worth derives from their renunciation and their association with "the living one in their midst" (Saying 52).

Saying 56

Jesus said, "Whoever has come to know the world has discovered a carcass, [2]and whoever has discovered a carcass, of that person the world is not worthy."

The connection with the previous statement revolves about the word "worthy." The subject has switched from Jesus to the seeker. Two statements construct an understanding of the world: the world is a carcass, and anyone who recognizes the world for what it is recognizes it as dead and decaying. Whoever has discovered that carcass has so far surpassed the world which it represents that the world no longer is worthy to house that person.

The two actions are equated: "to come to know the world" is "to discover a carcass." To know and to discover mutually interpret one another so that knowledge comes through discovery. The sort of knowledge propounded here revolves about both experience and experiment. The emotional factor characterized as discovering a carcass underscores the experiential dimension and suggests that the knowledge of the world is as shockingly graphic as finding the body of a dead animal. The linking of these unlikely elements (knowledge, discovery; world, carcass) emphasizes the challenging and experimental dimension of the wisdom presented because it totally displaces any of the natural discourse about the world while emphasizing the clear demarcation of the mundane world from the spiritual.

The striking carcass metaphor indicates the intensity of the conflict between the mundane world and the new world created by those who have learned to recognize themselves and to understand the world through spiritual eyes. The articulated system of values clearly locates the seeker as among living things and the world as among dead, and locates the value of the spiritual seeker as of higher worth than the world. The implication remains, of course, that the world does not recognize itself as dead and without value.

Saying 57

> Jesus said, "The Father's imperial rule is like a person who had [good] seed. [2]His enemy came during the night and sowed weeds among the good seed. [3]The person did not let the workers pull up the weeds, but said to them, 'No, otherwise you might go to pull up the weeds and pull up the wheat along with them.' [4]For on the day of the harvest the weeds will be conspicuous, and will be pulled up and burned."

This similitude (see also Matthew 13.24–30) compares the Father's Kingdom to a farmer whose good planting is subverted by an enemy who introduces weeds to the field. In order to avoid ruining the good wheat, the farmer with good seed allows the weeds and the wheat to grow up together until harvest time when the nature of each sort of plant will be evident and the weeds may be gathered and destroyed. The narrative follows a very tight logic of mixing the good with the bad until the nature of each is evident, and at the narrative level the actions are plausible. The point seems to say that both good and bad will grow up together until the day of judgment when the true nature of each will be disclosed and punishment and reward bestowed.

In the context of these sayings, the similitude seems odd. This parable does not address life in the world, but the realities of the Father's Kingdom. The similitude ascribes the mixing of good and evil within the Father's Kingdom, not within the world (as it is implied in Matthew's version of the story). The judgment that concludes the parable will function within the Kingdom, not in the world, so that the Kingdom itself will be purged of the bad seed, while the good seed will be obvious. This would imply that the seekers and the interpreters of the sayings do not live apart from the people who would be characterized as "weeds" but that they all live together for the time being, awaiting separation only at the end.

The argument suggests the inadvisability of making judgments too early. In the Kingdom good seekers and bad will grow up together until proper discernment may occur. The Father and the Father's enemy will both be able to do their work in the Kingdom, and the discernment about who belongs in which category will identify those who are the outgrowth of the good seed and those which the enemy planted. The emphasis here does not rest with a duality, a world of evil and a world of good, but with a world mixed of evil and good, a Kingdom capable of embracing (at least for a time) the plan of the enemy with sufficient grace to allow each seed to come to fruition.

Saying 58

Jesus said, "Blessed is [SV: Congratulations to] the person who has toiled and has found life."

Earlier (Saying 50) the lifestyle of these seekers was described as "motion and rest" in which the motion was identified with the activities of the seekers in these sayings. As it is articulated there and elsewhere, "rest" constitutes the goal toward which those interpreting the sayings progress. "Toil," on the other hand, describes the effort needed to achieve that goal. The process of interpreting the sayings, as well as seeking, finding, being disturbed, marveling and ruling (Saying 2), constitutes a vigorous work which overrules death and brings life. The one who has experienced that labor has experienced life energized and full of meaning.

The result of the labor continues the contrast of motion and rest: the hard labor, the toil and work result not in exhaustion but renewed life. The expectations about labor are reversed in order to offer an alternative understanding of hard labor. The substance of that hard work might include many different practices: the interpretation of the sayings (Sayings 1 and 2), the difficult work of withdrawing from family and social relations (Saying 55), the enduring of the conflict brought on by participation in this select society (Saying 16), and the difficult problems raised by the knowledge that the members of this interpretative community originate and are destined to live in the light (Saying 50). The toil, then, signifies the difficult, and yet rewarding, work of the seekers and hearers posited in these sayings.

This concept of hard work and toil is a commonplace of ascetical writings. The language deliberately metaphorizes ascetical activity as difficult physical labor. It places a high value on the labor necessary to transform and recreate self and society through ascetical effort. This saying emphasizes the potential for an ascetical interpretation of this sayings collection.

Saying 59

Jesus said, "Look to the living one as long as you live, otherwise you might die and then try to see the living one, and you will be unable to see."

The address here reaches again directly to the readers as "you." In this saying, Jesus admonishes and exhorts his readers as seekers to remain engaged with "the living one" because the seekers will only be able to see that one while they live. Oddly, Jesus does not identify himself as "the living one" but speaks of this person in the third person and at a distance from him. The readers, however, know that "the living one" is Jesus whose sayings in this collection makes his presence immediate and accessible. The narrator has promulgated this identification of Jesus and "the living one" by associating all "living" with the presence and sayings of Jesus (Sayings 37, 77, 82, 91, and 111) and this identification has made "the living one" a circumlocution for Jesus.

The juxtaposition of unexpected events continues in this saying in which living and dying contrasts with the capacity to see and the inability to see. Vision and life correlate: the live person should look to "the living one," because the dead will probably not be able to see. The hesitation suggests that it was believed that true seekers might be able to see after death, but without assurance of it, they should attend to the living one while alive. The discounting of death as a real phenomenon in the seeker's life emphasizes the high value placed on being a living person who does not taste death and who is engaged with "the living one." This saying affirms that true life after death may only be realized in this life, where death no longer has control over the interpreter of these sayings; therefore, after physical death there can be no more seeking for God.

Saying 60

> <He saw> a Samaritan carrying a lamb and going to Judea. ²He said to his disciples, " <Why does> that person <carry> around the lamb?" [SV: "< ... > that person < ... > around the lamb."] ³They said to him, "So that he may kill it and eat it." ⁴He said to them, "He will not eat it while it is alive, but only after he has killed it and it has become a carcass." ⁵They said, "Otherwise he can't do it." ⁶He said to them, "So also with you, seek for yourselves a place for rest, or you might become a carcass and be eaten."

There is a scribal problem (corrected above) with the text in verse 2, because the sense makes it clear that the person is carrying the lamb, not the lamb the person. The corrected text should probably read: "Why does that person carry around the lamb?"

The narrative dialogue begins with the tantalizing details about a Samaritan carrying a lamb to Judea. It holds the promise of discussing the conflict between Samaritans and Jews, and (with the mention of the lamb) their divergent cultic centers (Jerusalem and Mount Gerazim). These details set up expectations about social, religious, and cultural differences operating in the Near East.

The remaining dialogue does not actualize that promise. The details of the Samaritan and the travel to Judea receive no attention, while the presence of the lamb gathers up major themes of this sayings collection. Jesus questions the disciples about the Samaritan's intention in carrying the lamb. It is an odd question, one that does not bear any of the hostility generally evident in the questions the disciples put to Jesus. The answer the disciples give responds directly to the question which means that these interactions form a true dialogue, rather than the question functioning simply as a platform for some revelatory statement. So the disciples explain that the lamb will be killed and eaten. Jesus explains that the Samaritan will not eat it live, but will first kill it and make it a carcass; the disciples concur that it cannot be otherwise. This discussion of the carcass invokes the statement earlier (Saying 56) that the world is a carcass. The implication here is that the lamb represents the world which must be killed first before it can become food for spiritual people. The concurrence of the disciples indicates that they do indeed understand this proposition: the world is vainly carried about by people, because in the end, they will need to kill it to make it have value.

At the end of this dialogue, Jesus gives the revelatory statement addressed ambiguously to "you:" "So also with you, seek for yourselves a place for rest, or you might become a carcass and be eaten." Here the readers/seekers merge with the disciples in hearing the revelatory statement that is made a general principle. It contrasts the rest of the seekers with the fate of the sacrificial lamb. Seekers who are active like the Samaritan and connected to the world become vulnerable to being devoured. Those seekers who have found rest, however, cannot be devoured. Jesus twists the dialogue so that the lamb is not the world, but that the disciples might become lambs and be killed and eaten. The antidote to this potential slaughter and consumption revolves about finding a place of rest.

The combination of the theme of eating, becoming what you eat (as in Saying 7 about the lion and the human), the world as a carcass, and finding a place of rest makes for a complex set of interpretations. The complexity resides in the many details that the narrative provides and in the intertextual relations between this text and others in the collection. In the end, the saying warns the seekers (now aligned with the disciples) against becoming a carcass and being devoured. That warning places the conflict between the mundane world and the one created in these sayings at the table itself, in the very act of eating or being eaten.

Saying 61

Jesus said, "Two will recline on a couch; one will die, one will live." [2]Salome said, "Who are you, mister? You have climbed onto my couch and eaten from my table as a stranger [SV: as if you are from someone]." [3]Jesus said to her, "I am the one who exists in equality [SV: who comes from what is whole]. I was granted from the things of my Father." [4]"I am your disciple." [5]"For this reason I say, if one is equal [SV: <whole>], one will be filled with light, but if one is divided, one will be filled with darkness."

There are a number of problems with this text that need to be considered before commenting on it. The first relates to a problem of meaning in verse 2. Layton (1989: 75) concludes that the last phrase of verse 2 erroneously has the phrase "that you as from one have come" (the Scholars Version translates this as "as if you are from someone") and Lambdin omits it from his translation; however, Layton (1989: 74) also cites the Coptic scholar H. J. Polotsky who suggests that the Coptic phrase mistranslates the Greek phrase "as a stranger." Agreeing with Layton that there is some error in the text, I have adopted Polotsky's suggestion and supplied that meaning to the end of the verse, because the oddity of a stranger eating at a table makes more logical sense.

Another translation problem relates to the end of verse 3 with the Coptic phrase that Lambdin (Layton 1989: 75) translates as "I am he who exists from the undivided" and the Scholars Version translates as "I am one who comes from what is whole." Crum (1939: 606A) defines the Coptic word as "to make equal, level, or straight" which I translate as "equality." The point, it seems to me, relates to the stranger having status at Salome's table; Jesus announces his equality to the host even as a stranger. I have continued that translation strategy in verse 5: "if one is equal" which follows the correction suggested by Guillaumont (Layton 1989: 76).

Although this saying has needed some emendation and retranslation, it shows evidence of careful crafting. Jesus begins the conversation with Salome with a reference to division and death, and ends it with a reference to division and darkness. Division forms an envelope to a conversation about equality with a professed woman disciple.

A meal provides the setting for the narrative–which would be missed if one did not know that the proper posture for eating in antiquity was reclining. The first statement about division relates to two people eating together, one of whom will die and one of whom will live. This picks up the theme of division, of choice, of household strife which has been presented in earlier sayings (see Sayings 16 and 55, for example). This meal, however, does not follow the familiar household pattern; Jesus, as a stranger, joins Salome at the meal at her table. This open eating tradition reflects the earliest form of Christian activity (Crossan 1991: 341–44), and Jesus' attendance *as a stranger* prompts Salome to question his identity. With solitary itinerants as the model promulgated in these sayings (Patterson 1993: 196–214), this presence of strangers and of strangers who bring revelatory messages would not strike a reader as unusual. The nature of these sayings, mirroring the openness of the commensality, means that anyone may enter into the interpretative work and come into contact both with the living one in their midst and with the community of those who have gathered around the living one.

Jesus' revelatory response predicates that he is "the one who exists in equality," an equality that results from his having received a share of the Father's possessions ("I was granted from the things of my Father"). The stranger at the meal, then, prompts the revelation about equality, and about the one who has received a share of the Father's wealth and has come in equality. This again, provides a window into early Christian practice in which equality was stressed as the basis of membership in the new community (recall Paul, "neither male nor female" in Galatians 3.28–see Schüssler-Fiorenza 1983: 160–98), and it locates the seekers in these sayings as a community of equals.

Salome claims that equality for herself in announcing that she herself is a disciple. The transformative nature of the meal creates a level social setting (the verb means "to make level," as well as "to make equal") in which the participants become fully empowered as disciples. The claim of a woman to the category of "disciple" in itself surprises. This is one of the few places that any character at all is mentioned by name and the only place that indicates that women were part of the group called the "disciples" (for a fuller discussion of this see Buckley 1986: 99–104). The identification, while flattering to Salome, does not advance her status in the context of these sayings where the disciples (and the occasion of their questions) have been problematized by the negative characterization of the disciples' interaction with Jesus.

Jesus accepts Salome's announcement of her discipleship and adds the theological principle: those who are equal are filled with light, but those who make distinctions are filled with darkness. The division of person from person with which the saying opened, finds its ultimate meaning not in the division of one person from another, but in the transformative meal which makes all equal to one another. Those who participate in the meal, not only become equal, but are filled with light, enlightened. Those who are divided, separated from this community, are filled with darkness.

This saying presents important information about the community. Buckley (1986: 100) underscores the intimacy expressed in this scene–an intimacy uniting Salome and Jesus in discourse and fellowship. This dialogue constructs a narrative of a meal, of strangers becoming revealers, of affirmations of social and religious connection, and of enlightenment and equality among the seekers in this community. This narrative positively presents the role of a strong woman who questions Jesus while also claiming for herself a position as disciple. This positive attitude toward women invites an understanding of this community (and their understanding of Jesus) that included women and encouraged the leadership of women in their midst even when leadership itself is problematized.

Saying 62

Jesus said, "I disclose my mysteries to those [who are worthy] of [my] mysteries. [2]Do not let your left hand know what your right hand is doing."

The connection between these sayings hinges on the matter of disclosure. Jesus makes the general statement that he reveals his mysteries only to those worthy of receiving them. The mysteries, as the preserve of the worthy, relate to a select and preferred group of people. The metaphoric statement about the disclosure from one hand to the other transfers that restricted status of revelation to the personal level, so that the seekers must not disclose even to other parts of one's self, the activities of other parts of the person. If the person lives in a world bifurcated between mundane and spiritual, then the restraint of disclosure suggests that seekers ought not to discuss with outsiders what they know from their life in religious community. The theological principle underscores the importance of worthiness as a prerequisite for knowledge. The mysteries, the secret teaching and the careful training, must be maintained as the preserve of the few.

Both this hesitancy to disclose and the restrictive nature of the mystery language seem to be at odds with the rest of the sayings. Most sayings have an expansive view that anyone who seeks, or who begins the conflict with the world, or who withdraws, or who seeks rest— anyone, in short, with the right disposition may become a part of this group. The expansive ideology of most of the sayings seems to be severely restricted here. The ideology shows signs of shifting from a group of people who engage with the outside world in order to bring it light, to a group of people who withdraw from the outside world and condemn it as totally unworthy.

Saying 63

Jesus said, "There was a rich man who had a great deal of money. [2]He said, 'I shall invest my money so that I may sow, reap, plant, and fill my storehouses with produce, that I may lack nothing.' [3]These were the things he was thinking in his heart, but that very night he died. [4]Anyone here with two ears had better listen!"

Sayings 63–65 register a serious attack on the commercial aspects of living in the mundane world (see Patterson 1993: 48). These simple narratives are not provided any setting or any function: they are not presented as narrative descriptions of the reign of God (as Sayings 57, 76, 96–98, 107, and 109), but simply presented as short narratives (as also Saying 9) whose purpose simply is to instruct in Jesus' voice about the values and orientations of the narrator and the community of interpreters.

This narrative (cf. Luke 12.16–21), relating the fate of a rich farmer who intended to invest in order to produce even greater wealth, criticizes his investment in the world. The wealth the farmer seeks will indeed outlast him, rendering worldly wealth of more durability than the one who accumulates it. The saying affirms that those who invest in transitory wealth will in fact find themselves to be transitory. The narrative thoroughly rejects any such financially greedy accumulation.

The contrast between the extensive description of his wealth and his accumulation, as well as the narrative entry into his mental processes to show the depth of his greedy plans, contrast markedly with the simple, and succinct, statement "but that very night he died." The narrative development brings the readers to the point of savoring the prospect of the production of wealth, only to catch the readers up short. The narrative at once entices readers and comes abruptly to the end, only adding the final injunction as a sort of warning that says to the readers, "if you have heard such an interior dialogue within your own heart, beware."

The durability of the accumulated wealth over human durability provides an important perspective on the values of this community. There is no dualism or bifurcation between the spiritual and the physical realm, because this saying does not condemn wealth, or production of goods. It does, however, condemn the valuing of such activity over the discovery of true life. In the hierarchy of values presented in this saying, finding true life has a higher valuation than worldly wealth; life takes precedence over greed; filling the void by greed is decidedly more negative than searching for life. The activities of the world, so significantly criticized in these sayings, cannot provide the stability and the fulfillment which searching for the meaning in these sayings provides, and, therefore, such activities are ultimately futile.

Saying 64

Jesus said, "Someone was receiving guests. When he had prepared the dinner, he sent his slave to invite the guests. [2]The slave went to the first and said, 'My master invites you.' The first replied, [3]'Some merchants owe me money; they are coming to me tonight. I have to go and give them instructions. Please excuse me from dinner.' [4]The slave went to another and said, 'My master has invited you.' [5]The second said to the slave, 'I have bought a house, and I have been called away for a day. I shall have no time.' [6]The slave went to another and said, 'My master invites you.' [7]The third said to the slave, 'My friend is to be married, and I am to arrange the banquet. I shall not be able to come. Please excuse me from dinner.' [8]The slave went to another and said, 'My master invites you.' [9]The fourth said to the slave, 'I have bought an estate, and I am going to collect the rent. I shall not be able to come. Please excuse me.' [10]The slave returned and said to his master, 'Those whom you invited to dinner have asked to be excused.' [11]The master said to his slave, 'Go out on the streets and bring back whomever you find to have dinner.' [12]Buyers and merchants [will] not enter the places of my Father."

The problematizing of commercial enterprises emerges again as the subject of this narrative. The narrative itself (cf. the Synoptic Sayings Source Q 14.15–24) simply describes a servant who is sent out to invite four guests to a dinner, and each one of them makes an excuse for not being able to attend. The excuses all revolve about different worldly transactions that required immediate attention and that took priority over attendance at the dinner. The first refuses in order to collect debts from merchants; the second refuses because he has purchased a house; the third refuses in order to arrange a wedding banquet; and the fourth refuses because he has recently purchased an estate and needs to collect the rent. Each of these signifies a sort of social currency and business transaction that consumes the energy and attention of the invited guest. The conclusion of the saying states that people who engage in commerce will not find a place with the Father. Strangers are preferable to those who are too preoccupied with commerce to be available.

The dinner in this narrative does not seem to signify beyond simply providing the opportunity for criticizing those involved with commerce. It neither suggests an eschatological banquet, nor any other sort of intensified signification: it simply refers to the practice of the community constructed in these sayings to meet at meals. Since the meals, as in the Salome incident (Saying 61), become a time of revelation and empowerment, the invited guests to this dinner have both missed their true wealth and the revelation which was to come. Strangers are capable of receiving both. On the anthropological hierarchy of being, those involved in commerce rate below strangers, so that the entire system would be (from higher to lower): interpreters of the sayings, strangers who are available to others, those generally involved in the world, and finally "merchants and buyers." These sayings establish a very clear system of value and precedence.

Saying 65

He said, "A good person [SV: "A [...] person] owned a vineyard and rented it to some farmers, so they could work it and he could collect its crop from them. [2]He sent his *servant* [SV: slave] so the farmers would give him the vineyard's crop. [3]They grabbed the *servant* [SV: him], beat him, and almost killed him, and the *servant* [SV: slave] returned and told his master. [4]His master said, 'Perhaps he didn't know them.' [5]He sent another *servant* [SV: slave], and the farmers beat that one as well. [6]Then the master sent his own son and said, 'Perhaps they'll show my son some respect.' [7]Because the farmers knew that he was the heir to the vineyard, they grabbed him and killed him. [8]Anyone here with two ears had better listen!"

There are two distinct ways of reading this narrative. The first revolves about the simple narrative of the abuse of servants and the killing of the son of a landed farmer. The same themes of the previous two sayings emerge in this way of reading. This saying, however, reverses the social standing of the characters in the previous saying: rather than concerning the entitled purveyors of the world's goods, this narrative addresses the desire for wealth and worldly power among tenant farmers. The farmer makes himself vulnerable by engaging in the leasing of property for gain; this is not an unusual activity for a landowner. His involvement, however, meets the intense greed of the tenant farmers who abuse each one of the messengers, and kill the landowner's son. The message discourages people from investing their energy and human resources in commercial enterprises, on the one hand, and shows the greed and violence of those who desire wealth and power on the other. Neither set of people wins, both lose: the farmer loses the rent, has two badly abused servants, and loses his son; the tenants become killers. The way of commerce satisfied neither party.

The second way of reading this text is based upon an interpretation of a papyrological convention called *nomina sacra*. In the production of papyri among Christians in particular, divine names (such as "Jesus" or "God" or "Lord") and holy places (such as "Jerusalem") were abbreviated with the first and last letters of the word with a long line (called a superlinear stroke) drawn over the abbreviation (see Pestman 1994: 32). Sometimes the whole word would be written out in full, but a superlinear stroke added to indicate its divine or holy status (Bell 1972: 80–81). The word "servant" (SV: slave) above has been provided a superlinear stroke over the last three letters of the word (I have indicated it by using italics) in the Coptic papyrus document indicating that, at least to the last scribe, the two servants were divine figures. It is not possible to establish at what point the superlinear stroke entered the manuscript tradition: it could have been added to the Greek text and simply copied into the Coptic translation, or it could have been added simply to the Coptic version, even to only the last Coptic version. It provides an opportunity to follow an ancient interpreter's patterns of thought.

In the synoptic versions (Mark 12.1–12; Matthew 21.36–46; Luke 20.9–19) this narrative shows that the religious privilege of those who preceded Jesus and the community connected with him will be taken away from them and given to others (namely the Christians). The synoptic version takes this parable as indicating that the heir, Jesus, will be killed and that his killing will force the repudiation of the rights and privileges of those who killed him. This reading is further emphasized in the addition of the saying "The very stone which the builders rejected has become the head of the corner" from Psalm 118.22–23. The narrative emphasis, then, focuses upon Jesus as the killed son without any serious attention given to the other servants ("many" in Mark; "others" in Matthew; three in Luke) who are sent.

The narrative in this saying with the *nomina sacra* draws attention to the status of the first two servants. They are divine figures who are abused while performing the tasks given them by the property owner. The property owner, moreover, concludes that they were abused because they were "not recognized." This narrative indicates that they were not appreciated for who they were: the Coptic text seems to have inverted the pronouns in verse 4 so that "Perhaps he didn't know them" should be "Perhaps they didn't know him" in order to follow the story more carefully. Therefore, since they did not know the servant, the property owner sends his son who is killed. The subject of this narrative revolves about an inability to perceive the true status of the servants as divine figures, or perhaps even divinities. Those who are engaged in commerce, who till the land owned by others and refuse to give the produce to the rightful owner, entrap themselves in a cycle that prevents their ability to perceive divinity, or even to hear the message of the divine messengers. Ultimately they will kill, not just abuse, the son of the property owner: their cycle of greed will end in a cycle of violence and rejection.

The scribe who produced this papyrus acknowledged that the servants were divine agents whose abuse foreshadowed the violent attack on the son. This scribe understood the narrative not simply as a means of showing the necessary death of Jesus at the hands of previous religious leaders (as in the synoptic tradition), but as a complex series of divine messengers and divine projects that attempted to deal justly with the unruly tenants. For this scribe, those who preceded Jesus, and perhaps even every messenger of Jesus' work since the time of Jesus, participate in that divinity and form a progression of divine messages delivered to those in the world who are caught up in the commerce of daily living.

In introducing this second strategy of interpreting this saying, I do not mean to imply that this reading was that promulgated by the author. The superlinear stroke may have entered the manuscript tradition at any point up to and including the final Coptic version. However, it does provide an interesting perspective on a mid-fourth-century (or earlier) reading of the saying; a reading that may indeed reflect a wider range of interpretation than traditionally accompanies this parable.

Saying 66

> Jesus said, "Show me the stone that the builders rejected: that is the keystone."

This saying (based upon Psalm 118.22 and used in the synoptic tradition Mark 12.10–11 and parallels) valorizes rejection. Builders work in the world to create relatively stable and permanent structures, but in this saying (actually the basis of the wisdom tradition in Psalms and in the Markan passage with its parallels in Matthew 21.42 and Luke 20.17) the builders are unable to discern the true value of the material with which they work. Their lack of proper discernment makes them reject the very stone that becomes the keystone.

This saying bears much more force, because it is brought into relationship with Jesus through a demand. The saying hinges on discernment because Jesus demands to be shown the stone that the builders rejected: those to whom this saying is addressed may indeed perceive and find that which others have been unable to discern. Others, more discerning, will find the rejected stone and present it to Jesus who finds it appropriate as the keystone. The general orientation of the Biblical saying (in Psalm 118) has been made a specific point of interaction between Jesus and his discerning followers.

The valorization of rejection may in fact reflect the social situation of the interpreters of these sayings. Although they seem not to be valuable by those who cannot discern anyway, they indeed turn out to be the centerpiece of the new world construction. Rejection, then, becomes for this community a means of affirming their election and their special status in the new world, while simultaneously explaining why they are not fully valued by the world in which they live.

Saying 67

> Jesus said, "Those who know all [Coptic: the all], but are lacking in themselves, are utterly lacking."

This saying explores directly the subjectivity of the speakers. It problematizes those who have knowledge but who still understand themselves as deficient ("lacking in themselves"). It says that those who still perceive themselves as deficient, even though they are quite knowledgable, become totally deficient. Their self-understanding must, therefore, correlate with their knowledge; the inner and the outer, the knowledge of the self and the knowledge of the world must reflect one another (as in Saying 22).

There may be a suggestion in the Coptic that the knowledge carries more meaning than appears on the surface. The Coptic word translated above as "all" has a definite article so that properly it should be translated as "the all" or "the entirety." This construction seems to indicate that the knowledge refers to a more universal or cosmic knowledge, so that the saying suggests that those who know all the revelations of these sayings and understand the old world and the new thoroughly, and yet still perceive themselves as unempowered or deficient in standing, have not properly understood "the all". Seekers cannot claim the full knowledge while harboring deficient selves.

The emphasis of the saying rests not on the knowledge, but on the self-understanding of the seeker. Knowledge in itself does not benefit a person who otherwise remains deficient. The full and confident self-knowledge lends credence to other knowledge. Without that credence even the knowledge itself remains deficient. There is an interesting possibility that this saying engages in a polemic against those who "know" so that *gnosis* (knowledge) or gnostic theology is rejected. Collections of sayings need not be consistent: whereas there seems to be a promulgation of gnostic theology in Saying 28, this saying rejects *gnosis*.

Saying 68

Jesus said, "Blessed are [SV: Congratulations to] you when you are hated and persecuted; [2]and no place will be found, wherever you have been persecuted."

Just as Saying 66 valorized rejection, this one valorizes persecution. The blessings will come to those seekers who are hated and persecuted. This again shows the great disjunction between the world of these seekers and the world at large. The enmity which has been articulated as conflict erupts into thoroughgoing hatred. The seekers will not be welcomed, but consistently rejected.

The second verse does not make sense as it stands. Various suggestions for emending the text (summarized in Layton 1989: 78) propose first that it means that even though there is persecution and hatred around the seekers, eventually there will be a place where no persecution will take place (see Meyer 1992: 95–96). The statement, that is, refers to the eventual vindication of those who have been rejected in arriving at a place where rejection does not reach. The alternative has been to read it as universal rejection: there will be no place where the seekers have not been rejected (Quecke in Layton 1989: 78). The seekers will be persecuted and hated in every place. Since these sayings do not exhibit a tendency toward developing a spiritual geography of another world that will take precedence over the mundane world, and since there seems not to be a tendency toward dualism, the latter interpretation seems most likely. These seekers will experience persecution everywhere because the conflict between the interpreters of these sayings and those in the world is everywhere.

The seekers receive a blessing for their persecution. The struggle emergent from being part of a minority religious movement within a dominant religious culture sanctifies the seekers. The pre-eminent struggle to find the interpretation brings salutary effects even in the midst of tribulation. Here the toil (Saying 58) and struggle mingle to create the impression of a blessed life lived in adversity.

Saying 69

> Jesus said, "Blessed are [SV: Congratulations to] those who have been persecuted in their hearts: they are the ones who have truly come to know the Father. ^{2}Blessed are [SV: Congratulations to] those who go hungry, so the stomach of the one in want may be filled."

These two sayings are linked only by their similar constructions as macarisms ("Blessed are. . . . "). The first one blesses those who experience interior persecution as gaining true knowledge of the Father. The exterior persecution of the previous saying now becomes an interior persecution in this one. Those who enter not only the conflict with the non-spiritual around them, but also with the non-spiritual within themselves will gain true knowledge of God. True knowledge can only emerge from the conflict (see Saying 16) within the self or within the world; it does not come by any other sort of mastery. Knowledge, that is, emerges from the experience of conflict, rather than from reflection or mentation.

The second macarism discusses hunger. It states that the hungry will indeed be fed. It may be interpreted in two ways. In the first, the hungry will enable other hungry people to be fed because abstaining from food makes food available to others. This interpretation assumes that resources are limited and therefore that the ascetics of this community support one another by their food asceticism. There is a parallel to this understanding in Philo's "On the Contemplative Life" II.16. Another interpretation might suggest that the hungry themselves will be provided food to satisfy their desire. The desire and need for food will be fulfilled for those who go hungry, so that food deprivation will eventually lead to the provision of food. Neither of these sayings posits any future reality or world in which the knowledge of the Father and the filling of the hungry will take place: both these events are understood as present realities.

Just as the first part spiritualizes and internalizes conflict, so also the second (by association with the first macarism) suggests that the hunger itself is spiritualized and interiorized. This saying discusses and explores the relationship of deprivation and negation to desire and its satisfaction. Those who embrace their deprivation will find their desires fully satisfied. Deprivation creates desire and the satisfaction of desire follows the deprivation.

Saying 70

Jesus said, "If you bring forth what is within you, what you have will save you. [2]If you do not have that within you, what you do not have within you [will] kill you."

This saying explores the paradoxical relationship of life and death as a function of the possession of an interior substance. Salvation for those who have entered into the interpretation of these sayings derives from manifesting the interior understanding, so that salvation remains a function of the interpretative process and its transformative nature. The manifestation of this interior quality or understanding confers salvation on the seeker. This posits the origin of what saves as an interior reality, as something found within the person as the fount of salvation. It makes salvation come not from outside a person, but from within. The conduct of the inner knowledge effects salvation and brings life to the seeker.

The saying also states the opposite. Those who do not have this interior understanding, whose inner knowledge does not exist, will die. It is the interpretation of the sayings that brings life (as in Saying 1); death results for those who have not begun that process. There is no salvation apart from the inner knowledge, and there is no life. The transgression that brings death does not consist in an action, or in deeds or performances, but in a deficiency, a lack of understanding, an unwillingness to engage in the salvific interpretative process that brings life.

The saying enjoins the seeker to manifest outwardly the inner realities and in this way to find salvation. This process articulates a performance. The seeker is expected to do something ("bring forth") that will effect salvation. The performance relates to acting out interior realities so that what is invisible becomes visible and active. Conversely, the failure to perform this action will ultimately destroy the seeker. Knowledge, understanding, and wisdom all function as a performance rather than as a cognitive science.

Saying 71

Jesus said, "I will destroy [this] house, and no one will be able to build it [...]."

Although this saying is generally related to the destruction of the temple in the canonical tradition (Patterson 1993: 53–54), the house in this saying signifies the social arrangements that dominate in the mundane world: houses (whether of religious institutions or of social) provide families (or members) with protection. Jesus' statement that he "will destroy this house" points to the radical conflict between the houses of the world and the people who enter the new world posited in these sayings (Saying 16, for example). The two worlds cannot coexist; only one will be able to survive the conflict (see Saying 47). So Jesus announces not only the conflict, with the victory going to the new community, but also that the destruction is irreversible. Once that new society has developed, the old "house" will no longer be able to function: the new will totally destroy and replace the old.

The saying (even though it is fragmentary at the end) makes the seekers and readers bold in their self-understanding. They may understand themselves not simply as an additional dimension to a world that will persist in its usual ways, but as the founders of a new world, or as the seed of a new growth. Such an understanding would enable them to be fearless in their opposition to the world as it currently exists, and to be bold in their construction of a new self and a new society.

Saying 72

A [person said] to him, "Tell my brothers to divide my father's possessions with me." [2]He said to the person, "Mister, who made me a divider?" [3]He turned to his disciples and said to them, "I'm not a divider, am I?"

This saying contains an interesting set of narrative relationships. An unidentified and unspecified person asks Jesus to command his family to divide family possessions. The person appeals to Jesus as an authority who can impose a judgment upon others. Jesus does not reply to the request directly, but responds to the unidentified person with a question that addresses the underlying appeal to an authority: Jesus questions who gave him such authority to command others to divide their goods. The narrative then leaves this direct conversation and describes Jesus as turning to his disciples with a statement made ambivalent with the addition of a question: he states that he is not one to divide, but then appends "am I?" to it. This presents an oddity in these sayings where external or social power consistently receives negative assessment, while spiritual power has positive connotations. The narrative ambiguity about Jesus' status as a "divider" underscores the ambiguity about the status of Jesus in the community.

The answer that the readers or seekers interpreting these sayings might provide to Jesus' question would be "Yes." The conflict that Jesus has brought does indeed divide households and families in the battle between two diametrically opposed ways of understanding the true nature of the world. The problem with the initial request, that Jesus intervene in a family quarrel and divide the inheritance between the siblings, revolves about the centrality and importance of possessions. The readers have already heard that such possessions only bring death and destruction, and that they have no ultimate value (Sayings 63 and 47). So Jesus' refusal to divide property underscores that property has no value; nothing justifies the division of unworthy items among families. Moreover, the quarrel between the siblings has not revolved about the conflict between worlds, but about the argumentative greed of people investing in possessions. Jesus has not been made that kind of a divider, but one who brings conflict, fire, sword, war, as Saying 16 articulates it.

The narrative, with the curiously added-on question, seems to portray the confusion that results from engagement in the world of possessions and in the mixed world where disciples, seekers, and other people live together. Jesus literally talks around himself by confronting some, questioning others, making asides to the disciples, and even seemingly seeking to understand his own role in the process. The narrative then presents what is the opposite to those who have found rest.

Saying 73

> Jesus said, "The crop is huge but the workers are few, so beg the harvest boss to dispatch workers to the fields."

The next three sayings (73–75) all compare the many to the few, as a commentary on the relative number of those who are within as compared to those who are without in the movements. The first saying, with its parallel in the Synoptic Sayings Source Q 10.2, articulates the enormity of the early Jesus missions and the relative scarcity of missionaries. Three elements interrelate: an abundant crop, a scarcity of laborers, and the overseer's dispatch of more laborers. The request for more laborers indicates that the community experienced the potential work of the community as greater than those currently capable of performing the work. The abundance of the crop expresses the actual fruit of the community's activity in great excess to their ability to harvest, and this metaphoric structure provides some of the emotional content of the seekers of these sayings. A little of their work will produce an abundance of result, so much so that they will need to pray for more participants in the group to harvest the benefits. Although the laborers in this spiritual community are few, they still produce abundant benefits far in excess of what they themselves can handle. This portrays the work of this community positively, with rich resources and abundant results.

Saying 74

> He said, "Lord, there are many around the drinking trough, but there is nothing in the well."

The serious statement about the inverse relationship of mission to workers becomes a humorous statement about the emptiness of the majority of people. This saying shows the "many," the majority, as standing around an empty drinking trough. They resemble animals who cannot tell that water is not available. The derision of the outsiders by this group creates a strong solidarity among those who know that the cistern is empty. The empty well, as a description of the majority, aptly summarizes this community's understanding of outsiders.

The emptiness of the majority of people, and especially of people outside the community of those seeking the interpretation of these sayings, forms a significant theme in this Gospel (see Sayings 28 and 29, for example). The characterization of non-members of this group as empty, however, does not condemn them as ontologically evil or inherently corrupt. Emptiness implies the potential for being filled; the emptiness of the others implies that they may eventually begin the interior discovery that will show them to be filled, rich, and abundant. The characterization of the others holds out hope that they may change their ways and enter into a new style of living without their emptiness preventing them.

Saying 75

Jesus said, "There are many standing at the door, but those who are alone will enter the bridal suite."

The theme of the many and the few continues. This saying gives substantial definition to the few by identifying them as the solitaries (*monachos*) who will enter the bridal chamber (see Harl 1960; Klijn 1962; Griffith 1995). The initial contrast occurs between the many at the door and the solitary who will enter. The saying affirms the entitled status of the solitary.

The place of entry, however, presents a problem. The many stand outside and the solitary enters the bridal chamber, the place of marriage. The only other place in this collection of sayings where this term appears is in the narrative of the dinner in which one guest declines the invitation because his friend is getting married and he must manage the banquet (Saying 64). Since in that saying Jesus rejects the marriage-feast manager as one involved in the sort of commerce that will deny him entrance into the Father's place, it must be assumed that the marriage spoken of there and the bridal chamber here are two different places. It remains curious that the solitary would want to enter the bridal chamber, since marriage enmeshes people in the complexities of the world which these sayings reject. The bridal chamber here carries a surplus of meaning: it is the right place for the solitaries and the wrong place for the many who simply stand at the door. The bridal chamber or suite signifies the place where those who have become solitaries gather.

This bridal chamber metaphorizes the unity and merging of subjectivities which these saying promulgate, so that the solitary, by entering into the bridal chamber, joins the many others who have also become spiritual beings. The bridal chamber, in this sense, occupies a communal place similar to the language of the Kingdom of God or the Father's domain in the rest of the sayings: it is the place that mediates salvation, union, spiritualization, and life (see Valantasis 1995b), but it remains a place for very few, because only the solitaries may enter it.

Saying 76

Jesus said, "The Father's imperial rule is like a merchant who had a supply of merchandise and then found a pearl. [2]That merchant was prudent; he sold the merchandise and bought the single pearl for himself. So also with you, seek his treasure that is unfailing, that is enduring, where no moth comes to eat and no worm destroys."

There are actually two voices in this saying which indicates that the similitude between the merchant's activity and the Kingdom has been combined with a direct statement to the reader about seeking the enduring treasure. The two parts relate thematically and have been combined into a cohesive story with an attached moral.

The linguistic connection of the solitary and the pearl in the culminating sentence of the similitude provides the theological force to the saying. The merchant's discovery of the solitary pearl, now a redundant expression of the highly valued solitary life, warrants the sale of all the other merchandise.

There are two ways to read the relationship of the pearl to the merchandise. First, this solitary pearl finds itself enmeshed in the merchandized life of commerce: the general and comparatively worthless merchandise hides it from view. Or, the pearl may have been discovered in some other domain of the merchant's life, so that in discovering it, the merchant renounces all his other merchandise to secure the valuable item. In either of these options, the discerning merchant will both be able to recognize the value of the pearl and be skilled enough to purchase it. Only those capable of discerning will be enabled to clarify the realities around them and act accordingly; only the discerning will see the pearl in the midst of discordant materials, or realize the true value of the pearl in relationship to all other aspects of human existence.

The merchant here, in a reversal of the very negative attitude toward commerce and its worldly nature, has identified himself as one of the few spoken in the previous sayings. He manifests the discernment and wisdom that enables him to proceed and to advance in this spiritual life. This positive appraisal of commercial dealings tempers the negative ones in Sayings 63, 64, and 65.

The moral of this story ascribes shrewd investment in spiritual realities to the merchant. The readers and seekers must invest in imperishable goods, "unfailing" treasures that cannot be destroyed by the natural forces of the world (the moth and the worm). That investment in enduring treasures, however, does not happen with the shrewdness of one who goes after treasures (the similitude of the merchant would not permit that interpretation), but with the discernment of one who can recognize treasures of great value when they appear in the midst of discordant material or in relationship to lesser things. The Father's imperial rule, that is, must be found, not cultivated, and when it is found, all else must be divested in order to invest in it.

Saying 77

Jesus said, "I am the light that is over all things. I am all: from me all came forth, and to me all attained. ^{2}Split a piece of wood; I am there. ^{3}Lift up the stone, and you will find me there."

The attention shifts dramatically to a self-predication by Jesus. Most of the sayings do not concern a proper understanding of Jesus' identity, but a proper interpretation of the sayings so that the seekers come to understand themselves, the community formed of their common endeavors, and the world that they create by their struggles. Jesus' identity does not frequently become a topic of discussion, or even an issue in the community. This self-predication, however, makes up for much of the silence about Jesus. This saying presents three self-predications of Jesus as light, as the all, and as one found in nature.

Jesus calls himself light (cf. John 8.12), specifically "the light that is over all things." Light has figured in the sayings at various places as the place of origin of the seekers in these sayings (Saying 50), and a designation of the people interpreting the sayings (Sayings 50 and 83) they are filled with light (Saying 24), they do not hide the light, they manifest the light (Saying 32), and they proclaim what they see (Saying 6). Jesus identifies himself with that light, claiming not only the status of light, but also the status as the light which enables the discernment and sight of all things. This speaks of a universal sort of theology, not one restricted only to those who seek and read, but a light that flows over all things, a superior light that stands above all created things.

The second self-predication characterizes Jesus as "all" in two senses: as the origin of every existent being and as the fulfillment or goal of all existent beings. The self-predication develops a mythology that understands Jesus as the beginning and end of creation, as well as the one filling all creation. That God would be origin and destiny of creation has many parallels in Jewish wisdom traditions and in other early Christian literature. It is the panentheistic element that surprises and further articulates the mythology presented in the saying. It is not an unprecedented perspective in these sayings, however, because Jesus portrays himself as totally identified with the seekers (Saying 108) and as the one completely in their presence (Sayings 51 and 91). Such a collapse of differentiated identities between Jesus and the believers constitutes an important theological perspective in these sayings.

This universality, as light, also extends to Jesus' being. Jesus says: "I am all: from me all came forth, and to me all attained." The lack of differentiation of such things as the conflict brought in the world, the division that becomes central to the project of these sayings, enhances the universality of the self-revelation. Jesus the light has no boundaries; he is both source and destiny for everything. This vision correlates with similar emphasis on the union of two in a household, the solitary pearl, so that the understanding of Jesus as universally available, universally attainable, the source and destiny of all magnifies the significance of the mission that these sayings envision. No person, no place, no event can be outside the purview of the light.

The third self-predication ("Split a piece of wood.... Lift up the stone....") further emphasizes the panentheistic perspective in this saying, while making it impossible to ignore the panentheistic implications of the previous statements ("I am all"). The point simply is that Jesus not only *is* everything, but that he may be found in every place, even in a split piece of wood or under a stone. Such a conception of panentheism seems to operate in a different way from the other sayings in which interpretation by human beings living in community– which is a highly anthropomorphic enterprise–becomes a more cosmic and naturalistic characterization of the seekers' endeavors.

Saying 78

Jesus said, "Why have you come out to the countryside? To see a reed shaken by the wind? [2]And to see a person dressed in soft clothes, [like your] rulers and powerful ones? [3]They are dressed in soft clothes, and they cannot understand truth."

Without a narrative structure comparable to the application of this saying to John the Baptist in the Synoptic Sayings Source Q 7.24–26, this saying becomes a generalized confrontation of the readers by Jesus. The confrontation initially revolves about Jesus' questioning of their motives, their purpose, and their objectives. The saying as it stands here does not exhibit a self-referential modality regarding Jesus. In the synoptic gospels this saying is spoken by Jesus about John the Baptist, but here it seems to speak of someone (singular) whose identity is not explained. It is virtually impossible to explain who this person is who is like a shaken reed, or dressed in fine clothing, and who cannot understand.

As a general statement, however, this saying lacks definition and precision. The setting for the confrontative questioning is the "countryside" (which may be the desert, or simply outlying country) that stands in binary opposition to the city. In fact, the interaction of city with country plays an important role in the saying, because the mores of the city oppose the country environment of the saying. Initially, however, Jesus questions the readers or seekers about their withdrawal to the country, and he suggests two alternative rationales for their withdrawal.

Jesus cites the viewing of "a reed shaken by the wind" as the first possibility. This phrase lacks specificity, and it becomes a blank screen for projection. The seekers could have wanted to come out to observe nature, or they may have gone out to see an invisible wind shake a reed, or they may have gone out to observe the weaker parts of nature worked by the more forceful, or simply to see fragility manifest. The possible interpretations of the phrase multiply, but there is little narrative direction provided for selecting one over another.

Jesus leaves this alternative aside, however, when he presents the second alternative, one that forms the heart of the saying. Jesus suggests that the seekers went out "to see a person dressed in soft clothes." The soft clothes contrast negatively with the environment–they are anomalous. The people fashionably dressed contrast the lack of care that should be exhibited by the seekers (see Saying 36) with the careful construction of a persona by their "rulers and powerful ones." The contrast here revolves about the dominant and the periphery, the powerful and richly arrayed as opposed to the poor, the city versus the countryside. So this second alternative receives condemnatory treatment. Jesus condemns the form of clothing appropriate to "rulers and powerful ones," he rejects the trappings of authority and power and the mundane world in which clothing both matters and elevates the status of the wearer. Their preoccupation with these external things, as has been repeatedly stated in these sayings, renders them incapable of understanding the truth, because their engagement in the world prevents them from being free enough to understand, or disengaged enough to discern the truth. Such people, as this saying affirms, cannot become perceptive or achieve the sort of understanding the true seekers yearn for and which these sayings purvey.

By the end of the saying, the lack of definition, cohesion, and direction in the various statements of the saying become obvious. It moves from confrontation of the seekers, to a condemnation of the socially and politically powerful, from questioning about location to clothing and its signification, from the rejection of the rich and powerful to their characterization as beyond the capacity for truth. Without a narrative to give direction, the meaning of the saying simply devolves into a harangue.

Saying 79

A woman in the crowd said to him, "Blessed [SV: Lucky] are the womb that bore you and the breasts that fed you." [2]He said to [her], "Blessed [SV: Lucky] are those who have heard the word of the Father and have truly kept it. [3]For there will be days when you will say, 'Blessed [SV: Lucky] are the womb that has not conceived and the breasts that have not given milk.' "

Three separate statements comprise this saying: the woman's blessing, Jesus' response focusing on the reception of the word, and the prediction about future days. They form a neatly arranged sequence that coheres and mutually develops aspects of the other parts (cf. Luke 11.27–29 and 23.28–29).

The blessing from the woman in the crowd locates Jesus within the biological and social structure that elsewhere in these sayings he has rejected (see Saying 55). The woman rejoices in the good fortune of another woman whose son has done well, by blessing the nurturing womb (the womb is plural in ancient medicine) and the nourishing breasts. Her blessing emerged from the solidarity of woman to mother, but has as a result defined Jesus from a physical perspective alone.

Jesus counters her blessing with another blessing. It has the same form and follows directly upon the woman's in style, but not in content. Jesus' blessing redirects the subject: true nurturing (womb and breasts) consists of hearing and preserving the proclamation of the Father. The misplaced and merely physical blessing of the woman has been reformulated in terms of the hearing and responding to the word. Jesus' blessing refers to those who listen to the sayings, who interpret and preserve the words that they hear. Not only the subject of the blessing has shifted, but the direction has moved away from Jesus as a medium, to the hearers as the primary focus.

The final statement, in a mildly apocalyptic mode, points to the day when the blessing will be upon those who have not been productive in the physical sense. The blessing will be upon closed wombs and dry breasts that neither produce life nor nurture it. The harshness of the statement intensifies in relation to the happy blessing of the woman in the first section: not only is her blessing reformulated, but even what has given her joy has been taken away. The conflict which Jesus has brought between the normal way of the world and the new way of those interpreting the sayings does not allow even the romanticized joy of an enthusiastic follower to be unchecked by the new existence. The violence underscores the radical redefinition of categories of identity.

This saying may also be developing a theology of female asceticism. Saying 22 advanced the possibility that the male will no longer be male nor the female be female in a performance intended to construct a third alternative gender or cultural category for human beings. This strategy was followed by an ascetical recreation of the body "when you make eyes in place of an eye, a hand in place of a hand, a foot in place of a foot, an image in place of an image." The body's reconstruction correlates to the redefinition and articulation of the new gender. So in this final verse, Jesus blesses a "womb that has not conceived and the breasts that have not given milk" in a strategy consistent with the reformulation of female gender so that it is no longer female and with the reconstruction of the body through ascetical activity (see also Castelli 1986).

Saying 80

Jesus said, "Whoever has come to know the world has discovered the body [Coptic: *soma*], [2]and whoever has discovered the body [Coptic: *soma*], of that one the world is not worthy."

This saying repeats Saying 56 with the substitution of "body" (*soma*) for "carcass" (*toma*). The Greek loan-word (*soma*) could indeed be translated as corpse, carcass, or body, so that this saying may simply be a translation of the same Greek saying with two alternative Coptic renditions.

The saying valorizes the superior discernment of the true seeker. The principle that it articulates links knowledge to discovery, in a variation on the theme of Saying 2: those who through their interpretation of the sayings come to know the world will discover the body. The object of the knowledge ("the world") and the object of the discovery ("the body") give specificity and substance to that linking. Both objects ought to be viewed as problematized: neither one rates high valuation in the context of these sayings. The proper understanding of the world leads to a proper valuation of the body. The second part of the statement elaborates further by declaring that the discovery of the proper value of the body exhibits a superior posture in relationship to the world. The world ranks negatively ("is not worthy") before such a discerning person.

There is one intertext that may need to be investigated here which provides an interesting alternative to the interpretation I have just presented. The "body" may, in fact, refer to the corporate body, as Paul has used it in the Corinthian correspondence (1 Corinthians 12.12; 15.44). The body, correlative to Paul's Body of Christ, may be the counterpart to the world. The discerning person who knows the true nature of the world has discovered the true nature of spiritual community, the body, the society of spiritual people who have withdrawn from the mundane world in order to live a different life. Knowledge still links with discovery, but here in a totally positive statement. The ambiguity of the statement makes for multiple interpretations. This positive interpretation of the body encapsulates the theological perspective of the sayings in that the cosmos and world receive negative valuation in marked contrast to the seekers who engage in the sayings who become both immortal (Saying 1), divine (Saying 108), and invincible (Saying 32). The discovery of the spiritual body has at once recognized the world for what it is and found great worth.

Saying 81

Jesus said, "The one who has become wealthy should reign, [2]and the one who has power should renounce <it>."

The interpretation of this saying hinges on bringing to bear some of the themes of earlier sayings. The concept of reigning invokes the final phase of the seeking process delineated in Saying 2: the one who seeks will find, become troubled, be astonished, and rule. This saying then provides a particular understanding of reigning as the end result of the search for meaning and understanding through the sayings. Likewise the concept of wealth invokes the many statements valorizing poverty (Saying 54) and deprecating both the accumulation of money and the commercial processes that make it possible (Saying 64). The significance of wealth in this saying, then, must be referring not to the accumulation of financial and commercial resources, but to the spiritual wealth valorized in these sayings and promulgated by the values they present. The saying then may be interpreted as promoting the rule of those who have become rich in the knowledge purveyed in these sayings and of those who find their true wealth in the communities constructed around the sayings. The inversion of the meaning of "wealth" connects with the articulation of the concept of the "reign" to produce a consistent meaning.

The same strategy of inversion finds expression in the second verse: "the one who has power should renounce <it>." The saying directly states the inversion: the powerful should renounce their power. The acquisition of power has not been a theme of these sayings, while renunciation of business, worldly concerns, and family has. To these other renunciations, then, may be added power. The power receives no delimitation: it cannot be established to be power in any particular realm. The instruction to renounce power, then, stands as a general and universal rule. All power (presumably including spiritual power) must be renounced.

If these two sayings are related to one another, a further avenue of interpretation arises. My previous interpretation hinged on interpreting the "wealth" as an inversion, and identifying the one who reigns as the interpreter of the sayings. If, however, these sayings form a progression, the meaning may rest in a corollary to the seeking process of Saying 2. This correlative progression would be: accumulate wealth, become a ruler and amass power, renounce the power. Each of these statements would be taken literally to advance a particular way of entering into the lifestyle posited by these sayings.

Saying 82

> Jesus said, "Whoever is near me is near the fire, [2]and whoever is far from me is far from the <Father's> domain."

The precise meaning of this saying remains obscure because the reference to "fire" eludes specific definition. In this saying, however, the "fire" and the "Kingdom" function as a tautology, so that the fire stands in the same place in relationship to Jesus as the Kingdom. The difference between them is not found in themselves, but in the proximity to Jesus and the consequent proximity or distance from the fire and Jesus. Because of this parallel function, fire has completely positive associations.

The saying identifies the seekers' proximity to Jesus as determinative of being near the Kingdom. Contrarily, distance from Jesus translates to distance from the Kingdom. The ability to approach the fire, or to enter the Kingdom, derives from close proximity to Jesus.

Since the sayings collection constructs the presence of Jesus, this saying may not be so much self-referential to Jesus as to the voice of Jesus encapsulated in the sayings and refracted by their narrator. The self-referential strategy thus becomes an instrument directly addressing the authority of the collection of these sayings and the authority of their perspective. The one who comes close to the sayings and their interpretation draws near the fire and the Kingdom, but the one who remains distant from these sayings remains distant from the Kingdom and misses the fire of interpretation. In this way fire functions not only as a tautology to the Kingdom, but also as a metaphor for transformative interpretation.

Saying 83

> Jesus said, "Images are visible to people, but the light within them is hidden in the image of the Father's light. [2]He will be disclosed, but his image is hidden by his light."

This saying articulates a theology of iconographic representation. Images or icons (the Coptic uses the Greek loan-word *eikon*) present the physical representation to observer; the icon as a portrait makes the person visible to others, that is, it represents the person to others. Light makes that representation possible as well as making the icon visible. The light within the images, however, comes not from the physical representation itself, but from the presence connected with the Father's light. All light comes from the Father's light, and therefore the Father's light undergirds both the icon and its viewing. The presence in the iconographic representation derives from the greater presences that stand behind the physical representation. The light that seems present in the image refracts the light stored behind it, so that the light in the icon or portrait refracts the image of the Father's light. This describes a functional theology of iconographic representation for those with discernment about divine things: the theology developed here locates *all* light in the Father and maintains that all icons or images must use that light both for representation and as a medium of viewing.

That theology, however, does not apply to representations of the Father. The Father must be made visible directly, without a representation. A representation or image of the Father cannot be made because his light, as the origin of the light in other portraits, cannot be represented. A representation refracts that light, and the Father's originate light (according to this saying) cannot be refracted. Since the Father's light cannot be represented in the icons that represent others, then the revelation of the Father must be directly apprehended without the aid of images.

A third-century discourse on portraiture, evidenced in Porphyry's "Life and Works of Plotinus," may provide a justification for this interpretation. Plotinus refused to have his portrait painted by a student, he refused to be represented to others, preferring to be noetically (rather than iconically) present to others in his words. The words of Plotinus were refracted through Porphyry and his critical edition and biographical introduction. The words created the presence of Plotinus, so that portraits were redundant. So in this saying, the words reveal the image of the Father, and disclose the Father's light, so any representation beyond those words becomes redundant (Valantasis 1991: 35–61).

Saying 84

Jesus said, "When you see your likeness, you are happy. [2]But when you see your images that came into being before you and that neither die nor become visible, how much more you will have to bear!"

This saying connects with the previous one on the basis of their shared use of the word "image." The previous saying was presented in third-person address so that they spoke abstractly and generally about "images." In marked contrast, this saying speaks directly to the readers who are addressed in the second person ("you"). The previous saying related the theology of the images to light, while this one relates images to the emotional reaction of the seekers/readers. Their theological interests, therefore, are probably different.

The conjunction of "image" and "likeness" has a very specific intertext in the creation of human being in Genesis 1.26a where God says "Let us make humankind in our image, according to our likeness...." (NRSV). This saying may be understood as addressing the creation of humankind, and it appears to develop a theological anthropology for the people interpreting these sayings. This theological anthropology rests on a distinction between "images" and "likeness" and the seekers' ability to apprehend and respond to them.

The first part of the saying to the seekers makes a general statement: they are happy when they see their resemblance to God their creator. The statement presumes that the seekers will indeed recognize readily the divine likeness that they bear, and in recognizing it will rejoice in it. The anthropology posited here is at once positive and constructive.

In comparison to the next statement, the very positive anthropology of the first verse becomes shallow. The second statement characterizes the "images" as pre-existent, immortal, and hidden. The images are still visible, as was the likeness of the first statement, but now the character of what is visible has taken on a more developed theological character. The seekers will see the images that existed before them, the images that will not die (as they themselves will not taste death), and the images that will not "become visible." These "images" that the seekers will see bear a more immutable and eternal theological aspect, connecting them to the nature of the God who created them. The anthropology seems to indicate a dual understanding: a more shallow understanding among people who see their likeness to God and rejoice, and a more theological understanding of those who see the pre-existent, immortal, and invisible images. The saying adds weight to this sort of distinction by emphasizing the burden placed upon the more theologically adept in saying "how much more you will have to bear" in seeing those images. The seeker may view both the appearance and the image; there seems no restricted access to either one of the pair. Once the image has been seen, however, the seekers find a heightened awareness of its burden and concurrent responsibility. This burden results from the contrasting of the superficial with the intensely theological categories which describe the image.

The saying, then, describes the burden and wonder of the seeker awakening to the immortal, pre-existent, and invisible part of their lives.

This image connects the external divine forces to the internal, just as it was explained in the last saying. To experience that image carries the burden of living with the knowledge of its existence, activity, and presence.

Saying 85

Jesus said, "Adam came from great power and great wealth, but he was not worthy of you. ²For had he been worthy, [he would] not [have tasted] death."

There are not many explicit citings of biblical figures in these sayings, so this comment about Adam is unusual. It continues the previous reference to the creation of humankind in Genesis, and, therefore, continues to develop a theological anthropology for the seekers. Again, the direct address to the readers/seekers contrasts to the third-person reference to Adam, so that two levels of meaning are presented, one referring to Adam, the other referring to the participants in this community.

Jesus addresses this statement directly to the readers in order to contrast the readers/seekers and Adam. Adam's life originated in "a great power" and "a great wealth." These characterizations mark both Adam's origin in God and his superior status in creation. The characterizations suggest that Adam partakes of the divine image, likeness, and light presented in the immediately preceding sayings, and discussed in Saying 83. Adam stands at the apex of divine creation and empowerment, but in relation to the seekers in these sayings he receives a lower valuation. Adam contrasts negatively to the "you" of the saying.

The difference between the seekers ("you") and Adam revolves about the experience of death. Adam died; his divine origin and the great wealth with which he was endowed could not prevent him from experiencing death. The seekers in these sayings, those who interpret the sayings, will not experience death (as in Saying 1); their interpretative process guarantees that they will not die. The seekers do not reverse Adam's situation; they simply take precedence over Adam. Those who do not experience death have greater worth than those who do, including Adam. Had Adam been as worthy as the seekers in these sayings, he would not have experienced death; he would have been immortal like the members of this loosely formed community.

Saying 86

Jesus said, "[Foxes have] their dens and birds have their nests, [2]but human beings have no place to lie down and rest."

The series of sayings presenting contrasts continues; this saying contrasts animals to human beings. The habitat of animals contrasts drastically with that of human beings: foxes and birds naturally build homes, but humans do not. The contrast dramatizes the homing instincts of animals and the homelessness of humans. Unlike these animals, humans live as aliens in the world into which they are born: their alien status renders them without resources for sleeping and resting. By nature, the saying suggests, human beings live as aliens.

The presence of two specific terms raises further interpretative possibilities. The first term, phrased above as "human being," translates the Coptic and the Greek phrase (found also in Luke 9.58) that is usually translated into English as "the son of man." The point at which this phrase becomes a title of Jesus has been debated for a number of years (Koester 1982: II, 147–49). A consensus has emerged which supports the thesis that at the earliest chronological levels of these collected sayings of Jesus, the phrase was simply understood as a (Semitic?) circumlocution for "everyone" or "person", or, as it is translated in the Scholars Version, "human being." This early tradition provided the interpretative lens for the general interpretation above.

At some point, probably beginning in the mid-first century CE and certainly fully developed by the third and fourth centuries, the term "Son of Man" became an official title of Jesus. The contrast in the interpretation of the saying would then not revolve about the comparison of like creatures in the world (foxes, birds, humans), but rather it would revolve about the contrast of two creatures with natural homes (foxes and birds) with a divine figure who has no home. The issue, then, shifts from the alien status of all humanity to the specific itinerancy of Jesus, the Son of Man. The Son of Man (understand Jesus) moves about from place to place with no place to lie down and rest: the Son of Man functions as a homeless itinerant. The saying does not, in this interpretation, suggest that itinerancy for people in the community posited in these sayings, but presents it as a unique characteristic of Jesus in his role as Son of Man. Under the influence of a later theology of the title "Son of Man," the theological significance of the sayings has moved from an alien status for all humanity to the itinerant lifestyle of one particular divine figure.

The second term, translated above as "rest," also suggests an alternative reading of the saying. Rest has been an articulated goal of these sayings for those who seek. In the Greek version of Saying 2, rest culminates the entire process of struggle and functions as the final cause of all the other activities. Rest constitutes an important theological state for these sayings and the community built from interpreting them. The statement about rest, then, may have two distinct interpretations depending upon the precise referent to the term "son of man." In the first interpretation above, the natural human being, the creature correlative to foxes and birds, not only lacks a home, but also does not find rest. The rest in these sayings, that is, comes to seekers not by their nature or instinct, but through their cultivation of rest in the interpretation of the sayings. Rest remains, therefore, a status earned and not a natural predilection like foxes building dens and birds, nests.

In the second interpretation, the Son of Man (as a title for Jesus) lives as an itinerant incapable of finding rest. The theological category "rest" so necessary to the seekers in these sayings does not apply to Jesus himself. Seekers will find rest through living the life outlined in the sayings, but the Son of Man, as itinerant divine figure, will never find that rest. He exists in a category separate and distinct from human beings and other creatures.

Saying 87

Jesus said, "How miserable is the body that depends on a body, [2]and how miserable is the soul that depends on these two."

This saying, in the sequence of contrasts continuing to be made in this small section of sayings (Sayings 83–88), distinguishes between three human aspects (the body, the dependent body, and the soul) and characterizes the status of their relationship as miserable. The three-fold distinction presented here differentiates between the body and the dependent body which is the body that relies on other bodies. The body, in this distinction, suffers by the dependent body, and is made miserable. That is, the dependent body influences the body in such a way as to make it miserable. This does not necessarily imply that the body is negatively construed: only the body dependent upon another body bears negative connotations, so that bodies that are not dependent on other bodies would not be understood as miserable. The soul, moreover, also shares with both the body and the dependent body a relationship that renders it miserable. The two bodies, intertwined in their own need and limitations, hinder the soul and make it miserable.

The interlocking misery construes every kind of dependency negatively. Any form of dependency seems to receive negative appraisal, so that in every instance the one who depends on another becomes miserable. Dependency here would stand in contrast to the solitary ones who have found a source within them that frees them from such dependency and opens for them an unlimited source of knowledge and fulfillment.

Saying 88

Jesus said, "The messengers [Coptic: *angelos*] and the prophets will come to you and give you what belongs to you. [2]You, in turn, give them what you have, and say to yourselves, 'When will they come and take what belongs to them?'"

This saying describes an exchange between the direct address "you" of the sayings on one side and the angels and prophets on the other. The seekers stand at the very center of the activity, receiving from the angels and prophets, giving back to them what they have, and holding what belongs to them until they return to claim it. This central narrative role reflects the significant stature of the seekers.

The messengers (angels) who transmit messages from the divine and the oracular speakers (prophets) who speak words heard in the divine presence deliver to seekers what belongs to them, what (as Lambdin translates) "they (already) have." The subjectivity constructed in these sayings has acquired the knowledge of angels and prophets without their direct instruction, so that in the end these messengers and oracular speakers deliver to the seekers the messages and oracles they have already acquired and the things that properly belong to them. The seekers in turn transmit their messages and deliver their oracles to the angels and prophets; they bestow upon these emissaries and oracular voices the knowledge they have acquired. The exchange witnesses to the equality of their relationship, so that there is a mutuality of exchange of proper substances between the seekers on the one side and the angels and prophets on the other.

These seekers, moreover, surpass the knowledge even of angels and prophets in that they wonder why the angels and prophets have not come and taken what properly belongs to them. There is a curious positing of an interior question the seekers ask. The question, posited by Jesus in the course of the comparison of the seekers with the angels and prophets, has been presented as something they think, or wonder, about. It provides a precious window into the thinking processes of the seekers, who without any rancor or sense of superiority ask "When will they come and take what belongs to them?" The seekers, that is, find the angels and prophets lacking their full knowledge, but fully deserving of and entitled to having the fullness that the seekers have, and the seekers are eager to reciprocate.

Saying 89

Jesus said, "Why do you wash the outside of the cup? [2]Don't you understand that the one who made the inside is also the one who made the outside?"

At the literal level, this saying argues that it is unnecessary to wash the outside of cups (cf. the Synoptic Sayings Source Q 11.39–40) because both the inside and the outside of the cup were made by the same person. The saying appears confrontational because the question demands a rationale for the practice of washing the exterior of cups, while the statement dismisses any possibility of an acceptable rationale for the practice. So Jesus confronts the seekers regarding a practice neither acceptable to nor explicable by him.

Remaining on this level, the saying could refer simply to the practices surrounding the ritual purification of eating utensils. This would take the subject "the cups" as metonymically presenting eating utensils, and would dismiss the purification of those utensils on the basis that the same creator made both. Jesus thus would be rejecting ritual purificatory practices generally.

The language of the "inside" and the "outside," however, suggests other interpretative postures. The transformation of inside to outside, and outside to inside, constitutes a significant theme in these sayings. Saying 22, for example, lists the "making of the inside like the outside and the outside like the inside" as preliminary to entering the Kingdom. The language of inside and outside thematizes the unity of subjectivity promulgated in these sayings: the differentiation of inner self from outer self ignores the creation of all the selves by the same person. No differentiation may be made, the solitary remains unified. From the perspective of the seekers, the interior and the exterior remain the same, both function as a vital part of the seekers' self-understanding, and neither requires purification of any sort. Neither the practice of purification, nor the rationale for it, makes any sense in the context of these sayings and their interpretation. The saying, however, may properly refer to the seekers in these sayings who have no concern for externals and whose interior and exterior aspects are alike. The creator of both the interior and the exterior has rendered inappropriate any concern only for the exterior.

Saying 90

Jesus said, "Come to me, for my yoke is comfortable and my lordship is gentle, [2]and you will find rest for yourselves."

This saying (cf. Matthew 11.28–30) consists of three parts: a protreptic admonition or invitation, two justifications for the invitation, and a description of the result of accepting it. In a typical invitation of divine wisdom to faithfulness, the command extends a simple and direct invitation ("Come to me") to the seekers or readers of the sayings. The imperative mood makes the invitation general, because the implied "you" has no delimited boundaries. Jesus as a wisdom figure extends the invitation to anyone. The narrator identifies the voice as that of Jesus, but an ambiguity remains nonetheless. The narrative saying ("Jesus said") embeds the "me" of the imperative in a written collection of sayings. The admonition invites people to come to Jesus, but the collection of sayings, the narrated voice, mediates that Jesus (and his voice) to the readers, so that the readers and seekers find themselves attending to the narrated voice of Jesus in a collection of sayings. The ambiguity extends the limit of the invitation beyond that of Jesus alone as inviter, to that of Jesus and the saying as inviters of the seekers.

The two justifications for this invitation further this ambiguity. The comfortable or easy yoke signifies the working relationship between Jesus and his followers. The yoke joins the work animals together in order to make them submit to the task for which they have been appointed. It also signifies an increment of equality: those yoked together equally contribute to the necessary task. The yoke, then, establishes a comfortable conjunction of workers, goals, and tasks in an equitable way. The gentle or mild lordship follows from this statement: Jesus extends the invitation to enter into an equal relationship with him in the achievement of a common goal. Although Jesus has defined and inaugurated the parameters of the work (he has, after all, extended the invitation), he becomes one more partner in the tasks. This lordship, because of the equality of relationships, does not exercise rigid authority, but a gentle one among people conjoined for mutually effective work.

The goal also reflects this gentle lordship, for it is not Jesus who will provide them rest, but those who are yoked to Jesus in the work will find for themselves the rest that they seek. Rest defines the goal, a thematizing of the goal consistently presented in these sayings. The labor, then, moves not toward riches or productivity, but toward rest. The cessation of activity, the ending of the yoked work and the mild lordship, provides the final cause to the activity outlined.

Saying 91

They said to him, "Tell us who you are so that we may believe in you." [2]He said to them, "You examine [Coptic: *piraze*] the face of heaven and earth, but you have not come to know the one who is in your presence, and you do not know how to examine [Coptic: *piraze*] the present moment."

This saying returns to a form familiar from earlier sayings in which followers present Jesus with a question that shows their lack of understanding. Normally, disciples ask the question, but here it is a more general group of people ("they"). The question, however, exhibits more complexity than most of these sorts of questions heard earlier. These unidentified and generic people connect Jesus' identity with their willingness to believe. They demand of Jesus a self-revelation that would enable them to believe, and, thus, link faith and revelation (on faith versus knowledge see MacRae 1980: 126–33).

Jesus' answer reformulates the question by ignoring the correlation of revelation to faith, and by moving the inquisitors toward an understanding of the processes of examination and testing. Jesus' answer rejects faith as the primary category for seekers and adopts, rather, a concept of experience and understanding based on examination and proof. The Coptic employs the Greek loan-word *peirao* which means generally to test, to establish by proof, to experience, to become acquainted with something, or simply to attempt something. Research and understanding replace faith in Jesus' response, but the manner of that replacement also speaks of a very particular sort of understanding of Jesus and the world in which the seekers live.

Jesus tells these questioners that, although they have become acquainted with the knowledge of earth and heaven, they have not become acquainted with "the one who is in your presence." They have studied the external knowledges, or the sciences (as in Saying 3), but they have not learned about the one present to them in the sayings or in the voice of Jesus. Their knowledge does not suffice for them; they have knowledge, but not of the true knowledge available through the "presence" in these sayings. Not only does Jesus reprimand them for their lack of understanding of the presence, and the insufficiency of their understanding for knowledge of the enlivening and challenging presence, but he also says that their manner of study and examination lacks substance. These questioners do not know how to "examine the present moment." They lack the skills necessary to understand the moment in which they find themselves. These people lack knowledge, understanding of the presence, and skills whereby to progress.

Research, searching for the "presences," experiencing knowledge—these define the proper status of seekers in these sayings. Revelation exists in order precisely to lead one, not to faith, but to understanding; not to assurance, but to questions. The identity of Jesus works more as a locus of questioning than as a firm foundation for belief. True knowledge means to know Jesus, or to know the present moment, or to know "the one who is in your presence" (whether that one is Jesus or not), and the process of examining, searching, reading, understanding, and articulating will lead to this knowledge.

Saying 92:

Jesus said, "Seek and you will find. [2]In the past, however, I did not tell you the things about which you asked me then. Now I am willing to tell them, but you are not seeking them."

In Saying 2, a seeking that ends in finding inaugurates a process of spiritual transformation, and this thematization of spiritual desire persists throughout the sayings in this collection. The thematization constitutes the primary characterization of the subjectivity promulgated in these sayings. These people read the sayings and discover their interpretation, they seek after greater and more sophisticated knowledge and understanding, and in their seeking and finding they become transformed agents and empowered religious people. Jesus reiterates that subjectivity as the basis of this saying.

Jesus places this general statement (cf. the Synoptic Sayings Source Q 11.9–10) about the subjectivity of the seekers in these sayings into two different historical contexts: the past and the present. In the past, these seekers asked questions that Jesus did not answer. This peculiar statement stands out among the sayings. It seems not to apply to the more universal "you" of the sayings which articulates a distinction between the seekers and others. Nor does it indicate that the saying refers to the disciples who, while Jesus was still with them in the formative years of his earthly ministry, asked him questions that he refused to answer. Yet, Jesus's refusal to answer questions displays the strategy he usually employs against the ignorant disciples in these sayings rather than displaying the privileged questioning of the real seekers in these sayings.

In the second chronological context (the present), Jesus relates that now that he desires to answer their questions they no longer ask them. The former times have been succeeded by present times, marked by a cessation of questioning. In these times knowledge is available, but not sought; in the former times knowledge was desired, but not provided.

If the narrative of the ignorant disciples provides the context for this saying, then the disciples, who seem never to understand that their questions characterize them as lacking understanding, were kept ignorant during the earthly lifetime of Jesus, when they could not understand the answers Jesus would have provided. Now that Jesus could give them the knowledge, they do not seek it, either because they do not know that it is available, or because they are too ignorant to be able to access it. This saying alone in the collection develops the barest outlines of an historical narrative, one with a past and a present connected by some series of events (here questioning and the willingness to answer). The historical narrative explains why the people in the former times did not have the answers (and, presumably, some people do now): Jesus did not wish to give them the knowledge that they sought. It also explains why the progeny of the people in the former times remain in ignorance: Jesus now desires to answer their questions but they do not seek the answers. This saying suggests an historical rationale for the community of interpreters of these sayings to have knowledge from Jesus that others do not have, and it explains the reason that other followers of Jesus would not have the same sort of information and knowledge as they do. It also suggests a relationship between the interpreters of these sayings and the leaders of the great church, or the difference between the monks preserving these sayings and the prelates developing doctrinal statements.

Saying 93

"Don't give what is sacred to dogs, for they might throw them upon the manure pile. [2]Don't throw pearls [to] pigs, or they might ... it. [...]"

Just a few letters prevent a grammatical and lexical completion of this statement, but enough of it survives to be able to set forth its basic meaning. The saying valorizes the protection of sacred things by not giving them to unworthy people. The contrasts (sacred to dogs, pearls to pigs) have as their recipients animals unworthy of what they receive. Their unworthiness revolves about their inability to understand the worth of what they have been given. A dog does not understand sacredness and therefore does not honor it–rather, dishonors it by throwing it into the manure pile. Likewise the pigs should not be thrown pearls, or they would do something equally as inappropriate as the dogs. Their lack of understanding makes them unacceptable receptors of the riches possessed by the giver.

The presence of the giver provides the key to a reading in the context of these sayings. The seekers who have found, the interpreters of these sayings, find themselves in possession of great riches: they understand their own selves and their divine origin and divine destination, they have achieved an increment of divine power and exercise that power in the world in which they live. They have achieved a true wealth, found a pearl of great value. This saying instructs them to preserve that wealth and not to give it to people who will neither understand it, nor value it. Their knowledge should be reserved for the understanding alone.

Saying 94

Jesus [said], "One who seeks will find, [2]and for [one who knocks] it will be opened."

This saying (similar to the Synoptic Sayings Source Q 11.9–10, as well as to Sayings 2 and 92) links a sequence familiar to readers of these sayings about seeking and finding, to a new expression about knocking and opening. The two equations function tautologously because they present, under two different metaphoric expressions, the same guarantee of success. If the readers of these sayings begin to seek, they will indeed find that for which they seek, and likewise, anyone who knocks at a closed door (an apt euphemism for some of these sayings) that closed door will be opened for them. The mysteries which the seekers pursue will be made known to them.

Such sayings present the fulfillment of desire as immediate. The yearning and the desire will find their satisfaction in the inauguration of the processes described, not in a distant future, but with the speed of the opening of a door after someone knocks on it. The reward and the success follow immediately for those yearning; the fulfillment is not delayed.

An interesting avenue of interpretation emerges when Sayings 92, 93, and 94 are read together. Sayings 92 and 94 connect around the theme of seeking and finding. The statement that those who seek will find encloses a very negative portrayal of those who have failed to search (Saying 92.2) to whom the statement in Saying 93 may be applied. Those who do not search are like the dogs to whom the sacred should not be given and to the pigs to whom the pearls should not be thrown. However, for those who seek, the finding is guaranteed; the door will be opened to those who knock. The three sayings together form a well-developed and full articulation of the difference between true seeking and false, between the worthy followers and the unworthy.

Saying 95

[Jesus said], "If you have money, don't lend it at interest. ²Rather, give [it] to someone from whom you won't get it back."

This saying gathers two themes frequently addressed in these sayings: the devaluation of money and its accumulation, and the reversal of expectations among those who have personal resources. The normal mercantile process would dictate that money should be lent at interest to increase its quantity. This saying reverses that normal function and enjoins the possessor of money *not* to lend it at interest. A further inversion follows. Rather than lending at interest, the seekers should give their money away.

Jesus characterizes those to whom the money ought to be given as the one "from whom you won't get it back." This characterization redefines lending in the context of the community in which these sayings are interpreted. Lending money does not mean making money from money, but giving the money to someone who will not repay it. The social practice of manipulating money stands, but the meaning of that manipulation has been so totally changed as to constitute a complete reversal without denying the practice itself. Whereas in the sayings about fasting, alms-giving, and prayer, these pious practices were totally rejected, here lending is redefined, not rejected.

Saying 96

Jesus [said], "The Father's imperial rule is like [a] woman [2]who took a little leaven, [hid] it in dough, and made it into large loaves of bread. [3]Anyone here with two ears had better listen!"

This saying begins a series of three similitudes (Sayings 96, 97, and 98) for the Father's Kingdom (Doran 1987). Two of them compare the Kingdom to women performing traditionally gendered activities (Sayings 96 and 97) and the third likens the Kingdom to a man planning to kill someone (Saying 98). The comparison of the Kingdom to women indicates that the understanding of gender receives particular attention in these sayings.

The first similitude articulates the Father's rule as a woman baking bread with yeast. This saying has close parallels in the Synoptic Sayings Source Q 13.20–21, and therefore, derives from the earliest layer of the collections of the sayings of Jesus. In this earlier context, this saying describes performatively the action of the growth of the Kingdom. It begins as a hidden and perhaps even disreputable agent, if leaven is considered unclean (see Scott 1989: 324), that transforms the dough into large loaves. Its hidden nature points to the inconspicuousness of its presence (see Crossan 1973: 38); the Father's rule does not seem obvious at first, but its presence becomes manifest over time. The comparison to yeast in dough indicates that the Father's rule grows naturally; once it has been hidden in the dough, the activity of the Father's rule will transform and enliven in as natural and straightforward a way as yeast in dough, and dough to bread. This activity does not indicate a mystery or an unusual activity in the development of the Father's reign–it simply follows that where it is planted, it will grow. As a description of the early Jesus movement, this similitude posits a very positive and natural growth from a small, hidden group of people, to a large body capable of providing others with sustenance.

The comparison of the Kingdom to a woman performing a common household task indicates the relative ease with which these sayings deal with gender (see Till 1958–59: 455; Doran 1987). These sayings posit a new understanding of human spiritual subjectivity, and this new subjectivity redefines the nature of gender. Women's tasks in this community image the Father's Kingdom; the Father may favorably be compared to a woman; "the kingdom is likened not to the leaven, as in the Synoptics, but to the woman" (Wilson 1960: 96). This understanding of gender correlates to much of the recent scholarship on the historical Jesus and the early development of formative Christianity which claims that formative Christianity functioned as a gender-inclusive community with open table fellowship (Schüssler-Fiorenza 1983: 118–30; Mack 1988: 80–83; Crossan 1991: 303–53). This comparison, in the early period, then, would describe the relatively natural growth of the Jesus movement from a small inclusive group hidden in the dominant culture to a large community capable of feeding many.

The inclusion of women, however, does not exhaust the possibilities for interpreting this saying in later periods of the history of this text. In periods of patriarchal dominance, when the role and function of women had been significantly restricted and the former inclusive strategy of the early Jesus movement rejected and suppressed, this comparison stands as a reminder to the later Christians of the altered gender constructions of the earlier period. The Father may be likened to a woman because the subjectivity promulgated in these sayings recasts the binary gender construction of male and female into a third gender of the solitary who has made the male a female and the female a male. This new subjectivity, gendered as a third gender, a *tertium quid*, grows and develops like yeast hidden in dough. The new understanding of self naturally develops as a transformative personal agent, making the substance of existence into something alive and new. The saying points toward the new gender relationship available to those who interpret these sayings, or who seek for a new life.

It may also be that the community itself, a community living beyond death because of its favored interpretation of the sayings, may function as an agent of transformation, being hidden and invisible in the world at the start, but gradually growing and transforming the world by its presence. The communities made up of solitaries understood their relationship to the world through such metaphoric descriptions, and it assisted them to understand their own mission concretely and fully articulated, without restricting the possible arenas of transformation.

Saying 97

Jesus said, "The [Father's] imperial rule is like a woman who was carrying a [jar] full of meal. [2]While she was walking along [a] distant road, the handle of the jar broke and the meal spilled behind her [along] the road. [3]She didn't know it; she hadn't noticed a problem. [4]When she reached her house, she put the jar down and discovered that it was empty."

A narrative provides the substance of this second comparison of the Father's rule to a woman (see Doran 1987). The narrative portrays a woman carrying meal in a jar that broke allowing the meal to fall through the hole to the ground during her walk. At the end of her walk, she discovered the jar to be empty. The narrator provides no description of her interior state, or response to the situation–the narrative simply stands as a description of an action without any insight into the character.

The character, receiving no development, walks through the narrative completely unaware: the broken handle of the jar does not concern her, nor did she understand the implications of the broken jar. The narrator simply says that she did not have knowledge of the leak and that she did not notice a problem. Her walking about without understanding or knowledge provides the basis of interpreting the statement. This woman's plight describes the life of people who live their lives in the world: they carry jars they think are full, but discover, even after much activity, that they are empty. Unrecognized emptiness characterizes the life lived in the world whose resources (thought to be carefully stored) leak away fruitlessly.

That interpretation provides one avenue of exploration, another follows from the intertextual suggestions of the narrative. The storing of the meal recalls the narrative of the man who wanted to store more grain in order to amass his riches and rest, but he died that night (Saying 63). This intertextual reference underscores the vanity of provision for the future even before the jar breaks. Those who do not make provision for what they will eat do not need to carry jars full of meal.

The discovery of the emptiness invokes in a negative way the sayings that assure that those who discover the interpretation of the sayings will not taste death (Saying 1, but also Sayings 18, 19, 85, and 111). Here the discovery does not relate to the sayings, but to the emptiness of the world's containers. This intertextual reference suggests that the discovery of the fullness of the sayings correlates to the discovery of the emptiness of the things of the world.

Again, in a possible reversal, the spilling of the meal along the road recalls the narrative of the sower planting seed some of which falls on the roadside (Saying 9). The lack of direction and intention by the woman carrying the jar contrasts with the strong intention of the sower who spreads the seed extensively. The direction of those within the community, the seekers, contrasts with the indirection of those living in the world.

Without any interpretative direction provided either by Jesus or by the narrator, the interpretation of these sayings may advance along a variety of different (or even conflicting) strategies. The understanding of the Kingdom in this mode of discourse emerges from a playful, yet fully engaged, reading that develops aspects of the text narratively and intertextually.

Saying 98

Jesus said, "The Father's imperial rule is like a person who wanted to kill someone powerful. [2]While still at home he drew his sword and thrust it into the wall to find out whether his hand would go in. [3]Then he killed the powerful one."

The third similitude (see Doran 1987) presents a violent narrative of premeditated violence and murder: a person who intends to kill a powerful person practices at home by pushing his sword through the wall, and realizing that he was capable, goes out to kill the powerful person. The bare description, lacking any sort of comment that might provide insight into the rationale for such a plan and its implementation, defies any exploration of the underlying moral issues. Murder and its execution seem plausible activities to be practiced and carried out, so that, lacking all moral formulations, the point of the story seems to suggest that one practice beforehand and test one's ability before attempting to murder a powerful person. The practice described in the narrative makes the implementation of the murder-plot more attainable.

Another avenue of interpretation would take the murderous behavior as indicative of the conflict which Jesus claims to have brought to the world (Sayings 16 and 47). That conflict between the world envisioned by these texts and the normal world rages with intensity and dramatic power. It does not simply mean a struggle, but rather the practiced and deliberate struggle of a person against a powerful opposition. The seekers, fighting the world and its ways to the end, must test their metal, practice their swings, explore the limits of their ability to do battle, and then proceed to the killing of the world when they have shown their strength.

The careful deliberation and the practice of the killing on the wall make this murder performative. The actions perform the meaning, carry the meaning forward, so that the seekers understand that they do not simply oppose the world, but are called in private to practice and to consider the manner of their attack and then to perform it. Such performances show the crafted nature of the seekers' development of subjectivity. These performances construct the new person, and display the power and force of the new subjectivity so that the person and all who see her will be able to understand themselves and to know how they are to act and to think. The performances construct a subjectivity and assist people to be trained to live them out.

Saying 99

The disciples said to him, "Your brothers and your mother are standing outside." [2]He said to them, "Those here who do what my Father wants are my brothers and my mother. [3]They are the ones who will enter my Father's domain."

These sayings continually redefine common social and religious categories (see Sayings 55 and 25). Jesus redefines the family in this saying. The disciples, again in their mode of speaking in such a way as to show their consistent misunderstanding of Jesus, announce to Jesus that his mother and brothers stand nearby. Jesus replies to them that his brothers and mothers are those who do the Father's bidding; Jesus rejects biological relationship or social constructs of biological family in favor of a family based on those related to the Father's will. Again, the redefinition of the category allows the category "family" to stand, but provides a totally different understanding of the referent to the word.

The negative expression of the rejection of family hides the very positive message. Those who seek the Father's will become family to one another; the brothers and sisters consist of those who seek after the interpretation of the sayings and who have found a life beyond death. This new familial relationship does indeed redefine the way in which family is understood.

Saying 100

They showed Jesus a gold coin and said to him, "The Roman emperor's people demand taxes from us." [2]He said to them, "Give the emperor what belongs to the emperor, [3]give God what belongs to God, [4]and give me what is mine."

The majority of this saying has parallels in the synoptic gospels (Mark 12.13–17; Matthew 22.15–22; Luke 20.20–26). Only the last phrase ("and give me what is mine") lacks any parallel in the synoptic gospels.

The disengagement from the world of merchants and traders and investors means that money, coins, taxes, and any of the sort of traditional worldly activities become meaningless. The presentation of a coin to Jesus becomes an opportunity for a statement about the proper status of various realms of existence. The emperor, whose coin is presented to Jesus, owns the coin and should have it returned to him. Likewise the things that belong to God should be given back to God. The saying does not tell what belongs to God, nor does it define it further. The two realms, often portrayed in conflict, here find themselves as divergent worlds with different resources and ends which should be acknowledged. The third statement presents problems. Jesus says, "give me what is mine." Three different powers are presented: the Roman emperor, God, and Jesus. Each power receives what properly belongs to it.

The three-fold construction of power points to three groups, each with their proper domain. Jesus' group may well be the group interpreting these sayings: it is the textualized possession of those seeking to discover the meaning of the sayings and the voice of the speaker who proclaims the sayings recorded by Didymos Judas Thomas. In other words, what belongs to Jesus is the community of those who have entered a relationship with him through hearing and responding to the sayings. The interpreters, the interpretations, as well as the sayings themselves belong to Jesus and must be returned to him. The interpreters' origin and destiny are in God, a God who cannot be discovered until they withdraw from the world to become solitaries. The saying characterizes Caesar and his people as the world from which the seekers withdraw. The instrument of finding their destiny, and of the empowerment for withdrawal, is the voice of Jesus found in the sayings. This voice demands as much attention as Caesar and God.

Saying 101

"Whoever does not hate [father] and mother as I do cannot be my [disciple], [2]and whoever does [not] love [father and] mother as I do cannot be my [disciple]. [3]For my mother [. . .], but my true [mother] gave me life."

The redefinition of family comes to the fore again in this saying as in Saying 55. The rejection of parents, with its parallel in the Synoptic Sayings Source Q 14.26–27, presents a variation on a theme presented under the aegis of rejection of the entire family. Jesus defines discipleship as consisting of those who reject their socially given relationships to their father and mother. The conflict with biological paternity and maternity reflects the same violence as the conflict with the mundane world, and Jesus accepts disciples only among those capable of that radical renunciation (see Saying 47).

In the second verse, "love" replaces "hate" in the reformulation of the saying. Such a replacement of opposites in the same form performs the reversal in which these sayings frequently revel. The negation (hating father and mother) is negated in turn by its opposite, a positive (loving father and mother). This statement could be read ironically: true disciples love their parents as Jesus does, that is, they love them not at all. Or this strategy of reversal may be setting the stage for the distinction between kinds of mothers in the third verse: the disciples, that is, ought to love their true parents, their alternative and redefined parents, the parents who arise out of the community of the faithful in which they live. Such a reading exemplifies the redefinition and re-signification of categories effected in many of these sayings.

The final verse, incomplete as it is at a crucial point, clearly posits a distinction between two mothers. The fragmentary text only permits characterization of the mother marked as the "true" mother who gave Jesus life. The other mother receives no specific identification and her provision for Jesus cannot be recovered. The contrasting mothers further the contrasts of the previous two verses. The true disciples follow the true parents and find life.

Saying 102

> Jesus said, "Damn the Pharisees! They are like a dog sleeping in the cattle manger: the dog neither eats nor [lets] the cattle eat."

The controversy with Jewish religious leaders invokes the problematizing of hierarchy met elsewhere in the sayings (as in Sayings 3, 34, and 39). The clever characterization of the Pharisees likens them to "a dog sleeping in the cattle manger" and invokes a familiar Greek fable (Meyer 1992: 105). The hyperbolic statement describes them negatively as "dogs" and locates the center of their activity in the least likely of places, the cattle barn, a place not in the least associated with religious or spiritual leadership. The similitude maintains that dogs in the manger neither eat nor allow the cattle to eat. The prevention of feeding implies that the Pharisees as watch-dogs neither take provision, nor do they provide for others. Their leadership benefits neither themselves nor the ones they protect. The circumstances together with the particular roles have frustrated any potential for mutually satisfactory relationship. The Pharisees and those they guard find themselves stagnant and unable to break out of their circumstances.

This characterization of Pharisaic leadership (so consistent with the dominant Christian ideological construction of Pharisees and their practices) does not differ in tone from the characterization of the disciples in most of these sayings. The characterization differs for each: the disciples frequently represent shameless ignorance, whereas the Pharisees represent ineffectuality. They both receive negative attention, so that the seekers in these sayings come to distrust all hierarchical leadership, or, perhaps, all external hierarchical leadership.

Saying 103

Jesus said, "Blessed are [SV: Congratulations to] those who know where the rebels are going to attack. [They] can get going, collect their imperial resources, and be prepared before the rebels arrive."

The theme of surprise attack does not frequently occur in these sayings because the sayings lack an eschatological orientation. The preparedness for the rebels' invasion and attack here seems to strike an eschatological tone, but without an eschatological temporality. The content of the saying thwarts an eschatological reading because it shifts the attention from the time of attack to the place of attack. The ones who know its location will have the time to muster their resources and to prepare themselves for the invasion. The shift from the expected eschatological temporality ("when") to the locational character of the invasion ("where") drastically affects the saying and its understanding of the world, because the macarism guarantees adequate time for preparation, provided the persons know the place of attack. The emphasis on the adequate time for preparation underscores the positive understanding of the life of those who are interpreters of these sayings: there is no element of fear here, but a positive statement that when attacked, they will have had sufficient time to prepare to respond. Their success depends not on their timing, but on their knowledge of the enemy and the enemy's plans.

The preparation for those knowledgeable about the location of the invasion consists mostly of their reinforcement: the seekers will become active, gather the Kingdom (Lambdin, "domain"; Scholars Version "imperial resources") and prepare themselves. The curious phrase

"gather the kingdom" (as corrected by the scribe (Layton 1989: 90))
seems to signify that those prepared gather themselves, or are gathered
into, the Kingdom. This too functions locationally: the seekers find their
refuge in entering the Kingdom when they are about to be attacked:
they enter the Kingdom as the fortress place for their awaiting the
invasion. This reflects the superimposition of the Kingdom upon the
world as occupying the same space at the same time. The realized
eschatology of these sayings has forced a locational understanding of the
Kingdom as a place within the world to which seekers may retreat when
threatened.

Saying 104

> They said to Jesus, "Come, let us pray today, and let us fast." [2]Jesus
> said, "What sin have I committed, or how have I been undone?
> [3]Rather, when the groom leaves the bridal suite, then let people fast
> and pray."

The narrator does not identify the people who suggest that Jesus pray
and fast. From the content of their statement they clearly practice
fasting and prayer, and, therefore, they connect with people like the
disciples who ask about such practices in Saying 6. Their suggestion
receives no better or sympathetic response than Jesus gave to the earlier
disciples. Such performances clearly do not form important aspects of
the practice of the community reading these sayings.

Jesus repudiates the suggestion on the basis of two correlative
questions that discuss sin and defeat. Jesus connects the need for fasting
and prayer to the perpetration of sin, and to being vanquished. In the
context of these sayings fasting and prayer signify sinfulness and express
the world's victory over the seekers. Saying 14 makes the same
connection of sin and defeat with fasting and prayer. The presence of
these performances in a community marks the community as
disempowered, that is, a community that has not been able to
overcome its own deficiency and to reinstate themselves in their divine
origin.

Jesus confirms this sort of reading in the explanation he provides for
repudiating these performances: there will be no fasting when the
groom is in the bridal chamber; fasting and prayer will begin when the
groom leaves. In the context of the synoptic gospels which have the
parallels to this saying (Mark 2.19–20, Matthew 9.15, Luke 5.34–35),
this statement explains to later Christians why they are currently fasting

whereas earlier Christians did not fast. However, Jesus' repudiation of the practices of fasting and prayer in this saying hinges on the fact that wherever the sayings are read and interpreted Jesus is present. These sayings relate the living Jesus to individuals and communities who, when they have discovered the interpretation of the sayings, will not experience death (as in Saying 1). For this community, there will never be a time when the groom has left the nuptial chamber, because Jesus' voice perpetually speaks in the sayings read and interpreted. The seekers, moreover, understand themselves as those who have joined the groom in the bridal chamber, so that there will never be a time for fasting and prayer. The bridal chamber signifies the place of union and continual conversation with the living Jesus (Valantasis 1995a).

Among the monks who preserved these sayings in Egypt this saying would have been a confirmation of their mixed status. They would have indeed understood themselves as in the nuptial chamber, as initiates into the great mystery of union with Jesus, and as the solitaries who have entered into the Kingdom of the Father. But they would have also understood themselves as warriors, women and men who were continually on the verge of defeat by the demons, and whose sin prevented them from being able to live out their fully divine status. They would have located themselves positively among the sinful and defeated, while simultaneously rejoicing in the bridal chamber.

Saying 105

Jesus said, "Whoever knows the father and the mother will be called the child of a whore."

The problematizing of family continues here. Knowledge of parental identity points toward illegitimacy. For the seekers to know their parents would force them to be classified according to the standards recognized in the mundane world. Such knowledge presupposes an understanding of human engenderment and origins that masks the truly divine origin of the seekers. Such knowledge makes these seekers illegitimately cognizant of their true origin. From the perspective of those interpreting these sayings, such knowledge indicates their lesser status and their refusal to admit their true origin. The saying recalls the differentiation between the true mother and the other mother in Saying 101, so that the true mother gives life, whereas the biological mother remains a harlot who does not reveal the son's truly heavenly paternity.

Saying 106

> Jesus said, "When you make the two into one, you will become sons of (the) man [SV: children of Adam], [2]and when you say, 'Mountain, move from here!' it will move."

Three elements conjoin here: a statement about becoming one, the expression "sons of (the) man," and spiritual power over physical realities. The goal throughout these sayings has frequently been thematized as becoming a unitary person by making dual subjectivities (or worlds) into a unitary and fully empowered one (Sayings 4, 11, 43, 48, and 49). Although these verses may allude to some exterior myths such as the primordial human (Adam) or to the creation of the androgyne (Buckley 1986), the interpretation does not require external data. Two subjectivities have been posited in these sayings: one is the seekers who have become the solitaries; the other is the ignorant ones who continue to invest in worldly resources in one form or another. When these two subjectivities have become one, that is, when the worldly subjectivity has been incorporated and subsumed into the spiritual one developed through the interpretation of these sayings, then that unitary person achieves a higher level of power and authority. The unitary status enables them to become one of those in the category "sons of (the) man," that is, they take on the standing of one of those who stand in the same place as the "son of man" and they receive the power and authority of a person in that category. This same power and authority has been identified with Jesus earlier in these sayings (see the commentary on Saying 86). Their election as members of the "sons of (the) man" enable them to exercise divine power in the natural realm. Again, nothing divides the spiritual world from the physical world, because the empowered person may move physical entities. Divine power, then, emerges from this unitary presence in the world; the unitary subjectivity has elected the seekers to the category "sons of man;" and that election in turn provides power and authority to be exercised in the world.

Saying 107

> Jesus said, "The <Father's> imperial rule is like a shepherd who had a hundred sheep. [2]One of them, the largest, went astray. He left the ninety-nine and looked for the one until he found it. [3]After he had toiled, he said to the sheep, 'I love you more than the ninety-nine.'"

This narrative resembles in both tone and some details the earlier narrative about the catch of fish (Saying 8). The tone of both the narratives may best be described as ironic: the irony of a fisherman who throws away a whole catch for one large fish; and the irony of a shepherd who leaves ninety-nine sheep to fetch one. The characterization of both the fish and the sheep as large also connects them. These narratives of discovery provide an insight into the multifaceted experience of those for whom these sayings play a central role.

At least two alternative, but correlative, interpretations may be advanced. The first relates to the community. The one large sheep functioned as part of a dominant group of ninety-nine sheep. All the sheep originally formed one cohesive group, until the largest one "went astray"—a characterization that defines the dominant group's perspective on the one sheep. This structuring of the narrative provides the base that organizes the irony. The shepherd, whose responsibility at least (if he were hired) or whose wealth (if the sheep belonged to him) centered upon the ninety-nine, leaves the majority to find the one large sheep. The illogic of that action stands vividly in the narrative. From the perspective of the shepherd, the majority has less value than the one. The narrative lays out structures of valuation in sequence so that the reader may see true value in relationship to false value. That devaluation of the majority and the positive appraisal of the one large sheep takes on even more dramatic meaning in the last verses. The shepherd works hard at finding the one, and then professes a superior love for the one than for the many. The energy and dynamic of the relationship between the shepherd and the large sheep animates the story. The readers connect with the one, so that the message conveyed relates that they have value in excess of the dominant culture around them. That message communicates the value within the dominant religious culture of the one who "goes astray," who moves in another direction, who turns away from the fold to find a new direction. Those who withdraw form a community of intensity and love with the shepherd who among other possibilities could be either Jesus or the leaders of the community. The community's experience of election and love, so different from the experience of the dominant group, finds expression in the narrative.

A second alternative reading takes this corporate understanding of the narrative and applies it to the individual. These sayings betray an awareness of the interior conflict caused by withdrawing from the dominant culture, and they encourage seekers to enter the conflict, to withdraw from the dominant culture, and to strive to become unitary

and a solitary. The withdrawal of the one large sheep from the group–
which the group characterizes as "gone astray," but which for the large
sheep becomes the occasion of his election and the bestowal of the
shepherd's love–shows the movement of one creature toward the
solitude in which the solitary and the unitary life develop. The seeker
leaves behind the conflicting voices and demands of the group in favor
of a new path, one in which the seeker finds election and gratification.
The speaker of these sayings has expressed love for the one who has
withdrawn, and has sought that one out for extraordinary support. This
provides another window into the experience of the seekers who in the
process of losing themselves have also found themselves, and who in
withdrawing from the dominant religious culture have discovered a new
and intense relationship with Jesus.

Other details could open other possibilities for interpretation. Such
information as the "toil" of the shepherd, or the shepherd's continuous
looking for that which was lost, suggests an alternative perspective: in
the process of living out the life appointed them, they discovered that
they had lost something extremely valuable and went in search of it.
Their inner or spiritual life was lost, and now, having found it, the
seekers rejoice at the love they feel for that which they lost.

Saying 108

Jesus said, "Whoever drinks from my mouth will become like me; [2]I
myself shall become that person, [3]and the hidden things will be
revealed to him."

Lurking beneath the surface of many of these sayings lies the suggestion
that the seekers and Jesus become one and the same person. That
suggestion emerges from the intense identification of speaker of the
sayings and interpretation, from the emphasis on the transformation of
the two into the one, the emphasis on the defeat of death through
reading and interpreting the sayings, and the continual reference to
immortality and the exercise of power. These themes point toward the
identification of the seeker with the voice of the sayings. That suggestion
becomes explicit in this saying.

The mouth of Jesus has been metaphorized as a well from which
people drink the words that he speaks. The bubbling well or water
spring frequently signifies the mystagogue in religious initiation (as in
the Hermetic treatise from Nag Hammadi, Discourse on the Eighth
and Ninth (see commentary on Saying 13)) and that initiation transfers

power and identity from the divinity through the mystagogue to the initiant so that one identity lies over the others and merges with them (Valantasis 1991: 63–104). It signifies transformation, empowerment, and renewal. Jesus' statement, then, "whoever drinks from my mouth will become like me" fits into a common pattern of initiation and transformative empowerment. The textualized sayings come forth from that mouth, and the seekers drink of those sayings and become like Jesus. Through the mediation of the sayings envoiced in Jesus, the seeker adopts a new identity as the speaker of the sayings.

The union of mystagogue and initiant suggested in the first verse becomes explicit in the second. Jesus announces that he, the speaker of the sayings, will himself "become that person." This change in identity and status both for Jesus and for the initiant represents a dramatic theological postulate of these sayings. The living Jesus, the life bestowed in interpreting the sayings–these do not remain distant realities, but become the substance of a unitary identity. The subjectivity toward which the seekers move refracts Jesus' own subjectivity; the seekers become Jesus.

And finally, that empowerment and initiation conveys hidden knowledge to the seeker: "and the hidden things will be revealed to him." The power and status of the new common identity with Jesus exist not for power, but for knowledge and revelation. Through their union with the voice and speaker of these sayings, the seekers will come to understand and to know the hidden things.

Saying 109

Jesus said, "The <Father's> imperial rule is like a person who had a treasure hidden in his field but did not know it. [2]And [when] he died he left it to his [son]. The son [did] not know <about it either>. He took over the field and sold it. [3]The buyer went plowing, [discovered] the treasure, and began to lend money at interest to whomever he wished."

As in other similitudes the central focus here revolves about ignorance and discovery. Generations of landowners remained ignorant of the treasure hidden in the field. The son sold the field that he had inherited. The buyer worked the field himself, found the treasure while he was working, and immediately commenced lending money with interest. Ignorance and lack of understanding mark those who have not yet begun to search–they are the people in this world who have not become aware of their true identity and value. These ignorant people live according to the set patterns of the world: they inherit and they sell with no evidence of their own work. Their apparent wealth and lack of work keep them unaware of the treasure among them.

The buyer, however, works his land and discovers the hidden treasure. The true wealth discovered through his labor enabled him to increase the value of the treasure. A serious discrepancy emerges here: this saying seems to be completely positive about buying and selling as the means of true discovery, and about lending at interest as a fruit of that discovery. This positive valuation of commercial activity contrasts with its negative appraisal elsewhere (as in Saying 64). If the statement, then, ought to be taken figuratively, then the money working at earning interest mirrors the farmer's work in plowing and discovering the treasure. The emphasis, then, would focus upon the toil necessary to the discovery of one's hidden treasure.

Saying 110

Jesus said, "The one who has found the world, and has become wealthy, should renounce the world."

This saying consists of two interesting reversals. The first reversal posits that someone might find the world. In most of the sayings in this Gospel, seekers search and find when they sober up, or withdraw from the world, or enter the conflict with the world–the prospect of finding the world, then, seems ridiculous. Any person with any higher understanding would recognize that the world's wealth carries no value and, in fact, it really is not wealth at all. So this saying reverses the pattern of other sayings and portrays the opposite of the seeker's true search.

The second reversal (probably humorous) directs these wealthy seekers back to the renunciation which inaugurated their search in the first place. Only renunciation of the world and its wealth can lead the seeker to true discovery and to true wealth. The message is serious, but the tone is playful, because the reversal speaks to the inverse of the search and ends with commending the true search again.

Saying 111

Jesus said, "The heavens and the earth will roll up in your presence, [2]and whoever is living from the living one will not see death." [3]Does not Jesus say, "Those who have found themselves, of them the world is not worthy?"

This saying consists of two parts comprising three sayings and joined by narrative. The relatively seamless narrative structure of most of these sayings has consisted of a simple statement describing the speaker, either Jesus, or the disciples, or "they," or Salome, or Simon Peter. Only in the Prologue does the narrative voice display itself sufficiently to discover a narrative perspective. Here, however, the narrative voice answers somewhat defensively by quoting a saying of Jesus as a question to the readers. The comment "Did not Jesus say" breaks the invisibility of the narration so that the readers (and seekers) understand that the perspective on the sayings has more structure and literary work than appears in the dominant formula "Jesus said."

The first part links two sayings as though they were related to one another: an apocalyptic saying about the "rolling up" of the heavens and the earth in the presence of the readers/seekers, and a variation on the theme that the seekers will not experience death. The apocalyptic saying describes the end times when the whole creation will be changed. That transformation, whether cataclysmic or not, will occur in the presence of the readers/seekers in these sayings. Locationally, the readers remain outside as observers to the rolling up of the heavens and the earth; the apocalypse happens before them, but without affecting them.

The next saying has been placed beside this apocalyptic saying as an explanation. The saying itself ("whoever is living from the living one will not see death") forms a parallel to the saying about those who discover the interpretation of these sayings will not taste death (Saying 1). The underlying precept maintains that those who have heard the living words of the living Jesus will not experience death. Life comes to them from their engagement with the words and sayings spoken to them and interpreted by them. This community experiences itself as fully alive and beyond the reach of death. They, then, would indeed be spectators at the apocalypse, because they would not be affected by it in any way. Their life insures that they will not see death for themselves, but will watch the heavens and the earth be rolled up.

These claims are deliberate and intended to be taken literally; these seekers do indeed know that they will not die–they will neither see death or taste death. Neither the seekers, nor Jesus, speak of this immortality as figurative or metaphorical. The narrative defensiveness relates to the tendency toward metaphorization and spiritualization of the sayings, and the narrator intrudes with a defensive question addressed directly to the readers and the seekers of the text. "Does not Jesus say" argues for a literal interpretation, and the saying which follows underscores that those who think figuratively and metaphorically resemble the world that is being rolled up before them and they are not worthy of the true seekers. The seekers have found themselves: after Saying 108, this finding of self cannot be defined without reference to the identification of the seeker with Jesus. They are one person, united. The seekers have become divine, and of such divine subjectivities the world is not worthy. The defensiveness may in fact relate to these provocative claims by the seekers and readers of these sayings. The world does not recognize their status, and therefore, the world cannot have a correlative value.

Saying 112

Jesus said, "Damn the flesh that depends on the soul. [2]Damn the soul that depends on the flesh."

This saying condemns the problematic relationship of flesh on soul and soul on flesh. That problematic relationship revolves about the question of the dependency of one upon the other (see the commentary on Saying 87), not about the independent status of the flesh or the soul. The saying differentiates between the flesh and the soul in suggesting their polar opposition one to another, but it is their dependent interaction that locks them in debilitating relationship. The saying does not assert that the salvation of the flesh resides in the soul, because the flesh dependent upon the soul receives condemnation. Likewise, the soul's dependence upon the flesh does not support the soul's salvation in that the soul that depends of the flesh links the higher aspect of human anthropology to the most transient. Such a soul dependent on the weaker member will not succeed. Dependence of these elements inhibits their natural development.

The goal, then, moves toward independence. The saying posits the capacity of a flesh not to be dependent upon the soul, so that the life of the flesh and the life of the soul could develop in parallel, but different, directions. Likewise the saying posits the potential independence of soul from flesh, so that unencumbered by embodiment the soul may develop in a direction different from the body. Each realm will be able to live and develop according to its nature, provided that they remain independent and not dependent upon each other.

The saying forces the seekers to reorient themselves to their understanding of the body and the soul and the relationship of the two. In condemning dependency, and advocating independence, seekers find themselves of necessity considering their own levels of dependence in their bodies and in their souls. This perspective is consistent with the positive appraisal of the body as a site for proving personal worth (Sayings 56 and 80).

Saying 113

His disciples said to him, "When will the <Father's> imperial rule come?" [2]"It will not come by watching for it. [3]It will not be said, 'Look, here!' or 'Look, there!' [4]Rather, the Father's imperial rule is spread out upon the earth, and people don't see it."

The determined reluctance to acknowledge an apocalyptic interpretation of the Father's Kingdom emerges here as well. The disciples, again in their capacity of asking questions that indicate their lack of understanding, address the Father's Kingdom temporally. They want to know when it will happen. Jesus repudiates their temporal understanding, and indicates that the Kingdom will not appear before people as something to which they could direct their eyes or point their fingers (this same theme has been propounded in Saying 3). The Kingdom does not exist spatially or temporally apart from the seekers in these sayings (compare this to Saying 103). Instead of this understanding, Jesus posits a Kingdom that already exists in the world, but that remains invisible to people in the world. The Kingdom does not function as an apocalyptic vision (see also Saying 91), or a temporal end, but as a state of being congruent with the existent world and present for those capable of seeing it (see Patterson 1993: 208–13). Jesus observes that the difficulty resides with people's inability to see it as it exists before them.

This saying underscores the fact that these sayings do not promulgate a dualistic view of the world. The world and the Kingdom exist together without separation, although there remains a clear distinction between them. This understanding of the world, so different from most of the orthodox and gnostic theological positions, requires constant redefinition of categories. The definition of the categories remains locked in dualism and binary oppositions of flesh/soul, world/Kingdom, earth/heaven, so that any attempt to break out of that dualism and posit monism (as these sayings continually reiterate in different forms) requires significant redefinition. That redefinition, however, rests in an experience, in one of transformation through interpreting the sayings. That experience provides the basis for the articulation of a new subjectivity, new social relations, and a new conceptualization of the world. In short, that redefinition makes these sayings ascetical.

Saying 114

Simon Peter said to them, "Make Mary leave us, for females don't deserve life." [2]Jesus said, "Look, I will guide her to make her male, so that she too may become a living spirit resembling you males. [3]For every female who makes herself male will enter the domain of heaven."

This saying consists of three parts. In the first part, Peter complains about Mary's presence: "Simon Peter said to them: 'Make Mary leave us, for females don't deserve life.'" The presence of Peter here has often been interpreted as symbolic of the emerging catholic church, but such a symbolic reading need not provide the starting point. The denigration of women as unworthy of life and as not deserving participation in the community sets the stage. Simon Peter's objection, however, is made to a larger group of males (the "us" is plural) and seems not to be addressed to Jesus alone. Simon Peter's predominantly male community seems peripherally to have included Mary, whom he would like to reject from the community. Peter here represents the sort of male community described in the Nag Hammadi Hermetic treatise Discourse on the Eighth and Ninth in which all of the characters and functions are male, even female roles are played by males (Valantasis 1991: 83–84).

In the second part, Jesus responds to Simon Peter with an offer: "Jesus said, 'Look, I will guide her to make her male, so that she too may become a living spirit resembling you males.'" Jesus finds a way to include the women in the community as it is defined by Simon Peter by his taking on the role of mystagogue and effecting through his guidance a form of gendered transformation. In the Hermetic literature the male mystagogues are frequently described as "pregnant" or as "giving birth to a brotherhood." The mystagogue in Discourse on the Eighth and Ninth says, for example: "Indeed the understanding dwells in you; in me (it is) as though the power were pregnant. For when I conceived from the fountain that flowed to me, I gave birth" (52.16–20; NHLE 322). This gendered transformation exactly invokes for women the possibility of attaining the status open only to the other (just as the Hermetic men could take on the gendered functions of women). That Jesus is a mystagogue, a sort of third gender, is made clear by the characterization of Peter and his group as "you males" (not "us males," if Jesus were including himself in the category). Jesus tells Simon Peter (not Mary) that he himself will provide whatever is necessary for Mary to become a full member of the community (in this case articulated as "make herself male" and "resembling...males"). The dominant category, however, seems not to be either the woman or the man, nor even the task of becoming male, but the task of becoming a "living spirit" which merely "resembles you males". Jesus the mystagogue may function in relationship to both males in their formation and females in their formation, and both formations are equally transformative, both formations lead toward becoming "a living spirit."

The third section of the saying articulates a general principle: "For every female who makes herself male will enter the domain of heaven." The task of making the male into the female, and both into a single one, has been articulated before in these sayings (Saying 22). This task of creating something that is neither male nor female has been presented as a goal for all the seekers posited in these sayings. Here Jesus makes that articulated goal explicit for women. It does not seem to manifest a degree of misogyny, but makes the stated goal specifically for women as well. It does not say that Jesus will make her male, nor that the community will recreate her, but that any female "who makes herself male" will receive the benefits accorded to those males and females who have become a new gender in this community. Females perform this recreation on themselves in order to enter the Kingdom; but it is no different from those males who must become female, and then become a single one. The understanding of gender in these sayings establishes the "single one" as the primary category supervening the masculine and feminine genders altogether: so that the seekers "make male and female into a single one, so that the male will not be male nor the female be female" (Saying 22).

The Title

The Gospel According to Thomas

This title contrasts with the Prologue. The Prologue describes the genre of the work as "secret sayings." The sayings originate in a "living Jesus" and have been recorded by Didymos Judas Thomas. The identification of the work as a collection of sayings directs the readers to a particular kind of interpretative endeavor. The interpretative strategy must embrace each saying in their isolation and particularity and all the sayings as a cohesive text constructed to provide consistent meaning. The readers and interpreters of sayings, that is, construct their own narrative and theology linking the individual sayings into a cohesive text. In that strategy, the readers mirror the activity of the recorder of the sayings who has already constructed a meaningful meta-text of collected individual sayings. The recorder has also constructed a voice for that meta-text and described that voice as the "living Jesus" whose speaking conveys life, meaning, knowledge, immortality, and all the riches of the Kingdom.

Now that process of interpretation receives the meta-genre designation as gospel. It is impossible chronologically to identify the point at which these interpreted sayings became a gospel. The interaction of genre with meta-genre certainly implies a two-fold chronology in which the sayings were collected and interpreted (or at least some of them were) and later that collection was best understood in the genre of gospel (in my reckoning sometime during the first decade of the second century).

There is a performative aspect here that is important. The interpretative process, the challenge of the sayings and their modality of inversion, constitutes a performance of meaning. Knowledge emerges from an action of interpreting. The collection of sayings under the authorship of Jesus and editorship of Didymos Judas Thomas demand a performance to unlock their individual and collected meaning. It requires work and toil to perform these and to discover (note it is not to learn) the interpretation. These sayings demand activity. The Gospel of Thomas' contribution to the genre gospel may in fact revolve about this performative aspect. The gospel proclaimed in these sayings retains its performative dynamic, a dynamic lost when the primary modality of proclamation becomes predominantly narrative. Whereas a narrative defines carefully the actors and their actions, sayings simply float meaning without careful definition or careful control. This Gospel proclaims the priority of living voice over narrative, of textualized presence over narrative definition. The Gospel remains performative.

Bibliography

Attridge, Harold W. (1989) "Appendix: The Greek Fragments", pp. 96–128 in *Nag Hammadi Codex II, 2–7, together with XIII, 2*, Brit. Lib. Or.4926(1), and P. Oxy. 1, 654, 655*, ed. Bentley Layton, Nag Hammadi Studies 20, Leiden: E. J. Brill.

Baker, Aelred (1964) "Pseudo-Macarius and the Gospel of Thomas", *Vigiliae christianae* 18: 215–25.

—— (1965) "Fasting to the World", *Journal of Biblical Literature* 84: 291–94.

—— (1965–66) "The 'Gospel of Thomas' and the Syriac 'Liber Graduum' ", *New Testament Studies* 12: 49–55.

Bell, H. Idris (ed.) (1972) *Jews and Christians in Egypt: The Jewish Troubles in Alexandria and the Athanasian Controversy* (originally published 1924), Westport, CT: Greenwood Press.

Bianchi, Ugo (ed.) (1967) *The Origins of Gnosticism: Colloquium of Messina 13–18 April 1966*, Studies in the History of Religions (Supplement to *Numen*) 12, Leiden: E. J. Brill.

Brakke, David (1995) *Athanasius and the Politics of Asceticism*, Oxford Early Christian Studies, Oxford: Clarendon Press.

Brown, Raymond E. (1962–63) "The Gospel of Thomas and St. John's Gospel", *New Testament Studies* 9: 155–77.

Buckley, Jorunn Jacobsen (1986) *Female Fault and Fulfilment in Gnosticism*, Chapel Hill, NC: University of North Carolina Press.

Cameron, Ron (ed.) (1982) *The Other Gospels: Non-Canonical Gospel Texts*, Philadelphia, PA: The Westminster Press.

—— (1986) "Parable and Interpretation in the Gospel of Thomas", *Forum* 2: 3–39.

Castelli, Elizabeth (1986) "Virginity and its Meaning for Women's Sexuality in Early Christianity", *Journal of Feminist Studies in Religion* 2: 61–88.

Crossan, John Dominic (1973) *In Parables: The Challenge of the Historical Jesus*, San Francisco: Harper & Row.

—— (1991) *The Historical Jesus: The Life of a Mediterranean Jewish Peasant*, New York: HarperSanFrancisco.

Crum, W. E. (1939) *A Coptic Dictionary*, Oxford: Clarendon Press.

Cullman, Oscar (1962) "The Gospel of Thomas and the Problem of the Age of the Tradition Contained Therein", trans. Balmer H. Kelley, *Interpretation* 16: 418–38.

Davies, Steven L. (1983) *The Gospel of Thomas and Christian Wisdom*, New York: The Seabury Press.

Desjardins, Michel (1992) "Where was the Gospel of Thomas Written?", *Toronto Journal of Theology* 8: 121–33.

Doran, Robert (1987) "A Complex of Parables: GTh 96–98", *Novum Testamentum* 29: 347–52.

Elm, Susanna (1994) *"Virgins of God": The Making of Asceticism in Late Antiquity*, Oxford Classical Monographs, Oxford: Clarendon Press.

Fallon, Francis T. and Ron Cameron (1988) "The Gospel of Thomas: A Forschungsbericht and Analysis", *Aufstieg und Niedergang der römischen Welt* II, 25.6: 4195–251, Berlin: Walter de Gruyter, 1988.

Fieger, Michael (1991) *Das Thomasevangelium: Einleitung, Kommentar, und Systematik*, Münster: Aschendorff.

Filoramo, Giovanni (1990) *A History of Gnosticism*, trans. Anthony Alcock, Oxford: Basil Blackwell.

Frend, W. H. C. (1967) "The Gospel of Thomas: Is Rehabilitation Possible?", *Journal of Theological Studies*, n.s. 18: 13–26.

Gärtner, Beril (1961) *The Theology of the Gospel of Thomas*, trans. Eric J. Sharpe, London: Collins.

Glasson, T. F. (1976–77) "The Gospel of Thomas 3, and Deuteronomy xxx, 11–14", *Expository Times* 78: 151–52.

Grant, Robert M. and David Noel Freedman (1960) *The Secret Sayings of Jesus*, London: Collins.

Grenfell, B. P. and A. S. Hunt (1897). ΛΟΓΙΑ ΙΗΣΟΥ: Sayings of Our Lord, Egypt Exploration Fund, London: Frowde.

—— (1904) *New Sayings of Jesus and Fragment of a Lost Gospel from Oxyrhynchus*, Egypt Exploration Fund, London: Frowde.

Griffith, Sidney H. (1995) "Asceticism in the Church of Syria: The Hermeneutics of Early Syrian Monasticism", pp. 220–45 in V. Wimbush and R. Valantasis (eds) *Asceticism*, New York: Oxford University Press.

Grobel, Kendrick (1961–62) "How Gnostic is the Gospel of Thomas?", *New Testament Studies* 8: 367–73.

Haenchen, Ernst (1961) *Die Botschaft des Thomas-Evangeliums*, Berlin: Alfred Töpelmann.

—— (1961–62) "Literature Um Thomasevangelium", *Theologische Rundschau* 27: 147–78, 306–38.

Harl, Marguerite (1960) "A propos des Logia de Jésus: Le sens du mot *Monachos*", *Revue d'études Grecques* 73: 464–74.

Hedrick, Charles W. (1994) *Parables as Poetic Fictions: The Creative Voice of Jesus*, Peabody, MA: Hendrickson Publishers.

Jackson, Howard M. (1985) *The Lion Becomes Man: The Gnostic Leontomorphic Creator and the Platonic Tradition*, Society of Biblical Literature Dissertation Series 81, Atlanta, GA: Scholars Press.

Jonas, Hans (1963) *The Gnostic Religion: The Message of the Alien God and the Beginnings of Christianity* (2nd edn, enlarged), Boston, MA: Beacon Press.

Kaestli, Jean-Daniel (1979) "L'Évangile de Thomas: Son importance pour l'étude des paroles de Jésus et du gnosticisme chrétien", *Études théologiques et religieuses* 54: 375–96.

Kasser, Rodolphe (1961) *L'Évangile selon Thomas: Présentation et commentaire théologique*, Neuchâtel (Switzerland): Éditions Delachaux et Niestlé.

Klijn, A. F. J. (1962) "The 'Single One' in the Gospel of Thomas", *Journal of Biblical Literature* 81: 271–78.

Kloppenborg, John S. (1987) *The Formation of Q: Trajectories in Ancient Wisdom Collections*, Studies in Antiquity and Christianity, Philadelphia, PA: Fortress Press.

Koester, Helmut (1980) "Gnostic Writings as Witnesses for the Development of the Sayings Tradition", I: 238–56 in *The Rediscovery of Gnosticism: Proceedings of the International Conference on Gnosticism at Yale, New Haven Connecticut, March 28– 31, 1978*, Studies in the History of Religions 41, Leiden: E. J. Brill.

—— (1982) *Introduction to the New Testament* (two vols), Hermeneia Foundations and Facets, Philadelphia, PA: Fortress Press.

—— (1989) "Introduction", pp. 38–49 in Layton, B. (1989) *Nag Hammadi Codex II, 2–7, together with XIII, 2*, Brit. Lib. Or. 4926(1), and P. Oxy. 1, 654, 655*, Nag Hammadi Studies 20, Leiden: E. J. Brill.

—— (1990a) *Ancient Christian Gospels: Their History and Development*. Philadelphia, PA: Trinity Press International.

—— (1990b) "Q and Its Relatives", pp. 49–63 in *Christian Origins and Christian Beginnings: In Honor of James M. Robinson*, ed. James E. Goehring, Charles W. Hedrick, Jack T. Sanders, Sonoma, CA: Polebridge Press.

—— (1992) "The Story of the Johannine Tradition", *Sewanee Theological Review* 36: 17–32.

Layton, Bentley (ed.) (1981) *The Rediscovery of Gnosticism: Proceedings of the International Conference on Gnosticism at Yale, New Haven, Connecticut, March 28–31, 1978*, Studies in the History of Religions 41 (2 vols), Leiden: E. J. Brill.

—— (ed.) (1989) *Nag Hammadi Codex II, 2–7, together with XIII, 2*, Brit. Lib. Or. 4926(1), and P. Oxy. 1, 654, 655*, Nag Hammadi Studies 20, Leiden: E. J. Brill.

Lelyveld, Margaretha (1987) *Les Logia de la vie dans l'Évangile selon Thomas: à la recherche d'une tradition et d'une rédaction*, Nag Hammadi Studies 34, Leiden: E. J. Brill.

Lincoln, Bruce (1977) "Thomas-Gospel and Thomas-Community: A New Approach to a Familiar Text", *Novum Testamentum* 19: 65–76.

Mack, Burton L. (1988) *A Myth of Innocence: Mark and Christian Origins*, Philadelphia, PA: Fortress Press.

—— (1993) *The Lost Gospel: The Book of Q and Christian Origins*, New York: HarperSanFrancisco.

MacRae, George (1960) "The Gospel of Thomas–*Logia Iesou*?", *Catholic Biblical Quarterly* 22: 56–70.

—— (1980) "Why the Church Rejected Gnosticism," pp. 126–133 in *Jewish and Christian Self-Definition: Volume One: The Shaping of Christianity in the Second and Third Centuries*. Philadelphia, PA: Fortress Press.

Ménard, Jacques-É (1975) *L'Évangile selon Thomas*, Nag Hammadi Studies 5, Leiden: E. J. Brill.

Meyer, Marvin (1985) "Making Mary Male: The Categories of 'Male' and 'Female' in the Gospel of Thomas", *New Testament Studies* 31: 554–70.

—— (1990) "The Beginning of the Gospel of Thomas", *Semeia* 52: 161–73.

—— (trans. and ed.) (1992) *The Gospel of Thomas: The Hidden Sayings of Jesus*, New York: HarperSanFrancisco.

Miller, Robert J. (ed.) (1992) *The Complete Gospels*, Sonoma, CA: Polebridge Press.

Montefiore, Hugh (1960/61) "A Comparison of the Parables of the Gospel According to Thomas and of the Synoptic Gospels", *New Testament Studies* 7: 220–48.

Patterson, Stephen J. (1991) "Paul and the Jesus Tradition: It is Time for Another Look", *Harvard Theological Review* 84: 23–41.

—— (1992) "The Gospel of Thomas and the Synoptic Tradition: A Forschungsbericht and Critique", *Forum* 8, 1–2: 45–97.

—— (1993) *The Gospel of Thomas and Jesus*, Sonoma, CA: Polebridge Press.

Pestman, P. W. (1994) *The New Papyrological Primer* (2nd revised edn), Leiden: E. J. Brill.

Quispel, Gilles (1957) "The Gospel of Thomas and the New Testament", *Vigiliae christianae* 11: 189–207.

—— (1965) "L'Évangile selon Thomas et les origines de l'ascèse chrétienne", pp. 35–52 in *Aspects du Judéo-Chrétianisme (Colloque de Strasbourg 23–25 avril 1964)*, Paris: Presses Universitaires de France.

—— (1969) "Gnosis and the New Sayings of Jesus", *Eranos Jahrbuch* 38: 261–96.

—— (1981) "The *Gospel of Thomas* Revisited", pp. 218–66 in *Colloque International sur les textes de Nag Hammadi, 1*, ed. Bernard Barc, Quebec: Les Presses de l'Université Laval.

Rewolinski, Edward (1996) Private communication.

Richardson, Cyril C. (1973) "The Gospel of Thomas: Gnostic or Encratite?", pp. 65–76 in *The Heritage of the Early Church: Essays in Honor of Georges Florovsky*, ed. David Neiman and Margaret Schatkin, Orientalia Christiana Analecta 195, Rome: Pont. Institutum Studiorum Orientalium.

Riley, G. J. (1994) "The *Gospel of Thomas* in Recent Scholarship", *Currents in Research: Biblical Studies* 2: 227–52.

—— (1995) *Resurrection Reconsidered: Thomas and John in Controversy*, Minneapolis, MN: Fortress Press.

Robinson, James M. (1971a) "LOGOI SOPHON: On the Gattung of Q", pp. 71–113 in *Trajectories through Early Christianity*, ed. James M. Robinson and Helmut Koester, Philadelphia, PA: Fortress Press.

—— (1971b) "Kerygma and History in the New Testament", pp. 20–70 in *Trajectories through Early Christianity*, ed. James M. Robinson and Helmut Koester, Philadelphia, PA: Fortress Press.

—— (1979) "The Discovery of the Nag Hammadi Codices", *Biblical Archeologist* 42: 206–24.

—— (ed.) (1988) *Nag Hammadi Library in English* (3rd edn), San Francisco: Harper & Row.

Rudolph, Kurt (1977) *Gnosis: The Nature and History of Gnosticism*, trans. Robert McLachlan Wilson, San Francisco: Harper & Row.

Schoedel, William R. (1960) "Naasene Themes in the Coptic Gospel of Thomas", *Vigiliae christianae* 14: 225–34.

—— (1985) *Ignatius of Antioch: A Commentary on the Letters of Ignatius of Antioch*, Philadelphia, PA: Fortress Press.

Schrage, W. (1964) *Das Verhältnis des Thomas-Evangeliums zur sunoptischen Tradition und zu den koptischen Evangelienübersetzunger. Zugleich ein Beitrag zur gnostischen Synoptikerdeutung*, Berlin: Töpelmann.

Schüssler-Fiorenza, Elizabeth (1983) *In Memory of Her: A Feminist Theological Reconstruction of Christian Origins*, New York: Crossroad.

Scott, Bernard Brandon (1989) *Hear Then the Parable: A Commentary on the Parables of Jesus*, Minneapolis, MN: Fortress Press.

Till, Walter C. (1958–59) "New Sayings of Jesus in the Recently Discovered Coptic 'Gospel of Thomas' ", *Bulletin of the John Rylands Library* 41: 446–56.

Turner, H. E. W. and Hugh Montefiore (1962) *Thomas and the Evangelists*, Naperville, IL: Alec R. Allenson, Inc.

Valantasis, Richard (1990) "Adam's Body: Uncovering Esoteric Tradition in the *Apocryphon of John* and Origen's *Dialogue with Heraclides*", *The Second Century* 7: 150–62.

—— (1991) *Spiritual Guides of the Third Century*, Harvard Dissertations in Religion 27, Minneapolis, MN: Fortress Press.

—— (1995a) "Constructions of Power in Asceticism", *Journal of the American Academy of Religion* 63: 775–821.

—— (1995b) "The Nuptial Chamber Revisited: The *Acts of Thomas* and Cultural Intertextuality", pp. 380–393 in *Society of Biblical Literature 1995 Seminar Papers*, ed. Eugene H. Lovering, Jr., Atlanta, GA: Scholars Press.

Via, Dan O. (1967) *The Parables: Their Literary and Existential Dimension*, Philadelphia, PA: Fortress Press.

Walls, A. F. (1962) " 'Stone' and 'Wood' in Oxyrhynchus Papyrus I", *Vigiliae christianae* 16: 71–76.

Ward, Benedicta, SLG (trans) (1975) *The Sayings of the Desert Fathers: The Alphabetical Collection*, Kalamazoo, MI: Cistercian Publications.

Wills, Lawrence M. (1990) *The Jew in the Court of the Foreign King: Ancient Jewish Court Legends*, Harvard Dissertations in Religion 26, Minneapolis, MN: Fortress Press.

Wilson, R. McL. (1960) *Studies in the Gospel of Thomas*, London: A. R. Mowbray & Co. Ltd.

Index

condition, human 103 *see also*
anthropology, body
conflict 10, 21, 70, 77, 79, 82, 179;
brought by Jesus 139, 151, 159; in
world 19, 83, 129, 133, 141, 150;
interior and exterior 148, 187–8; of
Samaritans and Jews 136
confrontation 157, 169
confusion 116
consistency 96
construction 7; of body and gender
95, 177; of desire 115; of identity
51, 126, 150; of meaning 37, 88,
106; *see also* anthropology,
asceticism, body, community
content of sayings 70 *see also* sayings
context 13, 51, 52, 80–1, 119
contradiction 45 *see also* conflict,
literary analysis
control, narrative 51, 78, 115 *see also*
narrative
controversy 128, 182
conversation 185 *see also*
communication, strategies
Coptic 1, 12, 27, 49
Corinthians, First 15, 84, 94, 160
corporate identity 97, 107–8, 187 *see
also* body, community, identity
corruption, inherent 153
cosmic dimensions 147, 156
cosmology 12
countryside 156–8
court, writing and scribes of 15 *see also*
scribes
creation 9, 72, 164, 165; mythology of
13, 128, 156; *see also* mythology,
world
creature, of flesh 81
critique, of narrative 17 *see also*
communication, strategies
crops 67, 92–4, 143–5, 152
cross 16, 132–3 *see also* Jesus
Crossan, John Dominic 16, 26, 79
crucifixion 8, 16, 19 *see also* cross, Jesus
cult 82, 97, 131–2, 137 *see also*
performances, practices, ritual
culture, religious 22, 23, 30, 187
curing 44, 106–7

damnation 38, 182–3, 192–3
darkness 38–9, 128 *see also* light
date, of Gospel of Thomas 12–21
deacon 18 *see also* bishop, Church,
community, leadership
dead, the 70–3, 130
death 133, 135–6; and division 138;
and salvation 149–50; no tasting of
10, 11, 32, 54, 85–7, 87–90, 165;
not experiencing 21, 108, 190–2; of
Jesus 8, 132; rich man 141–2; *see
also* Jesus, immortality, living,
readers, seekers
deathlessness 32 *see also* immortality
deeds 140–1 *see also* actions,
performances, practices
defeat 11, 184
deficiency 74, 111, 117, 146–7, 149,
152 *see also* value, world
defiling 78–81
degradation 38 *see also* value
deities 104–5 *see also* divinity
delusion 42
demanding, of taxes 180–1
dens 166–7
departure, from world 102–3 *see also*
ascent, world
dependence 46, 47, 167–8, 192–3 *see
also* body, individual
deprivation 117, 149
derision 152
descent 41
desert 49
design, graphic 50 *see also* scribes, texts
desire 47, 68, 102, 124, 128, 144, 149,
174; and motivation 85, 97; of
seeker 46, 114–15, 172, 181; *see also*
readers, seekers, yearning
destiny 9, 125–7, 156, 181 *see also*
mythology, origins
destruction 45, 150
devaluation 75, 175 *see also* value
development of identity 127, 192 *see
also* identity, readers, seekers
devouring 137
dialogue 16, 19–20, 85, 92; of Jesus
with disciples 75, 136–8, 138–40;
see also communication, genre,
literary analysis, strategies

Gospel of Truth 1
Gospels 1, 2, 9, 16, 21, 25, 29, 114, 124
grain 67
grapes 121–2
grapevine 116–17
great commission (Mt 28. 16–20), 39 *see also* Gospels
greatness of seeker 122–3 *see also* value
greed 141, 144
Greek fragments 27, 29–48 *see also* texts
Grenfell, B.P. 29
groom 184–5 *see also* bridal chamber, fasting
growth 91, 176 *see also* development
guardianship 69
guarding 69–70, 92–4, 183
guests 142–3
guidance 33–4, 62, 65, 80; by leaders, 58–9, 194–5; by sayings 23, 47, 55; spiritual 10, 24, 76, 109–10; *see also* formation, initiation
guide 9, 41, 52, 76, 110

hands 84–5, 95–6, 110–11, 117, 140–1, 159, 179–80
handle, broken 177–9
happiness 163–5
harm 78–81
harmony 125
harvest 121–2, 134
hatred 10, 118–20, 147–8; of family 132, 181–2; *see also* renunciation
haven 45
healing 78–81, 100
hearing 7, 9, 45, 84–5, 108–9, 114–15, 158–9
heart 84–5, 102–3, 121–2, 141–2, 148–9
heaven 70–3, 120–1, 171–2, 190–2
Hedrick, Charles 26
heir 143–5
Heresiologists 3, 14, 57 *see also* gnosticism
heresy 24, 60 *see also* Gnosticism
Hermas, The Shepherd of 61
Hermeticism 188–9, 194

hidden things 11, 35, 115–16, 189–90; images 162–3, 164; things, revelation of 62, 188–9; *see also* esotericism, exotericism, revelation
hiding 45, 107–8, 108–9, 176–7
Hieracas 24
hierarchy 24, 35, 39, 76, 81, 96, 120–1, 142, 182; and Church order 18, 19, 21; of being 38, 64, 89, 122, 143; *see also* anthropology, leadership, world
hill 45
hindrances 99, 167
history 122, 130
holes 109–10
Holy Spirit 120–1 *see also* Trinity
home 44, 106–7, 166, 179–80 *see also* community, family
homelessness 11, 166 *see also* itinerancy
honoring 123–4 *see also* value
horses 123–4
hospitality 44, 46, 78–81, 142–3 *see also* practices
hostility 41, 118–19, 128, 137, 147–8 *see also* conflict
house 82, 110–11, 124–5, 142–3, 177–9 *see also* family, home
household 83, 111, 125, 139, 151 *see also* family, home
humans 38, 64–5, 65–7, 81, 112, 166–7 *see also* anthropology, readers, seekers, transformation
hunger 10, 148–9 *see also* abstinence, asceticism, fasting, food, renunciation
Hunt, A.S. 29

icon 124 *see also* images, portaiture
identification 98, 136, 188–9 *see also* Jesus, union
identity 10–12, 21, 23, 38, 44, 55, 70, 93, 111, 129, 131, 157, 185, 190 ; and asceticism 22, 23, 111; and Jesus 9, 118–20, 126, 139, 155, 171; corporate 42, 99, 105–6, 107, 187; new 8, 10, 55, 113, 126, 159; *see also* anthropology, community, formation, person, subjectivity